PRAISE FOR
OFFICER CLEMMONS

"Clemmons's thoroughly delightful, inspiring story will speak particularly to artists in marginalized communities."
—*Publishers Weekly* (starred review)

"A heartwarming story that explores the power of friendship as well as race, sexuality, talent, and identity." —*Kirkus Reviews*

"Full of resonant moments and artistic insights . . . Clemmons' memoir is often disarming in its intimacy and honesty."
—Nicholas Cannarioto, NPR

"*Officer Clemmons* offers us a look into the life of a man who may have once been overlooked, and is only now being appreciated for his unique and rippling influence on our society through friendship and a ferocious commitment to individuality."
—Ashley C. Ford, author of *Somebody's Daughter*

"*Officer Clemmons* is a window into a time that is rapidly being forgotten, a history of blackness and queerness, and perhaps most especially of beauty." —Carvell Wallace, author of *The Sixth Man*

T0005755

OFFICER CLEMMONS

A Memoir

Dr. François S. Clemmons

New York  Catapult

To *Fred and Joanne Rogers*

And to my beloved *Lawanna Boswell,*
whose light shone bright in my life

Some names have been changed to protect identities.

Kind permission to reprint photographs is courtesy of
the author and The Fred Rogers Foundation

Hardcover ISBN: 978-1-948226-70-7
Paperback ISBN: 978-1-64622-057-1

Cover design by Nicole Caputo
Book design by Wah-Ming Chang

Library of Congress Control Number: 2019947925

Printed in the United States of America
1 3 5 7 9 10 8 6 4 2

CONTENTS

OFFICER CLEMMONS

INTRODUCTION

Dear Fred,
My guardian angels, spirit guides, ancestors, literary agent, and many friends and acquaintances have urged me to write this book for over twenty years. I've been amazed by the unabashed curiosity that is readily shown by folks—those close to me, as well as outright strangers. I'm most frequently asked, "Was he really like that?" meaning your television persona. Usually my initial response is simply "Yes!"

Early on, I fully grasped your enormous popularity, and at the same time, I learned about your unusual and immense patience. It's so amazing to me that even during dinner as we'd travel across the country, I'd watch you permit complete strangers to greet you, interrupt meals, and tell you their life stories. You would stop eating and patiently wait to sign your name and a gentle message that they might request. You never got angry or annoyed.

The questions from your fans rarely stop with "Was he really like that?" So, I simply put on the patience, like I saw you wear so often, and prepare to listen.

"What was it like to work with him?" they continue. "Is he that nice?" "Does he ever get angry?" "Was he a Christian?" "Did he go to church and preach?" "Was he gay?" It's mostly the men or fathers who ask that last question, and usually in private.

"Was he really a Navy SEAL?" "Was he married?" "Did he have children?" "How long did you work with him?" "Where was the show filmed?" "Where did he live?" Sometimes they want to know, "What was his wife like?" "How'd you meet him?" "Did you make a lot of money?" Some of these questions I can answer easily. Others are more complicated.

When children used to ask me about you, they wanted to know less about the man himself and all about the Neighborhood of Make-Believe: the trolley, the different puppets, the piano player. Some children asked if the Neighborhood was real, but my all-time favorite question from children was, "How did you get out of the television?"

Questions from your many fans partially motivated me to write this book, but the other reason is its uniqueness. Before I started writing, I sat down with twelve or so biographies, prayer books, quotes by you, and songbooks. I googled you extensively and looked at other publications by or about you. I scrutinized everything so I could compare them to what I was attempting to do. I also began the long process of going through my personal archives. I reread our old letters, sifted through photos, and found newspaper clippings and memorabilia I had collected over the years. I wanted to spark a deep impression of the man I wanted to summon in this book. As often as possible, I spent time speaking with numerous educators and academics who had studied your program, either with their students or with their own children. In some cases, with their grandchildren, nieces, and nephews.

After all of this, I concluded that there was one thing in particular that stood out: none of the other publications were authored by a black, gay, ordained person of the theater who had worked intimately with you for over thirty years! Because of that, I felt that I could bring a singularly unique perspective to those years that no one else has. My perspective would offer far more than a one-time encounter at the local restaurant, or even hours spent in a research library. Our relationship was sustained, intense, and elbow-to-elbow. For me, you fulfilled the role of mentor, fan, and surrogate father.

But something was missing. As I wrote about you and your impact on me, I realized that I needed to start from the beginning—from *my* beginning. Not only how music brought us together, but how it saved me at a tender age. I wish I had been able to tell you some of the stories in this memoir before your death.

Fred, you were a *real* person to me. It's important to me that others know that. Lord knows you had your successes and failures like anybody else. But you taught through example not to live down in the *valley of disappointment*. That we all must learn to rise up and start over again. You practiced it and you helped me to practice it, particularly regarding my biological family. You taught me forgiveness and love. For you, forgiveness and love were action verbs, and it was imperative to live their true meaning one day at a time. Because of you, I was able to seek reconciliation with my father, my stepfather, and my mother—even after their deaths.

The most beautiful gift you gave me, however, was to help me accept that there are no accidents and that our unusual friendship was meant to be. You believed in life after death and that when the time came, we'd reunite in some place. I believe this too.

Until we meet again,
François

PART I

Little Buttercup

The Younger Years

WHEN I WAS BORN IN 1945, THE SANDERS-Scarborough clan had lived for several generations in the sprawling, blanched little town of Blackwater, Mississippi, just north of Meridian, in the backwater region near the Okatibbee Reservoir and the Alabama border. If you weren't a cotton farmer, a sharecropper, or a smithy who worked for white folks, there wasn't much for you to do there. Some folks got along raising chickens and guinea fowl; some did light farming but could not prosper. Each year they fell further in debt to the landowner, Ol' Mastuh Sanders.

Twice in our clan's memory, the floods had come in late spring, and no one had been able to plant in time for a summer crop. The seed money was wasted. But most folks stayed on because they didn't have anyplace else to go. It seemed better to be around your own folks—to scratch out a living in the tired earth—than to move to some strange place where folks called you mister and missus and didn't know your nickname, or your granddaddy's name, or how your uncle Jeb had lost one finger in the smithy on Mastuh Sanders's homestead, or even who to call for a county fair game of baseball. New folks wouldn't know nothin' at all about you. That was no way to live, so folks stayed on, hard as it was.

To my great-grandmama, this is what seemed important and what made her call this place home. She was also tired. Laura Mae Sanders Pinman had raised thirteen children of her own and found herself surrounded by grandchildren and great-grandchildren, including my older brother Willie Jr., me, and my twin sisters Betty and Barbara. She raised the children when their mamas couldn't do it. And the children just kept coming. She would cook. She would clean. She would wash and pray. She worked and didn't slow down for old memories to catch her.

The Old Homestead on Mastuh Sanders's land had been falling apart for as long as she could remember. Every shutter was hanging down or gone. The paint she helped apply when she was a young girl had never been refreshed; it was barely visible. If she could ever get the front door of the sagging porch to close, it might help to keep the marsh rats from invading the kitchen on hot summer nights. She was always mindful not to leave food out where they could get it; and she felt constant dread that those rats might crawl into the bedrooms of one of her grandchildren— her grans—and bite one of her darlings. When it rained, every bucket and pot in the house was used to catch water from the leaky roof.

There were many causes for sadness in her life, but the way people tell it, the greatest sadness of all was when her last husband was killed. Noah Leon Pinman could work hard and was good with his hands. He had a quick smile with pretty teeth. He had been her third husband and had stayed around The Homestead the longest.

My own mama, Inez Delois, would sometimes tell me and my brother the story, later on after we had moved up north, to give us an idea of how it was down south in the old days.

The way she told it, everybody knew that Great-Grandmama Laura Mae was Ol' Mastuh Sanders's woman. He came by to see her every week. Noah Leon Pinman knew it too. Even though he had agreed to work the farm for Ol' Mastuh Sanders, he hadn't agreed to anything else. Still, Noah Leon went on about his business farming and, with the help of the kids, year after year, got the planting and harvesting done. There was always some fence that needed mending, or some field that needed watering. He kept the children busy, and they all worked together from sunup to sundown.

Most of the time, Noah Leon just ignored Ol' Mastuh Sanders and his late afternoon visits. Great-Grandmama Laura Mae used to wonder how it was that Noah Leon always seemed to know when Ol' Mastuh Sanders was coming and just disappeared into the fields. She tried to ignore it too. She had been going with Ol' Mastuh Sanders for so long that it just seemed natural to her. She didn't know any other way. Mama Inez said that her grandmama, Lily Mae, had told Laura Mae to go with Ol' Mastuh Sanders when she was a young girl, and it had been that way ever since.

Laura Mae's mama, Lily Mae, had been a slave on the Sanders plantation all her life and had always been "worried" by the white men who came by the place. That's just the way it was, and she was no different from any of the other colored girls around there, even if she had wanted to say something.

One day, Noah Leon asked her to come to town with him and not go with Ol' Mastuh Sanders when he came by. She just looked at him and kept on with her cooking and cleaning.

When Ol' Mastuh Sanders came by the old house that night, Noah Leon stuck around. Laura Mae pulled off her apron and headscarf, wiped her face with her hands, and straightened her simple dress as she had always done when Mastuh Sanders came. She walked slowly out of the house, down the path, and past the barn.

She didn't like leaving and going with Mastuh Sanders, but if she didn't go, she knew they couldn't stay in the Old Homestead any longer. She didn't know where they would go. This place was home. This was the only home she had ever known.

Just past the barn, Mastuh Sanders walked closer and spoke to her as he always did. He asked her how she was feeling and if she was glad to see him. She tried to smile and said yes, as she always did. He told her he had wanted to stop by and see her earlier that week, but his work and family had kept him away. He had been saying that for more than twenty years, and Laura Mae had stopped listening. That night, she was troubled by the pounding of her heart and the sharp voice calling to her from the house. It was Noah Leon, telling her to come back to him and leave Ol' Mastuh Sanders.

Ol' Mastuh Sanders was still talking to her as she tried to block the hurt and anguish of Noah Leon's voice out of her ears. His voice grew louder, and she realized, suddenly, that he was standing close by. She wheeled around and stared at him. Noah Leon had a big chopping cleaver raised over his head, and he was coming toward Ol' Mastuh Sanders.

She screamed as she heard the shots ring out. Noah stood motionless and stunned. Ol' Mastuh Sanders had reached into his overalls pocket, pulled out his pistol, and shot Noah Leon point-blank, three times without stopping.

Everybody knew that he carried that pistol. He sometimes used it on sick livestock and stray rabbits. Didn't Noah Leon know it? Laura Mae never had time to speak, it happened so fast.

Noah Leon was on the ground at her feet, bleeding from his chest and stomach. A crowd quickly gathered around them.

"Stand back!" Ol' Mastuh Sanders barked. "Let him lay

there! Nobody touch him. Let the slimy bastard lay there where he belongs: in the dirt. I never liked him anyway."

They all stood there; nobody moved, not even the babies. They were all afraid of Ol' Mastuh Sanders and knew that he would shoot any one of them just as quick as he had shot Noah Leon. He looked around, and his eyes stopped on Great-Grandmama Laura Mae. She started crying, fell to her knees, and crawled over to Noah Leon's body. Blessedly, he'd died before he hit the ground.

Laura Mae gathered what was left of him and rocked him gently in her arms as she cried and wailed. She rocked him as though he were her baby and he was only asleep. Ol' Mastuh Sanders told everyone to leave him be and to not bury him. Silently, everyone backed away while Ol' Mastuh Sanders stood there over Laura Mae, who was crying and rocking Noah Leon's body. She looked pitiful and helpless, there on her knees, while Noah Leon's blood slowly soaked the front of her dress.

After mumbling something to Laura Mae and getting no response, Ol' Mastuh Sanders just shook his head, turned, and walked away, putting his gun back in his pocket. He walked away without looking back, past the barn and up the path to the Old Homestead. He moved silently around the side, got on his horse, and rode away.

My mother remembered Great-Grandmama Laura Mae sobbing and wailing in the yard for the rest of that evening. She was still there hours later when Aunt Coradelle and Cousin Dina Mae walked over to her, called to her softly, and carried her to the house.

After dark, some of the men went back for Noah Leon's body and carried it into the house. They laid him out and cleaned off the blood. Great-Grandmama Laura Mae insisted on being in charge of everything. She gave him his last bath with love and great patience as she talked to herself and anyone there listening. She kissed his body and rubbed him with Vaseline and the lanolin oil she used for her hair. When they had finished cleaning him and dressed him in overalls, she sat with him all night and continued to talk and sing and pray.

She sat for the rest of the night with one hand holding the Bible in her lap and her other on him. When people began to wake up in the morning, before the rooster crowed, they found her still in silent vigil with her Bible.

She stayed in her trance, weeping quietly, until some of Noah Leon's people arrived from Louisiana. They wanted to take his body back home to be buried, but she wouldn't hear any of it. Finally, she allowed him to be buried on a little hill by the creek. She put up a wooden cross. That way she could see him every day and take food and flowers to his grave. That was the way she wanted it, and no one could change her mind. Noah Leon's people went home without him.

When Ol' Mastuh Sanders came back, weeks, maybe months later, it wasn't to see Great-Grandmama Laura Mae. It was to introduce Mr. Slim Hawkins to everyone as the new overseer for the plantation. That time Great-Grandmama Laura Mae never came out of the house. Ol' Mastuh Sanders waited for her a long time, but she never came out. He stood around his horse and the trough looking and just waiting. After that, he came to the Old Homestead to talk to Slim about the crops and to discuss planting, but he never came to "worry" Great-Grandmama Laura Mae again. Those days were over when Noah Leon died.

Nothing much was ever said of Noah Leon's death. No

questions, no investigations, no detectives, no county sheriffs, no coroner's report, no trial. That's what I remember most about my mother's telling of Great-Grandmama Laura Mae's story. Everybody knew something, and nobody said anything.

How long it took before things returned to normal, nobody knew. It just happened.

Laura Mae's third daughter, my Grandmama Minnie, bore six children: Lula Bea, Abraham, my mother Inez Delois, Catherine, Minnie Laura, and Levi. All these babies were left in the country with their grandmother while Minnie went to town to earn money as a domestic for white folks. Minnie had married Saul Scarborough when she was fifteen, and she bore him those six children before he lost his mind.

When I was a child, Granddaddy Saul did little except sit in the old rocking chair and dip snuff or chew tobacco. He wore the same weathered overalls every single day until he had to get a new pair. By the time I was three years old, he was already using a cane to get around. I remember him telling me that the cane could talk. When we were alone, the cane would tell me fanciful stories of raccoon hunting and catfish fetching down by the creek. Granddaddy Saul's arthritis and rheumatism bothered him most of the time, and he had frequent migraine headaches, but nothing seemed to bother him when we went walking in the woods and that cane was busy talking. As we walked out beyond the hedges and down by the fields, he would hold my hand for a while. Then he would let me hold onto the side of his overalls so I could keep up. He seemed just like everyone else to me; he always seemed fine.

Every morning when I woke up, I'd go looking for him. I'd always find him sitting and rocking by himself or staring off into space or talking with the chickens in the yard. When I found him, I would stand by him and talk to the chickens too. After a time, we would go off walking together.

All the big people who came to the house were bossy to me and said that I was kin to all of them. Even when they came from far away and I didn't know them, they said I had some of their blood. Then they would hug me and kiss me and call me Little Angel and Little Buttercup, as if they knew me. I didn't like that.

If I could find Granddaddy Saul, we would go out walking for a long time. I would stay with him until the big strangers left. When we'd come back, it would be after dark and the dogs would bark and jump up, licking and greeting us. Everybody would fuss at Granddaddy Saul for keeping me away so long. I never complained because he fed me corn bread and sorghum from a can, and we talked to the cane. When I told my brother Willie Jr. that the cane could talk, he said it wasn't true because Granddaddy Saul never asked the cane to talk to him.

At night, while I lay on my pallet, I could hear my Great-Grandmama Laura Mae fussing at him about that talking cane and those tales he told. She said she knew he wasn't telling the truth and shouldn't be fooling me like that. That was when I had the revelation that Granddaddy Saul hadn't told Great-Grandmama Laura Mae or Willie Jr. or my mother that the cane could talk. This was a deep secret between him and me.

Granddaddy Saul taught me that to hear the cane talk, we had to be quiet. Sometimes we were quiet for so long that I fell asleep. Granddaddy Saul would wake me up to tell me that I'd missed the talking. I didn't like it that I had fallen asleep under a shady tree in the midday sun and had missed my important encounter with the talking cane. I would promise Granddaddy Saul and myself that I wouldn't fall asleep again.

When I managed to stay awake, the cane would tell me of clever animals that lived in the woods and outfoxed the old plantation master and ate his chickens. It told me about the deer and the rabbit and the fox, the bear and the coyote, the turtle, and the grasshopper that lived deep in the woods. I'd listen anxiously, hardly blinking my eyes and holding my breath.

Sometimes Granddaddy Saul and I would sing songs with the cane. We'd sing about flying, fishing, marching, and stealing honey from the bees. It never occurred to me that the cane wasn't singing when Granddaddy Saul was singing.

One day when we were out walking and I wanted the cane to talk, we waited a long time. After a while, we sat down by the banks of the Wateechee Creek and continued to wait and listen. Finally, Granddaddy Saul told me to hold the tips of my thumb and index finger together in each hand, close my eyes real tight, and make a wish that the cane would talk to us. I closed my eyes, and slowly the cane began to talk.

It told me of kings and queens who were my oldest kin, peoples in an ancient civilization called *Afrique*. The cane talked about tropical jungle places and described strange, ferocious, growling animals large enough to eat the fox and possum and jackrabbit and deer and me. The cane talked of a great *Afrique* warrior who was strong enough to kill the big animals with a spear and knife. He would skin and cook them over a fire. Then he would eat them and share them with his kinfolk. He wasn't afraid and would protect me from the big animals. The warrior, a mighty leader who was loved by his people, was named Shakti Binge. I told Granddaddy Saul that one day I would take him with me to *Afrique*. He smiled and rubbed my head and said that he would wait.

One day, my mother called me in from chasing the chickens and told me to stay in the house. It had been raining all day, letting up only for brief moments. There was water everywhere, and we all huddled under quilts and kept our socks on to try to stay warm. The rain continued steadily, and the pounding of the water on the roof and the wind battering the side of the house made us look at each other in fear. I stood between Great-Grandmama Laura Mae and Granddaddy Saul. My brother and Mr. Slim Hawkins stood behind Mama Inez and my daddy, Willie Son. Cousin Dina Mae and her four kids and Lula Bea and her six kids were all huddled nearby looking out the window and wondering like the rest of us. It had been raining off and on for well over a week. The rain was affecting everything. Daddy said that the factory didn't have any work for him.

Grandmama Minnie Green arrived home from town soaking wet. I heard her voice before I actually saw her. She said that everybody in town was talking about the rising water and the rain. Her feet were muddy, and she was carrying her shoes. She said that she'd had to walk the last five miles because Ol' Mr. Carmichael was afraid his mules and wagon wouldn't make it through the waterlogged roads. There were snakes everywhere, she said. She was almost bitten when she accidentally stepped on a rattler.

That whole day, the men huddled and smoked, and they checked on the animals in the barn so many times I knew it was a way to get away from the houseful of ladies and kids. They grumbled and hunched over as they walked through the rain, reaching in their pockets for their matches, pipes, tobacco, and snuff. Nobody had a good feeling about this water. The men had to mull over what to do if the rain got worse. There were few choices because there was no higher ground anywhere.

Mr. Elijah Sanders Jr., Ol' Mastuh Sanders's oldest son, who ran the plantation, appeared through the trees, leading his horse and holding his coat tightly to his chest. He was soaked to the bone. He called out to Great-Grandmama Laura Mae and drawled his news, "I reckon we may be movin' up the valley a piece to higher ground if this rain keep comin' up. My ol' missus up the road's been gatherin' everything to move first thing in the mornin' with this water not stoppin'. Y'all best be packin' and gettin' ready. Just don't know what this water's goin' to do."

Great-Grandmama Laura Mae let him know that we all intended to stay—if the house held up. Elijah said he'd be leaving in the morning and bid her goodbye.

Despite the best efforts of Great-Grandmama Laura Mae, her sons and daughters, their sons and daughters, and Mr. Slim Hawkins, the Old Homestead couldn't withstand the heavy downpour. The rains kept coming and the water got higher. By morning, the brick-and-stone supports began to sink and lean. Everybody began to feel unsafe. We gathered all the dry things we could, wrapped food in old sacks and quilts, pulled out small precious things we could carry (like Laura Mae's Bible), and began the long, muddy trek to higher ground. As we walked, we kept looking back at the sagging Old Homestead and wondered when, if ever, we might return. Would the house still be there? Great-Grandmama Laura Mae looked longingly at the knoll where Noah Leon Pinman was buried and tried to hide her tears. Those closest to her knew her anguish at leaving Noah Leon's body behind.

Our progress was slow and slippery. Everybody was soon

soaked and muddy. Snakes and mosquitoes were everywhere, and most of the paths had been washed out. Sagging trees and heavy, hanging branches were strewn along the way. All conversations slowed and finally stopped as we all moved farther and farther away from home, from stability, from our roots. By midday we had covered several miles, but nobody knew where we were. We were lost and confused.

Time and time again, Great-Grandmama Laura Mae would refer to that torturous journey as *The New Flood Days*, and everybody who heard would nod, look at one another, and sigh knowingly. That journey tested us all. The torrential rains kept coming. The clouds of circling, biting mosquitoes; the slithering snakes; and sodden, fallen branches were everywhere.

All through those first awful days, Granddaddy Saul wandered off the path and couldn't keep pace with the group. At first, my cousin Lemiel was told to watch over him. He had to go fetch him from his wandering. But after a time, with all the mosquitoes, snakes, and panicked stray animals, and with more people joining our trek north, it got harder to keep track of Granddaddy Saul. Twice my cousin went looking for him through the crowd, which grew ever bigger, more raggedy, and disorganized. Luckily, my cousin found a local farmer who allowed Granddaddy Saul to ride on the back of his mule-drawn wagon.

But then someone noticed that Saul wasn't riding anymore. What had happened to him? Where had he gone? Nobody knew. We all searched frantically, but there was no trace of him. Later, someone found his cane alongside a gulch. No one was surprised that there was no trace of him in this torrential rain. No footprints, no clothes, no body—nothing. Only his cane, lying there by itself on the stream bank.

When I saw the cane, I knew that something bad had happened to my granddaddy, but nobody told me anything. I cried and screamed until they gave me the cane for comfort. For days I lugged it along with me, urging it to talk, fluctuating between asking it to tell me where my granddaddy was and imploring it to tell me more stories of *Afrique* and the warrior Shakti Binga. I didn't sleep, didn't eat. I was lonely and listless, watching, listening, and waiting.

One night while I was asleep on the march to Alabama, the women in my family banded together and took the cane away from me. "For your own good," they said.

I grew silent. I withdrew. It just wasn't worth trying to talk about it. The loss of my beloved Granddaddy Saul and the magical cane was simply too much for me. Even though I was only four years old, I grieved deeply. I was inconsolable.

Then one day, I began to sing. No one had heard me sing before except my granddaddy. Great-Grandmama Laura Mae, Grandmama Minnie Green, and my mother all looked at me and at each other. I sang the songs I had sung with Granddaddy Saul and the magical cane. I didn't really know what I was singing about or whether my songs made sense to anyone. I sang because it eased my pain. Singing, I found my Little Buttercup self, my center, my home. It was Granddaddy's legacy: I was singing the music he taught me, the music of the cane.

✦

WHILE I WAS GRIEVING FOR MY LOST GRANDDADDY, our group traveled a long way. I had heard the talk. People said *Alabama* enough times that I wondered if it was a new world.

Where and what was *Alabama*? They said I was born in Alabama; we had left when I was too little to know.

I heard my daddy say that he knew people and had a few relatives in the area. He felt that our family could make a fresh start working in the factories and that he could give up farming. Willie Son had a plan for himself and his family.

Some members of the clan knew they weren't going back to Meridian, Mississippi, again anytime soon. There was talk about how bad it had gotten. They'd heard news from the area. The floods were worse than anyone had seen. It seemed we had all been lucky to leave the Old Homestead when we did, lucky to get out with our lives and what few belongings we had. Word among the clan was that the Old Homestead was no longer even there. The relentless rains had washed it from its moorings. They said it seemed like it just floated away. No reason to go back—no love, no land, no house, no loss.

For days the motley, undisciplined caravan continued east until it eventually came to rest at a village called Aliceville. Some wanted to settle there. Others were still eager to move on, maybe north. The Sanders-Scarborough clan decided to meet and talk it over. The rain had stopped. The sun had come out. People hung their wet clothes on dry branches and sat down. The old folks smoked, and everybody relaxed. Everyone knew that we couldn't continue to travel and live a nomadic life much longer. It was beginning to wear all of us down.

My daddy finally spoke up. He had some people in Tuscaloosa who had come up from Mobile and Baton Rouge, and they were now doing very well working in the sawmill and furniture factories of Tuscaloosa and Birmingham. Daddy had been itching to go back there and work and live. He and Mama had lived there when they were first married, but Mama had made him bring her, my brother, and me to Mississippi, to her own people. He wanted to go back to Tuscaloosa. He was sure they could all find work there. He didn't see a future for himself and our family in sharecropping. He wanted to explore something else.

As the family sat around the low, gently snapping campfire every night, everyone was uneasy with the uncertainty they faced. They wrestled for days with the thorny issue of what to do next and how best to do it. Ideas were thrown back and forth for quite some time before they reluctantly consented to give my daddy's idea number one priority. Without exception, they had misgivings about moving to another strange city and attempting to make it home. Some said out loud that they just might be better off staying exactly where they were. However, that idea was soon dismissed. It was finally decided one evening that my daddy, accompanied by Cousin Lemiel and Uncle Josiah, would go to Tuscaloosa.

✦

OUR HOUSE WAS NOISY. I HATED THE NOISE. I USED TO go outside and sing to myself. At first, I sang quietly, but the farther I got from the house, the louder I sang. I sang all the way to Big Mama's, Minnie Green's, house and then she sang with me. In no time, I forgot about the noise in my house and my parents' frequent arguments. I never told Big Mama they were arguing. I knew she wouldn't like it, so I sang and pretended I was happy.

In those days in Tuscaloosa, Big Mama would ask me to sing for anybody who came by the house. When she would take me back home, nobody was arguing, and I could pretend I was happy

again. It was during those times I would think about running
away to Big Mama's house forever. But no matter how much I
sang, she kept taking me back home.

My brother, my sisters, and I were sleeping one morning
when we were suddenly awakened by a horrific scream. I sat up
in my bed and remained perfectly still, listening. The scream
came again and again. It was my mother calling for help. I heard
another heavier, deeper voice yelling something I couldn't quite
make out. It was my daddy. He sounded equally upset and angry.

The loud commotion and the sound of breaking glass terrified me, and I began to cry. Willie Jr. dashed up from the bed
and ran to the bedroom door. The next thing I knew, my cousin
Dina Mae and my aunt Minnie Laura came rushing in. They
scooped my sisters and me up with our blankets still around us,
took Willie Jr. by his hands and shoulders, and rushed us out of
the house. I kept asking what was happening and calling for my
mother. I saw the flashing lights of the police cars and people
beginning to gather in front of my house.

Aunt Minnie Laura and Cousin Dina Mae ran as fast they
could to get us away from the house. We didn't talk until we arrived at the house where Great-Grandmama Laura Mae and the
rest of the Sanders-Scarborough clan were living.

Great-Grandmama Laura Mae finally quieted everyone
down, and Cousin Dina Mae and Aunt Minnie Laura began to
recount what had happened. Over the years, I would hear the
story many times from many mouths; it became part of our family's least favorite memories.

Mama and Daddy, along with several of their kinfolk, had
gone dancing a block or so down the street at a local juke joint
called Joe's Cradle Rocker. The place was crowded, and people

were having fun. One of the locals named Johnny Damon started flirting with my mother and asked her to dance. She declined and told him she was married. At the time, my daddy was at the bar getting something for them to drink. When he came back to the table, Johnny Damon excused himself and said pointedly to my mother that he hoped to see her around. She turned her head and never even answered him, but my daddy was all questions as he sat down again with the drinks. His anger and jealousy couldn't be assuaged by anyone at the table.

Through the excitement of the evening, the incident was soon forgotten by everyone, it seemed, except my daddy. He continued to drink and badger my mother for the rest of the evening.

As they walked home, my mother lingered a little behind everyone else and remained quiet. She had never seen her husband this way. My daddy was light and casual with the boys as he bantered and teased back and forth with everyone on the way home. But once inside the house, he turned into a monster. He slapped her, assaulted her, and accused her of flirting with this strange man whom she had never even seen before. In shock and panic, she begged him not to hurt her and denied his charge of her being a flirt. The slaps and cursing got worse until she fled the house, only to have him follow her and demand that she return to the house and the children. She did, not knowing what would happen to her next.

When she woke up the next morning, he was back at it again. Eventually, out of self-defense, she ran into the kitchen and grabbed one of the carving knives on the countertop. This time when he came after her, she lashed out with the knife and it drew blood. He began to hit her and grabbed her by the hair. She lashed out again with the knife and again drew blood. He screamed and yelled, backing up and knocking over glasses, pots, and pans. She fled from the kitchen with him in pursuit.

This battle continued until several of the neighboring men entered the house and tried to break up the bloody fight. Daddy, in his bloody, frenzied state, refused to stop, and my mother continued to wield the knife. More neighbors arrived, and a few successfully pulled them apart. It was then that Cousin Dina Mae and Aunt Minnie Laura had arrived and rescued my siblings and me. The house was in shambles, with blood everywhere. The police arrived, and efforts to restore calm were finally successful. My daddy would spend several weeks in St. Martin De Porres, the local black hospital, recovering from several serious knife wounds. His chest was covered with stitches; he'd have the scars for the rest of his life.

Mama's features showed the results of Daddy's anger. She had a swollen nose and two black eyes. There were lacerations on her face and hands, and patches of her hair were missing. As if that weren't enough, my mother sank fast and invisibly into a black, surly all-enveloping funk that she would carry with her for the rest of her life. Years later, when I would think about that day and about my mother, I would realize that her heart had been broken and she didn't know how to deal with that—or how to ask anyone to help her deal with it.

In retrospect, I'm also aware that my daddy was incredibly controlling, and he saw my mother as more his chattel than his wife.

After Cousin Dina Mae and Aunt Minnie Laura told this horrific tale, Great-Grandmama Laura Mae became enraged. She went into her bedroom and gathered her gun; she was dressed in a flash. She informed the family that several of them were to accompany her to my mother and daddy's house. She intended to go and get her granddaughter.

When the group arrived at the house, the crowd parted in the face of this formidable feminine energy. Great-Grandmama Laura Mae's presence was foreboding and unfriendly. No one wanted to block her way. She moved through the crowd, up the front porch, through the front door, and into the front room. The sight of my bruised and beaten mother made her cry out sharply in alarm and disbelief. She embraced her grandchild and cursed the forces that had allowed this evil to happen.

She insisted that my mother come immediately with her and never return to this house again. She was taking her beloved grandchild home. Nobody stood in her way as the somber parade moved out the front door and down the street. My great-grandmama's head was held high as she led the procession of her family's clan out of that house of iniquity.

I was sitting on Aunt Emma's front living room floor, rocking and singing to myself, when the group returned to Aunt Emma's house. My brother told me not to be afraid—Mama and Daddy were fighting, but Great-Grandmama Laura Mae would take care of everything. I stared at him and kept singing. *Why were they fighting?* I thought. I watched as they made my mother as comfortable as possible until Aunt Emma picked me up off the floor and began to rock me in her lap. Anxiously, I sucked my thumb and turned my head into her ample bosom. I fell asleep wishing for and calling for Granddaddy Saul. I was looking for the cane and trying to sing. I needed to sing.

It took a while for my mother to recover from the shock and trauma of her ordeal with my daddy. Although she could walk and got dressed every day, she didn't leave the house, and no one insisted that she go out. For some weeks, everything was done for her. Great-Grandmama Laura Mae fussed over her and combed her hair every day and massaged it with healing oil she had made. She held her in her arms often and rubbed her skin and face as she talked to her and told her how beautiful she was. She whispered stories of how she should live her life.

PART II

Youngstown

AFTER THE BRUTAL FIGHT BETWEEN MY PARENTS, Great-Grandmama Laura Mae hatched a plan that she decided to reveal only to the other women in the family.

"I been listening to the radio and prayin' to God and thinking," she said. "I'm tired of these no 'count men, and Willie Son's the wors' of 'em all. My baby Inez is near 'bout well and ready to move on. I been thinkin' about goin' far 'way from here! Maybe, goin' up north somewhere. Tryin' to settle down. Maybe, we could get jobs in one of the factories and work and save some money and build a house for ourselves. We don't need no mens to do that."

Every eye in the room was on her. Everybody was listening, but nobody said a word. Then, just as suddenly, came shock and doubt. Confused questions were thick in the room. They had just gotten to Tuscaloosa, and now Great-Grandmama Laura Mae was talking about going somewhere else? They weren't ready to think about packing up and moving on. They hadn't even settled down here yet. If the suggestion had come from anybody else, they would have all been laughing and howling, holding their sides, covering their mouths, and slapping their thighs in ridicule. But this suggestion had come from our matriarch—leader of the clan herself—and therefore could only be taken very seriously. So, they agreed and began saving up as much money as they could, which Great-Grandmama Laura Mae squirreled away in an old tin can she kept hidden in her room, concealed by layers of clothes and knickknacks.

Time flowed from days to weeks, from weeks to months, and then to the first year. My daddy regretted deeply what he had done. He really did love my mother and wished to be reunited. However, Great-Grandmama Laura Mae prevented him from finding my mother and talking to her at every turn.

In his efforts to woo my mother back to him, daddy gave money for my mother, my brother, and me to my aunts and to the other ladies of the house. He didn't know it, but the money he gave to the ladies wound up in Great-Grandmama Laura Mae's tin can, saved toward their secret trip up north. My daddy didn't know he was helping the plan to be rid of him forever. In his heart, he felt he had changed. He didn't go out much anymore and had practically stopped drinking. He wanted to show my mother that he could be the upright, gentle, loving man she had married.

When the women saved five thousand dollars, they decided it was finally time to announce their plan to the men. It was followed by doubt and shocked silence. The first question was "Where y'all goin' get duh money?"

"We done already saved duh money, from you and you and you and everybody here," announced Great-Grandmama Laura Mae, pointing to everyone in the room and silencing the doubting curious. For most of the men in the room, it wasn't a horrible thing—just not their idea! The men were accustomed to feeling as though they were leading and not being pulled around by their noses. How could all of this "money saving" have gone on without so much as a hint of it to them? It just didn't make sense.

They were prepared, however, to take full advantage of an attractive idea. Many of them had harbored fantasies of going north to get away from the racism oozing out of the schools and businesses. But just as the men were becoming used to the idea and throwing suggestions back and forth, someone asked, "Where Willie Jr. and Little Buttercup?"

The entire assemblage fell silent. All eyes were on Great-Grandmama. Something was definitely wrong. My cousin Cindy Lou spoke up.

"Willie Son was here. He took them home, he said. He said to tell Aunt Inez he wanted to talk to her and to come home and tend to them if she wants to."

My mother gave out a shrill cry and collapsed, sobbing, "Bring my babies back. I want my babies! God have mercy and don't let him hurt my babies. Somebody help me to get my babies back!" She got up and lunged for the door. Some of the men restrained her and told her they were going to my daddy's house to get us back.

Several possible plans of action were being entertained and debated when Great-Grandmama Laura Mae came out of her room. No one had really noticed when she left the front room to go to her room and get her pistol. She emerged and said, "I'm goin' to get my great-grandbabies. I'll be back." Of course, the rest of the family followed her down the street.

As they approached my old home, everyone could see my daddy standing at the top of the porch looking at them defiantly. He was holding my brother and me, restraining us from running to jump into my mother's arms.

"Give me my babies," my mother screamed. "Please don't hurt my babies. I'll do anything you want, just let my babies go!"

"I want you to come home and be my wife again, Inez. I love you very much, and I'm sorry for what I did. Cain't you give me another chance?" Willie Son pleaded.

"You done had plenty enough chance," Great-Grandmama Laura Mae responded. "I'm not goin' to let you do to my grandchile what you did before. Let my great-grandbabies come home now. I'm not goin' to play with you, Willie Son. If'n you don' let my babies go, Willie Son, I'm goin' to shoot you."

"Aw, shut up, you meddlin' ol' lady. Why don't you mind your own business and leave my wife to me?" my daddy said.

"If'n you had treated Inez like a wife, she would still be with you. But you forgot who you were—just a man—and had to attack my baby for some stupid jealousy. I'm not going to stand for it. If'n you don't let my great-grandbabies go, I'm goin' to kill you, Willie Son, and I mean it. Let those babies go!" She was furious.

Then Great-Grandmama Laura Mae reached for her pistol and the crowd fell away. She aimed and shot one round that hit my daddy square in his shoulder, and he collapsed on the porch, releasing my brother and me.

Great-Grandmama Laura Mae walked slowly up the steps, her gun pointed at him the whole time. She looked at him and said, "I'm not goin' kill ya, 'cause you my babies' daddy, but I want you to know dat if you ever come 'round my house again and messes wid my babies, I'll kill ya. I'm bound on dat and ya haves my word."

Great-Grandmama Laura Mae stared at the wounded Willie Son and turned away. She put her pistol back in her bosom and descended the stairs.

A siren could be heard in the distance. Someone had reported the shooting. In just a short while, my daddy would be recuperating in the same hospital as a year ago, looking at the same four walls and asking himself the same question, "Why me, O Lord?"

◆

THE NEXT DAY, GREAT-GRANDMAMA LAURA MAE SENT the men to purchase tickets for the first contingent to take the train to Ohio. That group was to include my mother, my brother, my little sisters, and me. We were to leave immediately. Great-Grandmama would come along later, she said.

In Youngstown, Ohio, the cars were faster, and the noise was louder. There were a lot more people around, and I wasn't allowed to go out alone. I was enrolled in kindergarten. I didn't have any friends, nor was I looking for any. At school, they didn't think I could talk, or at least, not well. I chose to be silent. I had my own world of rules and regulations: success with no failure. In my mind, I spent my time with Granddaddy Saul, singing and minding his cane and letting the world go by. I moved away from the pain I carried from Alabama—the violence and the hurt.

◆

I HAD BEEN SHELTERED ALL MY LIFE AND WARNED TO BE wary of strangers. Now the rules were different. My daddy had been considered a friend, indeed, an intimate family member. He was someone I knew, yet he had proven to be very dangerous. I now had recurring nightmares of my parents fighting. My dreams conjured up the dangerous kitchen knife that my mother used in her fight against my daddy, and gradually it took on a life of its own. The knife would fly through the air, and the rising blood would be everywhere, threatening to drown me. I would wake up in a cold sweat, struggling to breathe. Sometimes my mother would wake me up and sit with me to hold and calm me. She said that I was howling and singing "nonsense songs," thrashing about. Because of those dreams and memories, even to this day, I'm wary of knives. As a child, I would insist on breaking my food into pieces with my hands, or with a fork, but never with a knife. My mother knew why and didn't insist. Sometimes she would cut up my food for me. Some people thought she was spoiling me. But she and I both knew that she was making it possible for me to relax and behave in a normal way. When I had to do chores, like cleaning up the kitchen, she would always wash the knives herself. I was in my late teens before I reached a point where I could peel potatoes and cut up vegetables without starting to shake. Today, it would be called PTSD, but back then it had no name—it was just something I had to manage and overcome.

✦

DESPITE MY ROUGH BEGINNINGS, YOUNGSTOWN—A bustling, dirty steel town of 150,000 people—started to feel like home fairly quickly. The streets were a combination of cobblestone and pavement, generally well kept. Streetlights worked, and the garbage was picked up regularly. It was easy to find out which neighborhoods were safe for a black boy at night. I knew exactly which churches welcomed me and my music. Even the movie theaters had a section for black people upstairs and white people downstairs. Though this was supposed to be the North, I learned about racial segregation well above the Mason-Dixon Line. One of the black neighborhoods in Youngstown was called The Bottom, and it went under the Oak Street Bridge as far as the East Side, on past McGuffey Boulevard. If I stayed in those areas, I was safe. We eventually wound up on Meadow Street, which was centrally located in The Bottom. There were lots of other kids to play with and a playground nearby where end-of-summer concerts were hosted. Even at my tender age, I was given a prominent part and sang and danced in all of them.

✦

IF THINGS HAD CONTINUED LIKE THAT, I PROBABLY would have been a very happy preteen, but my mother met and started dating Warren Boswell. His effect on all of us was noticeable immediately. I wish I could say that he was ugly and old, and loud and raucous. He was none of these things. He was an introvert, whose worst qualities came out when he drank too much, which, unfortunately, was too often. He was what you call an ugly drunk. When he was sober, you hardly knew he was in the house, except that he played a harmonica. You could hear it all over the house, gently playing what to me sounded like country and western tunes. He was not a well-educated man, but he took pride in reading the newspaper daily and watching the news on television every evening. Right from the beginning, my mother spent a lot of time doting on him: cooking for him, dressing him, and kissing him.

He was of average height, with black wavy hair and about my complexion. In many ways, he looked just like Daddy. We had such high hopes and expected him to be the presence that our real father never was. But we had one idea, and my mother had another. Looking back, I think she was trying to make up for the loss of my daddy. With him, her dreams had never come true. Maybe she would have a second chance with this man, who eventually became my stepfather.

Before long, my mother announced she was pregnant with my baby sister, Lawanna, and that Warren was going to come and live with us. I was jealous. Nobody had asked me how I felt about him. Nobody had asked me if she should marry him or get pregnant. It was all stated as a fact. I probably would have been fine with the whole thing, but nobody had asked. My mother started spending more and more time with Warren and excluding us kids. It was easy to conclude that we would be left out as long as he was around.

I began to look for activities away from home. I sang all over the neighborhood for civic organizations, ladies' groups, luncheon clubs, Kiwanis meetings, and even schools. The bonus was that some of them paid me, and I enjoyed my independence.

In the same way, I began to enjoy school. I decided to interact with the teacher and other children. Maybe I would have fun if I entered into the day-to-day business of the classroom instead of constantly retreating into my world with Granddaddy Saul and the cane.

But I thought about my Great-Grandmama Laura Mae almost every day. I also thought about my aunts and uncles and cousins, and especially about my Aunt Emma. Mama said she was sick. She and Great-Grandmama Laura Mae would be along later. I didn't ever think about my daddy. I didn't miss him. Mama told me he was trying to find us, and if he did, we'd have to move again. I hoped he'd never find us.

✦

MY COUSINS BELONGED TO THE MT. CARMEL BAPTIST Church on Oak Street, and we soon became regular members there too. In the early days, I met two of the most important musical influences in my young life there: Mrs. Jonathan Butler and Reverend Obadiah Rhodes. Mrs. Butler was the superintendent of the Sunday school and sang alto in the regular church choir. She loved my baby voice and encouraged me to sing from a tender age. She coached me on the hymns and spirituals and would sing them with me often. At home, Mama would encourage our singing for the Lord, and we would all join in. Poor Willie Jr. couldn't carry a tune in a bucket with a lid on it! But he loved singing as much as I did, and nobody had the heart to tell him he couldn't stay on key.

My family was a traditional Baptist, God-fearing one. And even before I truly understood what *homosexuality* meant, it was drilled into my brain that those men were *wrong* in the eyes of God.

One Saturday morning, my mother told us to wash up and dress in our Sunday best. My cousin Johnny Mae was getting married at Mt. Carmel. I'd never been to a wedding before. Everyone was excited, and the music was great. We sang along, and I enjoyed the steady parade of familiar faces marching down the center aisle to their seats, everyone dressed up in their finest outfits. Even people who didn't go to our church were there.

When I saw Johnny Mae coming down that aisle all dressed in white, my heart nearly stopped! I thought she was the most beautiful woman in the whole world. Even though I was only five years old, I knew that one day I would wear one of those dresses and look just as beautiful as my cousin. Later, when I told my mother my idea, she slapped me on the behind and told me not to be silly. "Boys don't wear wedding gowns," she said, and rolled her eyes at me. I tried not to show how disappointed I was and kept asking if I could be an exception. But she emphatically refused. She and the church found my deepest desires to be unacceptable.

Still, I found solace in the church. As I got older, I took on more and more responsibilities. I eventually became the choir director. By the time I was twelve, I had learned to read music at the Christ Mission after-school program. Rev. Obadiah Rhodes, our pastor, loved my singing. I seemed to have a gift for pleasing him and most of the ladies of the church. When I sang a solo, which was often, women and men alike would shout and throw canes, fans, hats, and purses around. People attributed all kinds of spiritual anointments and God-given gifts to my ability to deliver a song. I was singing for the Lord!

Knowing that "the hand of the Lord was upon" me made all the difference in the world to me. This knowledge gave me a power of concentration and single-mindedness that has stayed with me all my life.

✦

THROUGHOUT GRADE SCHOOL, I WAS ENCOURAGED BY my teachers and given lots of extra attention. I gained confidence musically, and my grades were pretty high. I not only got along with the other students, but also at some point I realized that I was, indeed, popular *and* a teacher's pet. It seemed they doted on the one that needed the most help and encouragement. I was teased a lot for that.

I recognized that some of the kids were jealous of my special status, so I always downplayed it. I even downplayed it with my siblings. I continued to work hard, but I stopped telling my friends how I did on exams, and I never showed off a high mark on returned papers. I sang as best I could, and I studied often. I became adept at avoiding any confrontations.

From grade to grade, I grew in confidence and performance. I never let myself say that I was special, but I knew that I was. If I had been a weaker person, my stepfather's growing anger would have turned me around, but the more he drank and the meaner he was, the stronger I became.

My mother seemed to ignore all of it, as though it wasn't happening. The first time he reached out and struck me, everything stopped. He said I had a "smart mouth." I said I was just telling him the truth. The second time, he knocked me down. It only took me a second for me to realize that telling the truth was dangerous. My mother always sided with Warren and further solidified his superior status in our home. It goes without saying that things were never the same again between us after that.

Warren's continued cruelty was a major factor in my decision to spend as much time away from home as possible. Nobody seemed to notice that I was staying after school with the choir director more and more. I learned every song from memory that my junior high music teacher would give me, and I started playing the clarinet. I started behaving one way at home and completely differently in school. I was so outgoing in school, it was maddening. At home, I fell into such a silence that often nobody knew I was around. I hid behind books: classics, poetry, romantic Western novels, *Rin Tin Tin*, other dog stories, and *The Adventures of Huckleberry Finn*. The local librarian became my best friend. Often, she suggested new books that I should read.

All of this was superseded by my study of the Bible. I quietly searched for some saving force that could take my stepfather out of my life. I leaned heavily on the Old Testament and the fire-and-brimstone God who had rescued Israel from Egypt. People saw me reading the Bible all the time, but seldom did they ask me specifically what I was reading. I struggled with the knowledge that I had grown to hate my stepfather, but I figured God would forgive me because I had given my heart and my talent to singing sacred Christian songs in praise of Jehovah and Jesus Christ. Nobody was perfect.

Even though I carried a copy of the Bible small enough to fit into my book bag, I wasn't thinking about the Bible all the time. Sometimes I would surprise myself when I realized I was thinking about boys. Nobody ever mentioned anything about being gay or straight, but I did hear sermons from time to time that laid out, in detail, what the preacher would call an *abomination* in Sodom and Gomorrah—men sleeping with men.

I wondered over and over if this warm feeling in the pit of my stomach for one of my buddies was sinful. I dared to bring the subject up several times with a couple of my friends, who quickly told me to put it out of my mind. It was not a subject that was supposed to be discussed, even among friends. Well then, whom *was* I supposed to discuss it with? I already knew that I could not divulge this secret to my brother and sisters. So, I prayed and kept this *warmth* to myself.

✦

I DIDN'T NEED A HIGH IQ TO NOTICE THAT MOST OF THE students in my class at Hayes Junior High School were white or Jewish even though the school was supposed to be integrated. Of the 1,300 or so students, ethnic groups were all about evenly divided: one-third white, one-third Jewish, and one-third black. I later learned that the school system utilized a track system, which was based partially on race and family economics. All the students in my class were white. All thirty-three, except for me. I was in the second track most of the time. Sometimes I was in the first track. In my view, it was unfair, and I often wondered how the officials in the public school system could justify their decision to segregate most of the black students.

This kind of subtle, systematic racism continued through junior high school and into high school. Because of my love of music, I continued to play in the band and sing in the choir. When my voice began to change, the kind junior high school music teacher, Miss Williams, insisted that I attend choir anyway and learn all the music until I could sing with the group again. Eventually, I went from boy alto to young tenor. I was hoarse a lot, but the period didn't last very long. In addition to singing in school, I also sang on variety shows and in talent contests and earned the nicknames Blue Bird and Moon River.

Without my parents' knowledge, I helped to start a rock 'n' roll singing group of six guys called The Jokers. We would practice on the walk home from Hayes Junior High or when we got to my friend Hiawatha's house. His parents didn't mind our singing at all. Our group only lasted three years, but it was one of the most fun things I've ever done. I became more aware of the songs of Ray Charles, Frankie Lymon, Little Anthony and the Imperials, The Coasters, Sam Cooke, and many others.

Hiawatha was dark, handsome, and six feet tall even in junior high. I felt he had a sweet baritone voice and even sweeter lips. I could have sung with him forever. He had a good sense of rhythm, as we used to make up routines like The Temptations or

Gladys Knight & The Pips. We'd move the furniture around his room so we could master the routines easier, and we'd sit in his room and listen for hours while his mother cleaned the house or cooked dinner. His daddy was a bus driver, and sometimes I'd run into him when I rode the Elm Street bus.

All of us guys would imitate the records. We'd put on a record and pretend we had microphones, or tie our heads up in do-rags, and move around like the Edsels or The Coasters or Little Anthony and The Imperials. I used to pretend that I was the lead singer. I wasn't surprised that I could do it.

Sometimes it was just Hiawatha and me, and I'd put on Dinah Washington or Etta James and sing just like them. Hiawatha loved it when I acted like Dinah Washington or Ruth Brown. He'd laugh real nice and say, "Stop it! Stop it! Stop it!" and then he'd smile some more and say, "Do it again!" And I would.

Hiawatha was an only child, and his parents doted on him. They were always telling him that he was special, "even though he was black." I used to listen to the way they talked to him and silently wished that my mother and stepfather would talk to me the same way. After a while, I realized that even though he was a really good singer, he was not very bright in school. In fact, he was worse academically than my brother, so I often helped him with his homework. He had terrible handwriting; I helped him with that. In a short time, his grades improved, and he began to enjoy studying. Partly because of that, his parents welcomed me into their home often.

In Hiawatha's room, as we sat or lay close on the bed, I'd imitate Ray Charles and Frankie Lymon. He'd sing lead on The Drifters' songs or on The Coasters' songs. We harmonized easily. He had a rich, low voice already, and I still sang high.

During those times, I realized that while I was singing like Dinah Washington or Ruth Brown, I was feeling very easy and "natural," like my mother or any woman. I didn't pretend I liked any girls, and I didn't want to hug or kiss any girls. I imagined myself walking "down the aisle of love" in my wedding dress, like my cousin, Johnny Mae. I was feeling really happy. When I sang then, I knew that my songs had feelings and not just pretend emotions. I was, for those few sweet moments, Mary Wells with her two lovers, like The Marvelettes, asking Mr. Postman for "a letter for me." Those were the kind of songs I could sing when I was walking home by myself or in my room with the door closed and nobody told me to act "regular" or not to act "like a girl!"

When Dinah Washington and Brook Benton came out with their famous duets, like "Baby, You've Got What It Takes," and "A Rockin' Good Way," I, of course, sang Dinah's part and Hiawatha sang Brook's part. It seemed as natural as anything to me. I knew right away that all of this was very different from church. Singing with Hiawatha made me feel sexy, and I sometimes looked longingly at him and wondered *what if* we could hold each other like Brook and Dinah did? What if we could kiss sometime like in the movies? But nothing ever happened, even when I slept over and we were in the same bed. He was warm and comforting next to me, but he always turned his back to me and went to sleep.

More and more, I became aware that this music and the closeness of my buddy was *sexy*. Rock 'n' roll was *sexy*. At first, I thought everyone felt the way I did. One day while singing and feeling sexy, I pulled him close to me and rubbed our crotches together. I pretended that we were grinding. I'd seen other guys do this with girls during the slow dances at socials. But Hiawatha let me know that grinding was really reserved only for "chicks." There were certain things we fellas could discuss, but we really wanted to get the girls alone to grind and do the rest. I didn't know what "the rest" was, but he talked about it so matter-of-factly that I pretended I did. I wanted to continue to be able to be close to him.

Hiawatha seemed to say all the right things about what men felt and what I was supposed to be happily learning to do. I just couldn't tell him that I was far more interested in *him* than any of my girl friends. I never wanted to call girls up and whisper to them on the phone or hang out with them and sing. I much preferred the two of us alone. But he was constantly reminding me that our singing was to attract the girls. He said that women would love us for being able to sing and look cool. He also said it would make me popular with the boys because they would be jealous of the way the girls felt about us. I thought about that for a long time.

"Singing can do all that?" I asked.

"Sure, man," he answered confidently. "You can have a different girl every night."

He silenced me with his enthusiasm. I couldn't possibly explain to him how little his proposal interested me. Never could I imagine spending the night with many different women. I'd be satisfied with one handsome guy like him. He was tall and dark and moved with a confidence that I found very attractive. I didn't need any women in my life as long as I could hang out with him every night. I kept singing, but it was clear to me that we were singing for very different reasons.

◆

By the time I was sixteen, I had learned to tamp down my feelings for the same sex, but I was still making discoveries of a different nature: a whole new fascinating, musical world I'd never even known existed. I loved pop music, but for a long time, I didn't tell my mother or any church members because I felt that they would scold me and object. One day, some of the parents of my fellow singers went to my mother and begged her to permit me to sing pop music publicly with The Jokers. They were obviously persuasive because she didn't explode or try to punish me. I was greatly relieved when she finally agreed.

During that time, I started to fully appreciate everything from Motown to gospel to traditional spirituals and hymns. All of us in The Jokers were black: we were the Motown crowd, and I sang the high parts, of course. The Jokers played a couple gigs out together, and sometimes we would even make five dollars per person, per gig. But it was mostly just some of my buddies hanging out and having fun. We even bought red matching outfits to sing together in! But I had to leave my clothes at Hiawatha's house because I didn't want my family to know I bought them, and I certainly didn't want them to see me in them. I knew they would tease me mercilessly.

Additionally, I gradually let it be known to the church ladies that I was interested in singing secular classical music, and not just fundamentalist Christian music. Ironically, these same grand old church ladies stepped in to help me out on other occasions. They even gently urged my mother to let me go to Stambaugh Auditorium to hear a recital by the famed mezzo-soprano Betty Allen, who was from the Youngstown area. She sang exquisitely, and my fate was sealed.

Betty sang loudly, without a microphone. I could hear her voice everywhere—in front of me and in back of me. I knew that my voice, even when I sang like a woman, sounded nothing like that. But the vibrations through my body thrilled me. You could have exploded dynamite in that seat, and I would not have moved for the rest of the concert. I didn't even venture out of the auditorium during intermission. I decided that one day I was going to sing at Stambaugh Auditorium, and I wouldn't use a microphone either.

After the concert, I was lucky enough to get a backstage introduction by Mrs. Gamble, one of the sorority ladies.

In every way, Betty Allen was bigger than life. I shall never forget the smooth brown powder makeup on her face and the rouge on her cheeks. She also had two pretty red combs in her full head of hair, one on each side near her ears. When she extended her hand to me, I saw her bright red polished fingernails. They were so long! I was swallowed up in her big smile.

Mrs. Gamble introduced me, saying, "This is our little François. He's in high school and wants to be a singer like you."

"Well, what do you sing, young man?" she asked.

"I sing spirituals like you." I didn't dare say more.

"Well, I'm sure you sing them very well. Keep up the good work, young man. I'll be looking out for you now." She was holding my hand the whole time! Finally, I was able to ask her for her autograph. She signed my program, *To François, the young singer from Youngstown, my hometown. See you in New York.*

I will never forget the kind, encouraging things she said to me. For the rest of my life, I hung on to the special words uttered to me by a total stranger at an important time during my development. Years later, I was able to connect with Betty Allen in New York City, and she proved to still be just as generous and supportive. She was very instrumental in bringing many black singers from all over the boroughs of New York City together to rehearse at the Harlem School of the Arts. Later, we were transported en masse to Berlin, Germany, to sing at the Theater des Westens in the history-making, all-black, complete version of George Gershwin's stunning production *Porgy and Bess*, as directed by Götz Friedrich.

✦

AS TIME WENT ON, I SAW WHAT I WAS BEING TAUGHT IN church and frequently in school were not enough to fully satisfy the growing artist deep inside of me. I wanted more than the vocational life frequently pushed toward me, or the church singing my mother wanted for me. There was something powerful and real outside of Youngstown, and I was going to get at it. Maybe my family, my church, and my school weren't going to help me get it, but I'd find a way. So help me God, if I had to leave walking, I was going to leave Youngstown.

By this time, it was very clear that Aunt Emma and Great-Grandmama Laura Mae were not going to come to the city to live. Aunt Emma had cancer, and Great-Grandmama Laura Mae had stayed down south to take care of her. I was disappointed, but I didn't feel I could do anything to change it, so I kept singing. Anytime I felt deep disappointment or hurt, I moved even more deeply into my music. Every opportunity I saw, I got out of the house to sing.

I still had a couple of years left to go before I could graduate high school, so I tried to make the best of it.

One of my buddies from the school choir, Mickey Wol-
sonovich, had a rough second-tenor voice that helped carry the
section for the weaker guys. We tenors could be a tight-knit
group as we struggled together to sing high notes, learn the new
music, and hold our own with the rest of the sections. We used
to hang out at Mickey's house all the time—it didn't matter that
I was the only black kid.

One day Mickey had to go to the Ukrainian Orthodox church
to be altar boy for an hour during mass. He invited us to come
along. None of us were Catholic, but we all felt that it would be
okay to just sit in the pews and wait for him to finish. When we
arrived at the church, everyone headed for the rear pews to sit
and wait. One of the priests came over to us and asked why we
were there. He seemed to be speaking directly to me.

"We're friends of Mickey's and we're going to wait for him to
finish so we can all sing together," we all said.

The priest looked directly at me and said, "You don't belong
here. Why don't you go home or wait outside?"

I didn't know what to say. I sat there as he stared, waiting for
me to move. I looked at the others, and none of them would let
their eyes meet mine. Slowly, I got up, practically in tears, and
shuffled reluctantly for the nearest exit. No one else moved. I
knew exactly what that priest had meant. That's the way it was
in Youngstown. Nobody had been so direct before, but I knew
my place and didn't try to fight it. I never set foot in that church
again.

I went on home and didn't mention to anyone what had happened to me. I knew my mother or stepfather couldn't do anything, so why make a fuss? I just tried to wipe it out of my mind
and get on with my life.

But I had trouble talking and singing with the guys the next time I saw them in school. I knew that they had let me down, and they knew it too. I moved my seat in choir and only spoke to them when I had to. Regardless of what they were thinking, they never mentioned the incident again. I never forgot it. We hit a racial divide that was too painful for me to renegotiate. They were part of the white world, and I was part of the black world. In spite of what some of my other close white friends did or said, I always knew what could happen if I was in the wrong place at the wrong time, and so I carried a wariness inside of me that they did not.

I wasn't wrong. When I was a junior it happened again—this time with my buddy Albert. Albert was in the bass section in the choir, and we enjoyed harmonizing together from time to time. One Friday night, Albert mentioned that there was a party at the VFW out on Midlothian Boulevard.

"Have you ever been there?" he asked.

I hadn't ever heard of it. Albert described it as a big crowd of people from all over—maybe some students from school—with beers and dancing: a lot of fun.

That sounded fine to me, so I agreed. There was a huge parking lot surrounding the VFW, already half full. The action was coming from a dilapidated old two-story brick building.

We parked a little way away and headed for the entrance. We walked in rhythm to the deep *thump, thump, thump* coming from inside that got louder as we neared the entrance.

When we got to the door, Albert knocked. The bouncer opened the door a crack and looked at us. I could smell the cigarette smoke and feel the visceral rush of the music as the vibrations shook the building. The sound was vintage Little Richard.

"How much is it to get in tonight?" Albert yelled, cupping his hands over his mouth.

"Five bucks for you," yelled back the bouncer, "but your buddy can't come in. Tell him to come back on Wednesday, Nigger Night!" His voice was harsh as he directed his refusal toward me. Someone from inside, a guy about thirty wearing tight jeans, came over and looked over the bouncer's shoulder. He joined in the bouncer's explanation.

"Yeah, nigger boy, this ain't Nigger Night. Check with your people and come back then. There's no niggers allowed here tonight!"

By his body language, I could tell that he wasn't even talking directly to me. He was yelling to Albert to tell me, as though I couldn't hear or understand the meaning of his words because of all the noise. It had never occurred to me or to Albert that blacks and whites didn't go to the VFW on the same nights. We stood there dumbfounded. I could tell that Albert wanted to go in. He had been planning on it for several days. I didn't want to spoil it for him.

"Look, Albert," I said, "why don't you take me home, and you can come on back and do your thing. I don't need to go in there tonight." I was already headed back for the car. It was too far to walk home, or I'd have offered to let Albert stay and gone home alone.

When Albert caught up with me in the parking lot, he was all apologies.

"I'm really sorry about this, man," he said. He was earnest. "I didn't know. Let's get out of here. We can head back to my place. I didn't want to go there anyway."

We sat in silence in the car. I didn't feel that it was Albert's fault, but he was white. I was sure that nothing like this had ever happened to him before. He said as much.

I knew that it wasn't just the VFW that discriminated against blacks. I heard the older folks talking, and I knew that it could happen all over town. It could happen in any white church, at my school, at certain community functions—like plays where blacks didn't audition because we knew we'd never be cast as anything except a maid or shoeshine boy. We also didn't go to the Northside swimming pool or the downtown YMCA. There were neighborhoods that were traditionally white and others that were all black. This brand of racism was not new to me. It was found all over the city, all over the state and country. One just swallowed and moved on.

Although Albert protested, I insisted that he take me home. As I got out of the car, he yelled, "Hey, man, I'll see you on Monday, okay?"

"Yeah, see you on Monday," I answered, desolate. As I walked into the house and up to my room, I knew that I was somehow a second-class citizen. He was my buddy, but he wasn't able to do anything about what had happened. This knowledge caused me to feel rage, a very different kind of rage than when I was angry with my parents. I was enraged enough to not want to live in the United States, to want to get away from it all. I didn't want any white friends. I wondered how I could manage that and finish my education. If I kept thinking about what had just happened, I wouldn't be able to work or practice or sleep. It was paralyzing.

I sat down, but I couldn't pray. I was mad at God too. My eyes glanced around my bedroom and rested on an old clarinet that I hadn't played for a while. I picked it up to try to forget what had just happened. After a few lame phrases, I heard banging on the ceiling downstairs and my stepfather's irate voice yelling at me.

"Stop that damned noise! It was nice and peaceful around here till you got back and started your noise. Stop that noise before I come up there and shove that damned clarinet down your throat."

Now my rage had a more immediate and visible enemy. I could hate him and know that one day I would do something about it. I was going to leave this tormentor and his house—this whole stupid town—and go as far as I could go. It was a bit more difficult for me to leave this country. That I'd have to work on, but I could distance myself from Warren.

Nothing like what had happened that night ever happened when I was with my black buddies. We just knew where to go and where not to go. We knew that we weren't going to change Youngstown, and we weren't trying. We wanted to be survivors. That meant not rocking the boat.

Back in school, Albert handled things very differently than Mickey. He kept referring to the incident and mentioned that he had told his parents.

"Would you come over and talk with Mom and Dad about it? I want them to know what happened. I'm not going to the VFW again. They're dead set against it. They made me promise. I wish you'd come over and talk with them sometime." He was serious.

I wanted to talk with them, but I felt that the real issue was talking to the actual racists who ran the VFW. Somebody should talk to *them*.

✦

My TICKET OUT OF YOUNGSTOWN APPEARED IN THE form of two unlikely people: Ms. Mary Lou Phillips and Professor Ron Gould. Mary Lou Phillips first met our family through Warren's mother, who needed to get approval for social security. (*Aid for the Aged* is what it was called in Ohio at the time.) Mary Lou came to the house to interview Warren and my mother to find out as much info as she could to qualify Warren's mother for Aid for the Aged. During one of Mary Lou's home visits, I came home from school and my mother introduced me as "my son François, who sings." She asked Mary Lou if she would like to hear a song. I certainly wasn't shy about singing, so I ended up singing a few songs for her right there in the living room. Mary Lou was impressed, and immediately suggested that I meet the organist-choirmaster from St. John's Episcopal Church, Ron Gould, and maybe take some voice lessons with him.

I waited to take my cue from my mother. This singing was not for the Baptist church, and I could just hear her saying "No!" Well, she surprised me and said I should do it if I really wanted to. The deal was set, and Mary Lou promised to be in touch with me soon to confirm a starting date. I was a bit suspicious of this white church, St. John's, but I was willing to give it a try. I wanted to learn to sing better.

My life changed drastically from the moment I met Professor Gould of Youngstown State University and St. John's Episcopal Church. Neither he nor Mary Lou were much older than I was, but their experience and world outlook was so vastly different from mine that sometimes I felt I was trying to communicate with aliens. They were both white and probably had never been discriminated against because of their color. I wondered if either of them could ever understand how wounded I'd felt at the VFW and the Ukrainian Catholic church.

I trusted them, but at the same time, I didn't trust them because we were so different. Yet, we shared so much through our love of music and the arts that I felt charmed and even entranced at times. It started out very professionally on a weekly basis, with Mary Lou paying for my voice lessons with Ron.

On Wednesdays, I was allowed to leave half an hour early from school and take my voice lesson at the church with Ron. He was a wonderful coach who taught me how to sing my first Schubert, Bach, Handel's *Messiah*, etc. Eventually Ron and his wife, Marsha, started inviting me to come home after the lesson for dinner. They didn't have children and served as a combination of big brother, sister, and parents for me. They lived within walking distance to my house, and Mary Lou didn't live far either. I could always go over to their houses to get away from fighting at my own home. They provided a sanctuary.

Within several months, my lessons increased in frequency to several times a week after school and sometimes on weekends, depending on my school studies and activities. Even though I grew up in the black Baptist Church, I reluctantly gave up conducting my Baptist church choir at Mt. Carmel and began singing in Ron's Episcopal church choir. I explained that I was leaving simply because I needed the money, and Mt. Carmel couldn't provide a weekly salary. My parents would never give me an allowance, so I had to earn my own money. Meanwhile, St. John's hired me as their tenor soloist and paid me twenty-five dollars per Sunday, no small chunk of change in those days. It paid very well for a high school student.

Ron and Mary Lou's influence gradually replaced the home

and church life I had grown up with. Ron seemed to be an expert on Italian, German, and French vocal music, especially for the tenor voice. Although I was studying Latin in school and was going to study French later, I didn't have a clue about how to sing any German, French, or Italian language songs. Mary Lou was an encyclopedia about popular performances, performers, and musical theater. Sometimes when the three of us were together, I spent the whole time listening and trying to figure out exactly what they were talking about. I would come away from our sessions feeling ecstatic and "high." Fortunately, they were natural teachers and spent hours and hours explaining to me America's musical traditions and our relationship to world music. Mary Lou especially loved reggae and jazz.

She was the first person to explain to me that American Negro spirituals were the foundation of all American music. It took a while for that to sink in. I had never heard that the slaves did anything of significance except work themselves to death on the plantations in the South and in white folks' homes in the northern states. *How could they have known anything about music?* I wondered.

"Slave songs were work songs, because the slaves were required to sing while they worked. They turned this horrible condition into a great song repertoire," Mary Lou explained. "I hope you'll always sing these songs, which you already sing so well. One day you'll do many concerts like Roland Hayes or Paul Robeson. Except I'm hoping you'll be able to do more in opera too. I think you have the flare for drama. You just need the right training."

Ron agreed. "We'll work on that more and more in the oratorios. That'll prepare you to do lots in opera. You must learn to let your voice teach you. I'll help you to listen to yourself. You mustn't sing heavy arias for your lyric tenor while you're young and still developing. I intend to start you with Handel's *Messiah* and eventually get to Bach's wonderful *Passions*. I'll see to it that you're ready before you go away to college."

This kind of talk exhilarated me.

In a town like Youngstown, blacks and whites did not traditionally mix like this. We were becoming friends, though I was still suspicious and sometimes fearful. I was afraid that they would eventually stop talking to me and reject me because of my skin color. How could these white people know so much about black music and black people? Why were they so eager to share this treasured knowledge with me? Nobody had ever spent so much time on my education. Certainly not my parents.

I gained a new level of confidence and polish under Ron's tutelage and nurturance. He paid a lot of attention to detail and wouldn't let me get away with any sloppiness. We would repeat a phrase a hundred times until he was satisfied that I was doing it correctly with the right color and inflections to the words. In many ways it wasn't hard for me. I had youth and stamina on my side. I worked until he said it was enough. I never complained, and he never gave up—it was his way of showing love and discipline. I needed both. It was clear to everyone that we had found something deep and special in our relationship. We began to have long conversations at dinner about what it took for a serious career in music.

For the first time, I seriously considered a college education with a major in music. Previously, my parents had urged me to take up tailoring or plumbing—a trade, so that I would always have a good job. I was always fond of cooking and had even considered becoming a chef.

There's no telling what I might have gotten into if I didn't have my faith and my love of music.

✦

MEANWHILE, MY HOME LIFE CONTINUED TO DISINTEgrate. My older brother and I continued to drift further apart—he was interested in boxing, and I hated violence. He and my stepfather butted heads, and before long, they were challenging each other physically with my mother trying to play referee.

My stepfather had managed to get into the steel mills as a laborer when he was barely seventeen and had stayed there all his working life. He went to the army for three years and returned to the mills right where he left off when he was discharged. He managed to stay sober during the weekdays, but he always found a bottle for the weekends.

The drunker he got, the more abusive he was toward my mother, and my brother had had enough. It all came to a climax one evening after dinner while I was upstairs in my room with the door closed, trying to study for a biology exam the next day. The noise downstairs became too raucous to ignore. My mother and sisters were trying to separate my stepfather and brother, who both seemed focused on a battle to the death. They were straining and cursing at each other as though they were outside in some alley. I tried to break up the fight, but I wound up being the punching bag. I put my hands over my head and fell to the floor. After I took a couple of solid kicks, I tried to get out of there but was unsuccessful. I was not being disciplined by a parent but beaten up by a *man* who had been trained to kill by Uncle Sam. His three years in the military were not wasted. If it weren't for the rest of my family, he could have killed me. The last thing I remember was a kick to my head over the right ear.

I only barely recall being dragged across the floor by my brother and my mother and hearing my stepfather cussing. I had done the unforgiveable. I had challenged him in trying to help my brother in the fight. I didn't move as my mother and several of the neighbors dabbed my bleeding head with towels. I tried to talk, but my mouth was full of teeth and a fat tongue, so I stopped. I just sat there and let them minister to me. Part of me wondered which was worse: being beat up by your stepfather or being thrown out of a white church for being black. I wouldn't have chosen either one, but my fate had generously given me both.

My brother ended up moving out, and several months later, he joined the army. I watched it all with confusion and anger. How could my mother allow this man, my stepfather, come into our lives and cause such havoc? At home, I became an introvert who walked on eggshells; I didn't ask any questions and never offered any information. It seemed too dangerous to even be happy. I suffered the indignities of occasional hits and kicks from my stepfather and mostly stayed away from home. I usually spent extra time at school with my music teacher, or with Ron and Mary Lou.

During this time, I was also spending more and more time away from the formal church, and I discovered that I still had a sense of my inner life and anointment; those gifts that had been so highly praised during the services at Mt. Carmel Baptist Church were still in me. My ability to turn a phrase and deliver the heart of a song didn't disappear. I loved music-making just as much as ever. I decided to try praying. It was reassuring to know that that Unknown Something that filled my church work was still with me.

Day after day, I would become still and call forth the wondrous sense of rightness and calm. So much for the church and formal Christianity. Meditating actually gave me courage to continue, on my own. This knowledge freed me more and more to be the true person I was, emerging from within. It was months and years before I was comfortable knowing that the God I loved and served actually was everywhere, that I could access Him anywhere and everywhere. What did this mean for me and my role in the church? Was this sense of transcendence also present in Schubert or Beethoven songs, within operatic arias, and paintings, and dance—all which often left me feeling hypnotized? I had to do some serious thinking about this. I did not take any of these questions to my mother or pastor. I needed to live alone with them for a while.

When I look back on that early spiritual awakening, I realize that I was separating myself from any formal dogma or church. In my humility, I still struggled with the fact that I carried a powerful spirituality that had nothing to do with any organized religion. I treated all religions the same but also found no fault with agnostics, atheists, Unitarians, Christian Scientists, Mormons, Baha'is, Buddhists, Religious Scientists, Earth Goddess Worshipper, Sikhs, Taoists—all manner of expressions were fine with me. Time and time again, people wanted me to be a judgmental, fundamentalist Christian singer who hated a lot of regular people, and I just couldn't do it. I was not there. It is not who I am. My message is simply one of inclusiveness and love. Period.

Despite this, my relationship with Mt. Carmel was about to be shattered.

Judging from all the talk, everyone around me was having sex. But I wasn't. So I dared to think that a few other people, like my sisters, were also "pure." After all, frequently when I went to church, they went with me. I blithely went along believing in the best of everybody because I was still a virgin. In my limited experience, sex never solved any problems. It seemed to create problems, especially for people who were not married to each other. In my opinion, sex was polluted and involved girls. I still hadn't solved the problem of being gay. I did not want to be intimate with girls.

I had read enough of the Bible to know all about adultery and fornication. If I could have physically washed my mind, I would have, but abstinence would have to suffice for me during those turbulent teenage years. I sincerely felt that my brother and sisters were as committed to purity and abstinence as I was. The fact that I was so naïve didn't really register with me until I was in school and heard several of my classmates talking about the fact that my fifteen-year-old sister was pregnant. I didn't know anything about it.

In spite of everything I heard, I really knew little or nothing about sex and still believed on some level that the stork was a central character in the process of procreation. I *wanted* to believe in the stork. It seemed so wholesome and magical. This other stuff about petting and grinding that I heard people talking about, especially Hiawatha, seemed messy and complicated. Over the years, I had not changed my mind. I was a stubborn Taurus who wanted to be clean and wholesome and angelic for God, so I clung to my fantasy.

Gossip and rumors are crafty demons that have immense power to ruin people's lives. They are often found in the least likely places.

My friend Elaine Logan pulled me aside and stage-whispered that the students were talking about the fact that my sister, one of the twins, was pregnant.

"How do people find these things out?!" I lashed out. "And who is spreading such scandalous gossip?" I was outraged. I lived with my sisters and hadn't seen or heard the first hint of one of them being pregnant. I promised Elaine that I'd ask at home about this just as soon as I could get to my mother.

It wasn't long before the sordid facts and all the horrific details were out. It read like a cheap soap opera, and I was profoundly saddened and shocked. It involved the new pastor at Mt. Carmel. It seemed that while I was spending so much time at the church singing, the new pastor was making another kind of music with both of my sisters. Only one became pregnant. Whatever he had said to my mother to justify his actions was never clear to me. My mother and stepfather kept me at a distance and would only discuss superficial details in my presence. There was no lawsuit or accusations of statutory rape. The pastor left town and moved back to Chicago; I never saw or heard from him again. The whole situation was so foul to me that I became even more silent and introverted. I was so disillusioned that I never went back to Mt. Carmel again.

I agonized over the obvious questions: How could God have allowed this to happen? Whose fault was it? What should or could have been done to prevent it from happening? How come one sister became pregnant and not the other sister? For days I silently raged against this God whom I loved so much. Again, in my life, someone whom I trusted implicitly, an authority in the Church, had betrayed me, to say nothing of my sisters' profound betrayal at his hands. On some level, I was also asking, *How could my sister not have known something like this could happen?* I hated the Bible; I hated the truth; I hated Christianity! So this was what sex and procreation was all about. I didn't want anything to do with it and vowed even more strongly to remain a virgin. All my illusions about the stork and fairy tales were utterly shattered. I was being forced to grow up.

I remember hearing Nina Simone sing this mournful song:

> *Trouble in mind, I'm blue*
> *But I won't be blue always*
>
> . . .
>
> *Let that 2:19 train*
> *Ease my troubled mind!*

I was troubled and blue too. Worse, I was a singing basket case of rage and confusion. I wanted to protect my sister from the scandal and gossip of nosy neighbors and false friends. My helplessness added to my pain and sense of worthlessness. Being a big brother had no special power or perks in this case. Over and over, I questioned my value to the family, to myself! Where were Great-Grandmama Laura Mae and Granddaddy Saul when I needed them? I wished I could just disappear.

My mother and Warren forced my sister to give up the baby, a little boy, for adoption. My sister didn't want to give him up, and it caused a tremendous rift in the family. After the pregnancy, my sisters were taken out of my mother and Warren's home and sent to live with a black Islamic family. Mary Lou Phillips was the caseworker; the girls told their stories to Mary Lou, and Mary Lou reported the situation to the authorities. I was always welcome to go over and see them in their new home. There were times when I tried to salvage my sisters' lives and ambition. I tried to get them to focus on school, but it was hopeless—I felt like I was talking to a wall. Over the years, we slowly drifted apart; the whole ordeal changed my family forever.

And speaking of change, I was at Elaine's house when I got the call that took my breath away. My mother didn't say much, just that Great-Grandmama Laura Mae had died quietly the night after her eightieth birthday gathering, amidst her family. The funeral was to be held next week. We weren't going to attend. After all these years, Mama was still afraid that we would have trouble with my daddy.

Great-Grandmama Laura Mae loomed as a powerful bigger-than-life legend in my mind, a giant. Her death affected me profoundly. I had felt she'd just live forever. Why should a legend die? Why should the passionate and powerful queen of my youth die? I felt her death disconnect me from my past. I felt abandoned and on my own even though I hadn't seen her in more than ten years. Elaine's family—the Logans—offered their sympathies and her father, Reverend Logan, even snuck me a drink of whiskey out of an oddly shaped brown bottle from some secret location. I cried while I washed dishes and wrestled with my thoughts. Later, I went for a long walk with Elaine. I tried to share with her the meaning of my Great-Grandmama Laura Mae's death. She had been the foundation, the bedrock of our family, and now it felt like we'd lost our mooring.

✦

I STARTED WRITING POETRY IN MY SOLITUDE. I WASN'T very good, but I found a way to express my pain. I continued to spend a lot of time away from home and joined the after-school creative writing club. James Baldwin was all the rage then, and I

read all his writings. His voice echoed my sentiment on national issues concerning race and power. It was whispered that he was gay,
and I wondered how he could be such a great writer and be gay. I
really didn't know of any other gay people or writers. According
to the church, being gay was a sin. It seemed like even *thinking* too
openly about being gay was a sin. I wondered if Baldwin had already done what I wanted to do. If he were around, I could ask him
what it felt like to be with another man. What it would be like to
take a man out on a date, to make love, to talk on the telephone. I
wondered if I'd ever know. If he was openly gay, did he have a special friendship ring from another man? Did they live like a couple?
How did people treat them? I knew he used to preach. What did
God have to say about all that? Was he still a Christian?

In the creative writing class, beyond reading novels and es-
says, we read our own work in class and offered polite criticism.
I was too sensitive to talk or write in any real depth about my
emerging sexuality or the racism I had experienced. I did write
about my family and my estrangement. I could talk about that.

I didn't date very much, just enough to keep the guys from
teasing me. Just like Hiawatha had said, I was very popular because of my singing and girls seemed to be constantly trying to
get my attention. I was set on being a virgin when I married and
dating cost money; I preferred to spend my money on music. I
was in love with the new black prima donna soprano Leontyne
Price, and I bought my first opera recordings of her and William
Warfield singing duets and arias from George Gershwin's *Porgy
and Bess.* For the most part, I avoided those insistent girls and
kept to my buddies and my studies.

I studied regularly with Professor Gould and began to prepare
myself for a liberal arts education with a major in music. Ron often

asked me if I wanted to teach music, but he made it clear that I was good enough to be a performance major. My high school music teacher, Mr. Miller, echoed that opinion. I was good enough to be a member of the boys' octet, which performed at school and throughout the community. I considered this valuable experience training for my career, and I took the responsibilities very seriously. Mr. Miller would often turn the choir or the tenors over to me to teach song parts. I didn't play the piano very well, but I could always play the tenor part in anthems and hymns. I would check the lax or marginal boys who were there often just for show. Even though I developed a good sense of humor, I took myself very seriously when it came to learning music. Many kids knew it and groaned when I took over the choir. Privately, Mr. Miller used to talk to me about taking it easy with the guys. But when he wanted the job done, he called on me. He often told me that I was better at teaching music than he was because I sang all the parts. I set the bar pretty high for the other students and showed them that if they were serious about singing, we could have the best choir in the state. When we went to the National Association of Teachers of Singing, Inc., (NATS) state singing contest in Columbus, Ohio, we received the highest rating every time. That kind of success was infectious, and many of the students tolerated my strictness because they liked the acclaim. I also got the highest rating for my solo singing.

✦

DURING MY SENIOR YEAR, THINGS CAME TO A HEAD FOR me with my stepfather at home. I had the habit of sneaking out of the house on evenings to attend performances at Stambaugh Auditorium. My parents' refusal to permit me to attend these exciting events seemed arbitrary to me. Most of my friends could go, and I felt resentful that I couldn't. There were touring opera productions or the Youngstown Symphony Orchestra in concert. These were very wholesome events and a great joy to me. One day when I tried to sneak back into the house without disturbing my parents, my stepfather was waiting for me. It seemed I had been missed early on after I had left, and no one knew exactly where I was. My stepfather didn't say very much, but the look in his eyes told me how much he disapproved. He began to beat me with a belt; I suffered under his vicious blows until he was finished. I just stood there; I didn't cry out or try to defend myself. The worst part was my mother never raised an objection. As I went to my room, I decided I would leave home. I was too old for this kind of humiliating discipline and would not allow myself to be treated this way again. For several months I could feel the physical effects of that beating. I didn't have a clue where I would go, but I had had enough of him and that house.

I spoke to my buddy Elaine of my dilemma, and her reaction was fast and helpful: "Come stay with us! My mom and dad love you, and I'll explain to them what happened."

The next day, Elaine said that her parents wanted to talk with me after school. I was so nervous that I almost didn't go, but Elaine insisted. Her parents were in their fifties and seemed more like grandparents to me than parents. They were kind and patient and listened to all I had to say. It occurred to me that Grandmama Laura Mae might look like Mrs. Logan . . . and I liked her even more for that reason. She seemed to be very wise and never in a hurry. Elaine was lucky to have a mother like that.

We discussed the circumstances of my family situation thoughtfully. It was finally agreed that I would bring my things on Saturday and become a member of their family for as long as I needed to stay there. Elaine would come by in the car. For the first time in months, maybe years, I began to relax. I slept that night knowing I would soon be free of the anxiety and stress that had become my daily family life.

When Saturday came, I got up early, gathered my things together, and stayed out of sight of my parents. I kept watching and listening and kept the door to my room closed. I turned on the radio to cover any noise. Dinah Washington was singing "Unforgettable." Nobody seemed to notice anything unusual. I prayed that they would leave the house before Elaine arrived so that I wouldn't have to fight or explain where I was going. After a while, I finally realized that their voices were gone. I heard the car drive down the side of the house and out to the street. I ran to the bathroom to see them turn left and head off. I instinctively felt that they would be gone for a while. I quickly called Elaine. Mrs. Logan told me that she had already left to pick me up. What timing!

Life in the Logan household had a really different energy and shape than our house. Everyone went to bed early—no exceptions! Everyone got up early because Mrs. Logan said so. She never called to me twice. I didn't want to do anything to change my good relationship with her. So I went to bed early and got used to being awakened whenever she called. However, I was rarely up before I had to be. I liked my sleep, but I also liked the attention. It was like someone wanted me to get up and be with them and share in family things. I ate breakfast with the whole family. Whatever Mrs. Logan cooked was fine with me. I helped cook and often washed the dishes. It was the least I could do considering how kind she was to me. Elaine's brother and sister were happy with this arrangement! There were no loud voices or fights. I seriously wondered if Reverend and Mrs. Logan ever had an argument. To me, their relationship was perfect. I was always treated fairly and kindly by everyone, including Prentiss, their only son, and Malvina Louise, their youngest daughter, who was quite a live wire. She loved popular music as much as I did, and we used to listen to Motown in secret.

There was no smoking, no drinking, and no dancing. Mrs. Logan had laid down the law. I was given my chores and expected to study hard after school and go to church every Sunday. So what else was new?

The dancing part was the hardest for me. I loved to jitterbug and do the twist. Both Elaine and I were pretty good at it. It was the one forbidden thing I kept doing, but only when the Logans were away or I practiced at my other friends' houses. Elaine kept our secret. She was like a sister to me and helped me to learn the new routines.

I found joy in fitting in with this new family. I kept asking myself why my family couldn't be like this. I couldn't imagine Reverend Logan drinking or hitting Mrs. Logan or coming in early in the morning from a night of boozing, playing cards, and whoring around. It felt like he was as faithful to Mrs. Logan as I wanted to one day be with my partner! I tried to show my admiration for him, although I never said it.

Most of the time the house was quiet and mellow except for lots of laughter and wholesome teasing. I soon learned the way they prayed and began to imitate them at dinnertime. It wasn't hard. They just said "Jesus Christ" and "in Jesus's name" a lot. It was easy to love the Logans. They gave me so much that I didn't mind one bit changing the way I prayed.

I continued in school as though nothing unusual was happening in my life. A general announcement went out from the principal's office for all seniors to make an appointment with our guidance counselors to map out a strategy for all those interested in entering college the next spring. Those interested would need to take the correct college entrance exams and send for application forms for admissions. I was interested in studying music at Oberlin College, Ohio State University, and Kent State University. Ron felt that Oberlin College would give me the solid musical grounding I sorely needed. There I could continue the work he and I had begun together. At the same time, Oberlin would not neglect the academic discipline Ron felt was so essential to a good liberal arts education. I made an appointment to see Ms. Kryzan and Mr. Balalis, our school counselors.

Earlier in the year, several of the guys in my gang, myself included, all of us black, had received packets of information encouraging us to select an Ohio vocational school in Youngstown or Columbus to obtain some kind of associate degree. Some of us had attended a meeting led by the counselors to hear about making concrete plans to become carpenters, bricklayers, plasterers, painters, and the like. I hadn't been able to attend because of my voice lessons with Ron. I simply dismissed the whole idea because by that time I knew that I was headed for music school. Ron and Mary Lou had encouraged me to think that way.

When I sat down in the office of my guidance counselors, I started talking about Oberlin College. Hardly a word was out of my mouth before I could sense that something was wrong. I couldn't ignore their dour faces as I shared with them my fascination with the famous liberal arts college and desire for a career in music. This was not the reception I had expected. They fidgeted and stammered, and finally Ms. Kryzan said, "Who encouraged you to consider going to college, and especially Oberlin? It's full of liberals! They have quite a reputation, you know!"

I responded, stunned, "My voice teacher said that I would be good at Oberlin. If I couldn't afford it there, I could always try to get a scholarship to Ohio State or Kent State University to study music. My grades are excellent, and I can always do a great audition. I'm working on Schubert's *Serenade* now and *Ah! So Pure* by von Flotow. Next, I'm going to learn some of Donizetti's *Lucia di Lammermoor.* I don't know anything about this reputation. I'm going to sing."

Everything stopped. Ms. Kryzan took the initiative: "Wait just a minute; wait a minute. Oberlin just might not be the place for a boy like you. In fact, college may not be the real answer for a boy like you—from your background. Who will support you?"

I suspected that she paused to let her words sink in. She continued, "Had you considered a vocational education or learning a practical trade that will guarantee that you will always be able to make a living and support your family? We had a meeting earlier this year for all the boys like you in the conference room. You should have attended."

She went on, "Some of the kids say that you can cook and maybe sew! Had you thought about being a short-order cook or tailor? Our programs here at Kaufman Vocational School are considered some of the best in the state. You could stay at home and finish in about nine months. You'd be perfect! Had you considered that? The way you're going, young man, you're setting yourself up for quite a disappointment. We can't just let you do that."

I listened in utter disbelief. They acted as though they hadn't heard a word I'd said. I had heard lots of things about me in my life that had hurt and confused me, but this one took the cake. Everything they implied about me said that a "boy like me" couldn't go to that expensive, upper-class, liberal arts college and succeed. I would make a good cook or tailor or carpenter, but not be a great singer.

Still in shock, I averted my eyes. I had heard the rumors about what the guidance counselors said to the black students who came to them for advice, but I naïvely never suspected they would treat me that way because of my excellent grades and my singing. Now I knew it for myself; I was wrong.

Slowly, I got up and left the room. I mused to myself that it was their turn to be shocked. I didn't look back. I kept thinking that if they knew what I was thinking, they'd never speak to me again. So, that's how it had to be: I had to make it on my own without their help. Later that day, I went to the library and got the address for Oberlin College and wrote to request an application for admission. Forget about Ms. Kryzan! Forget about Mr. Balalis! I would not let them determine whether I went to college. I would study music in college regardless if they approved of it or not. I never said a word about the incident to either Mr. Miller or Ron.

✦

THE SOUND OF MY NAME ON THE LOUDSPEAKER ONE morning at school shocked me. I was to report to the principal's office immediately.

What on earth have I done wrong? I kept asking myself all the way to the principal's office. When I arrived at the office, the secretary motioned for me to go right in. It was like the gathering of the Biblical judges. Everyone was there: the Logans, my mother and stepfather, Mary Lou, Ron, Mr. Miller, and the principal, Mr. Tear. I instinctively wanted to turn and run and just keep running. They sat somber and accusing, silent and knowing. I just knew I was going to be punished for leaving home without so much as a word to my parents. Mr. Tear indicated where I was to sit down. I was furious at having been called in front of everyone and at the possibility of being taken out of the Logans' home. If my anger could have leaped out of me and consumed my mother and stepfather, it would have been over immediately. I was going to have to endure this one. My ears burned with anxiety and confusion.

I sat down, lowered my head, and became very quiet. It was strange sitting in the same room with my mother and not wanting to be with her or touch her. I was grateful that my seat allowed me to look at Warren and keep an eye on his actions. Even in this setting, I was wary of him. I felt like a traitor to my mother. Mrs. Logan had become my new mother. I wondered if my mother knew I had deserted her. She loved Warren; I did not. I was determined not to be imprisoned by her love or stupidity. The way she sat, so correct, so cold and distant, made it difficult to imagine her in her former life with my daddy and my Grandmama Laura Mae. I couldn't meet her confused eyes.

Mrs. Logan reached over and squeezed my hand. It meant a lot. I felt she was trying to tell me something.

Finally, Mr. Tear broke the ice: "Young man, do you know why I've called you to this meeting?"

"Yes, sir," I said, looking straight ahead and not directly at anyone. "I have an idea that it's about me not being at home with my mother," I said hesitantly.

"It certainly is," he said, and stopped and waited. I could feel him looking at me. "Now, do you want to explain yourself?"

My mind was racing. Mr. Tear always impressed me as a patient man who was really interested in the students. I wanted to take a chance and tell him the truth. It hurt to be holding so much within.

"My stepfather beat me for going to a concert at Stambaugh Auditorium," I said. "I won't let him touch me again."

"You'll do as I say as long as you're in my house," snapped my stepfather. His words lashed at me like the strap he had used to beat me.

Very calmly, Mr. Tear asked him, "Why would you beat him for going to a concert?"

"If I tell him he has to stay at home, then he has to stay home. I'm responsible for him. He's a smart-mouth, and I'm going to break him of it. He knows he'll have to answer to me if he smart-mouths back to me. I won't stand for it!" For my stepfather, the matter was closed. He sat there glaring at me.

I glared back, finally able to look up. Anger made me fearless.

"He's not my boss," I shot back. "And I don't live in his house anymore." I was ready for battle. "If he ever puts his hands on me again, I'm going to hit him back," I said. "I'm not afraid of him!"

In seconds, the tense quiet of the room was replaced by the steamy rage of someone ready to do something violent. I was not going to be a bystander. My mother sat up in her chair and put her hands to her eyes as though she was going to cry.

"You'll do no such thing, young man!" Mr. Tear responded as he looked at me sternly. "Everyone just relax. We're going to take a couple of deep breaths and allow ourselves to think clearly. I intend for us to have an intelligent discussion, and I don't want to have to remind us again that we are in a school, and certain aggressive behaviors are inappropriate. Is that clear?" he asked, not expecting anyone to answer. "We'll conduct ourselves like mature adults as long as I'm in charge here. Now, I hope I've made my point here!"

During this lecture, I had stood up. My stepfather had stood up. We glared at each other with looks of pure hatred. Slowly, a kind of calm returned to the room.

"Look!" I said. I yanked at my shirttails, lifted up my shirt, and turned around. I had felt the marks when I bathed and had seen them in the mirror as I strained to see my back. I had been too ashamed to dress and undress for gym for a month because of the bruises and scarring. Everyone gasped, and the room was hushed. I let the sight of my injuries sink in so they could know what I felt and understand my shame. My rebellion had not developed in a vacuum.

Mr. Tear was the first to speak: "Mr. Boswell, what do you have to say for yourself? Under what circumstances was this kind of brutality justified?" My stepfather was silent. Everyone else in the room stared in disbelief.

Mary Lou spoke next: "If I go to the juvenile court, we can have him taken away from you, and you could be remanded to jail for child abuse! I had no idea. Inez, did you know about this? Why didn't you say something?"

My mother never responded. She lowered her eyes and wrung her hands over and over. She was crying openly now. Mrs. Logan moved over and tried to console her. She held her as a mother would hold her daughter. I wished that Mrs. Logan *were* my mother. She had hugged me a lot since I had come to live with her.

It was agreed that I would continue to live with the Logans. My mother continued to cry while Mrs. Logan helped me dress and stood next to me. The meeting ended. Mrs. Logan asked me if I had enough money for lunch and assured me that they would see me that evening for dinner. Neither my mother nor step-father said goodbye when I left.

Once my living situation was settled, I was finally free to devote all my time to preparing for my Oberlin audition. I couldn't wait to get out of Youngstown. I worked hard on the days before my audition and felt a special connection with the school. When the time came, the Logans gave me a worthy send-off, and Mr. Miller and I headed north.

It was like entering a new world. The town was very small and clean. So was the campus. There was no trace of the big-city ugliness of Youngstown, no mills or factories. The lawns were manicured, the buildings ivy-covered. Students walked around smiling and joking like they didn't have a care in the world. I felt drawn to this calm atmosphere. White people were everywhere. I wondered where the black people were. For a young man from the black ghetto of Youngstown, this was something completely different.

The audition went extremely well, and I felt that I had passed my first big hurdle. We'd be hearing from the college by mail.

A few weeks later, I was called into Mr. Tear's office again. But this time, I was to be pleasantly surprised. He asked me about my Oberlin audition and told me he was rooting for me—that it was his alma mater as well!

"Let me make a suggestion," he said. "I'd like for you to come to a meeting next Saturday in Boardman of the Oberlin Alumni Club. I've been telling them about you and your desire to attend our alma mater. They'd like to hear you sing. Maybe you could sing some of the songs you sang for your audition. If or when you get in, we may be able to work out some way to help you out financially. By the way, I especially like the way you sing those spirituals. Would you be willing to do that?"

Of course I agreed, and Ron agreed to accompany me on piano.

This time I left Mr. Tear's office on cloud nine. Who could have imagined? This was an opportunity of a lifetime, and I had every intention of making the best of it!

Time slowed to a crawl while I prepared to sing for the Oberlin Alumni Club. I walked around unable to talk or think about anything else. I needed scholarship help, or I simply would not be able to attend if they accepted me. I had written requesting many brochures and academic bulletins about the school and its history; still I asked a million questions of Ron, Mr. Miller, and Mary Lou. My school buddies all began to call me Oberlin. I loved it.

Around this time of year, the senior class would traditionally get together and decide on superlatives. I was surprised to be voted Most Likely to Succeed and Most Studious in my class even though I wasn't on the honor roll all the time. This vote and the last few classes kept me busy until the day of my performance.

Ron left no details to chance and even insisted on telling me what to wear and what to eat when I performed. On performance days, I was to talk less and be sure to be well rested from the day before. Next to breathing correctly, he felt that a good night's rest was absolutely essential to good singing. I tried never to disappoint him or myself. I drank lots of water and tea with lemon and kept some lozenges in my pockets for breath and throat health.

He told me it was torture to have to sing a duet with a singer who had bad breath.

The Saturday of my audition for the Oberlin Alumni Club, I was excited and nervous at once. Never had so much depended on a single concert as on this one. I did everything right the day before and got a good night's rest. That morning I slept late and didn't talk much before I had breakfast, fixed myself some tea, dressed in my new suit, and went to meet Ron.

The meeting was brought to order by its president, and I was introduced. I walked to the front to polite, warm applause. I thanked them for their invitation, introduced my teacher, and nodded to Ron that I was ready. I began (as I had at my Oberlin audition) with my Handel song: "Ombra mai fu" (There Was No Shade) from the opera Serse. The applause was warm and encouraging, but not intense. Next, I sang Schubert and then a Fauré song. The audience was warming up, and I felt that I might actually enjoy this. For my fourth song, I sang the aria from Martha by Friedrich von Flotow. Ron was very fond of it, and I sang it well. The members of the alumni club were smiling everywhere; they seemed to enjoy themselves too. I concluded with several spirituals, including "Steal Away" and "There Is a Balm in Gilead." The applause was sincere and long. I began to dare to hope that they would agree to help me attend Oberlin College. They thanked me, and Mr. Tear assured me that he'd be talking to me next week at school.

Waiting is never easy, and I'm worse at it than most people. It seemed to take forever for my Oberlin acceptance to arrive. When it came, even though it was contingent upon a successful live audition and a thorough examination in theory and sight singing, the Logan family and I celebrated. Mrs. Logan even baked a cake and put candles on it as though it were my birthday! In a way, it was.

A week later, Mr. Tear called me into his office to give me the good news. The Oberlin Alumni Club had decided that upon my final and complete acceptance to Oberlin they would be happy to offer me a full scholarship (tuition plus room and board) to Oberlin College for four years. They also offered to help me with books and supplies and only requested that I return home each spring to give a short performance for their spring meeting. I barely had words to express my gratitude.

When I received my letter stating that Oberlin had finally accepted me unconditionally for the incoming freshman class for September of 1963, my joy was boundless!

I worked all summer to get ready for Oberlin. Mr. Miller had put in a good word for me, and I was hired as a short-order cook at a Kentucky Fried Chicken/Wonder Boy restaurant. I worked overtime as often as I could and saved every dime.

Graduating and leaving home—the Logans' home—was difficult, but I was determined to put the best face on it. Everyone was so kind to me, especially the Logans, my school buddies, Mr. Miller, Mr. Tear, Ron and Marsha, and Mary Lou. But in spite of this, something was missing. I missed my Great-Grandmama Laura Mae. The news of her death still haunted me every day. I couldn't just accept it and get past it. The knowledge of her presence in Tuscaloosa had sustained me all through the fighting with my stepfather, through my mother's indifference and inability to protect or love me.

I found it hard to pray, but I kept trying. I wondered where God was in the midst of my crises with my parents and my unsettling move out of the house. Just living with this big silence was difficult. I kept my fears and questions to myself. I smiled when I wanted to cry. I kept busy when I just wanted to run away and be by myself and think. What good was a song without my Great-Grandmama Laura Mae and Granddaddy Saul? These were questions that I had no answers for, and they kept me awake at night. But I was determined to put them away and get on with making a life for myself. The Oberlin Alumni Club had placed their faith in me by giving me the full scholarship. I had to live up to it.

PART III

Off to College

I ARRIVED AT OBERLIN IN THE FALL OF 1963 WITH HIGH
hopes and a trunkful of clothes. Oberlin was the first college
in the United States to regularly admit African American students, beginning in 1835. It's also the oldest continuously operating coeducational institution. It was a hotbed of abolitionism
and a key stop along the Underground Railroad. It is thought
to have been stop number ninety-nine because it was so close to
Canada, which was number one hundred! From what I understood, both students and faculty were involved in the controver-
sial Oberlin-Wellington Rescue of a fugitive slave in 1858. One
historian called Oberlin "the town that started the Civil War."
A century later, many Oberlinians were deeply involved in the
civil rights movement and various peace and justice campaigns.
It seemed that I'd found my kind of people at last.

In this academic and artistic haven, during the first week of
orientation, I met my best friend, Thomas Jean-Pierre Pellaton
from Port Washington, New York, on Long Island. (Later he
was to become an ordained Episcopal minister.) We hit it off
right from the beginning. He had spent a year at a Connecti-
cut college and had transferred to Oberlin because of his love
for music. I found out later that he read assiduously and had
a nearly photographic memory. He had that New York savvy
and seemed to know everything going on in the conservatory
of music and the college. I, on the other hand, hadn't a clue
about how to get around and get involved. Jean-Pierre used his
extraordinary ability to remember dates and names and his

natural organizational skills to help me out. I soon became adept at keeping a daily calendar like he did, jotting down which campus activities I wanted to attend. Many events and concerts were free, and for those that required tickets, I could make purchases in advance. For the first time in my life, I found many other students, especially him, who were as interested in music as I was. They were as well prepared as I, and I soon found out that the competition was fierce. The choir held auditions. Jean-Pierre and I listened to many others sing before our turns came. After listening to wonderful singing for over an hour, I doubted that I would get in. I began to think of other organizations that I could enjoy. Jean-Pierre cautioned me to distract myself while we waited to find out the results of our auditions. We soon learned that we had both gotten in. We celebrated like hysterical little children.

During that fall semester, in October of 1963, it was officially announced that the Oberlin College Choir had been selected to represent the United States in a cultural exchange program with the Soviet Union. The tour was scheduled for March and April of the spring semester of following year, 1964. This was heady stuff for a guy whose family had only recently migrated from the cotton fields of the south to the urban north. We spent the entire first semester planning and learning repertoire. This affected the amount of time I had for the rest of my classes. I felt that I was studying *all the time*. High school had never been like this. One or two classes had been challenging, but I could coast for the rest. Not at Oberlin. My social life took time too.

After Jean-Pierre, my voice teacher, Ellen Repp, was the most significant person I met during my undergraduate days at Oberlin. Miss Repp was a salt-of-the-earth, tall Wagnerian goddess soprano type; I could imagine her standing proudly on stage with her war spear.

I used to walk by her studio in Warner Hall just to see if she was in, say hello, and apprise her of my progress on my latest vocal assignment. My need and hunger went far beyond songs and arias and knowing whether one entered stage left or stage right. This was a woman of the world. She and I could talk about life, struggles, relatives, hope, pain, humor, the arts, dance, and good food—just about anything. My weekly lessons with her were a discourse on life. It wasn't long before I was working with her almost every day.

She required that all her students come over on Saturday afternoons at least three times a month to listen to opera recordings or the live broadcast from the Metropolitan Opera. A dozen or so of us would sit around on chairs and on the floor as she explained sotto voce details she thought we should know. At about 4:00 p.m. each Saturday she would serve a special dessert as an enticement and reward. Those Saturdays stoked my dream to one day make a Metropolitan Opera debut.

My college choir rehearsals were also a revelation. The attitudes and accomplishments of this talented group made this my dream choir. The deceptively easygoing atmosphere was encouraged by our director, Professor Robert Fountain. He presented a friendly facade, but I recognized him as a benign tyrant. He seemed able to hear every mistake, every sluggish rhythm, every misaligned chord, and every wrong breath. It was impossible to sneak anything past him. I learned to do it right the first time and every time or at some point he'd mention it—not to embarrass, but to make it clear that he noticed, that he knew.

With little effort, I can recall his voice, his body language, his intense gaze, and his undisguised lust for perfection. In later years, I'd bring the same sense of purpose and concentration to my own group, the Harlem Spiritual Ensemble, but I'd get only mixed results. I could never push my professional ensemble the way he pushed us kids.

The work challenged my endurance, memory, learning skills, pitch accuracy, range, and rhythmic precision. Everything was tested.

I worked all four years at Oberlin to earn money for things I wanted to do. For a while, it was not uncommon for me to work a little at all three meals at the dining hall. Eventually, I settled on working during dinner. That's where I met my buddy, Carl Brown. Only in hindsight would I realize I had a crush on him. At first, I had to admit to myself that I was avoiding this friendly, jockish, big-man-on-campus kind of guy.

Carl played basketball and lacrosse and had a winning high school career in sports. There were rumors that he had dated all the hot girls on campus, but he wasn't arrogant or obnoxious. Life had dealt him a good hand, and he was just playing it.

When I finally got over my crush on him, I found him to be a sensitive, highly personable companion. When I had free moments, we began to spend time together just hanging out and enjoying each other's company. Occasionally, being with Carl was awkward, as girls would often vie for his attention and try to pull him away. Carl would have to decide whether to hang with me or live up to his reputation.

I also found another friend during that first semester, Selden Charles "Chuck" Dickinson. He was a tall Nordic type who played basketball and tried his hands at politics. He wasn't very successful, but he was a natural schmoozer. His good looks attracted admirers, and he could have a deep conversation with anyone, it seemed. We spent time together in the dorm and at meals.

Whenever I sang, Chuck and Carl were always in the audience, and they saw to it that other dorm buddies didn't forget to come either. Chuck's family lived in a Chicago suburb, and I was invited home with him for the Christmas holidays. That was an experience!

The Logans were disappointed when I called and told them I was not coming home to Youngstown for the holidays. It was a difficult decision, and now looking back, I realize that I was running away from what I used to be and toward what I was becoming. I didn't want to be the same young, confused adolescent I was before college. My mother had also begun to write me letters imploring me to come back home again; she and my stepfather were still together. Youngstown held many raw, toxic memories, and I wasn't sure what was emerging inside of me. During this soul-searching period, I made a firm promise to myself to never again allow anybody to tell me what to do. Never. I had to stay away from my past.

✦

IN 1964, I TRAVELED TO THE SOVIET UNION. SOME folks thought culture might be able to do what diplomacy had failed to do, so the Oberlin College Choir had been chosen by the powers in Washington, D.C., to ease some of the tensions of the Cold War between the bastion of democracy, the United States, and the godless totalitarian state, the Union of Soviet Socialist Republics. Americans had admired many Russian/Soviet writers, painters, conductors, and composers, institutions like the Bolshoi Opera and the Bolshoi Ballet, and other venerable Russian institutions for several centuries. Likewise, the everyday, common Russian couldn't get enough of the young pianist Van Cliburn, the black American expatriates (e.g., James Baldwin, Langston Hughes, and W. E. B. Du Bois), American Negro spiritual concerts, jazz, rock 'n' roll, modern dance, and our oh-so-common blue jeans.

Our choir was the first cultural emissary to the Russians, which would eventually include The Philadelphia Orchestra and a Broadway touring company of Gershwin's *Porgy and Bess*, featuring Leontyne Price and William Warfield in the title roles.

The United States had been involved in a Cold War with the Soviet Union since the end of World War II and the partitioning of Berlin and Germany into East and West. This cultural tour marked the beginning of a diplomatic thaw between the two superpowers. The choir prepared five programs for the tour with some minor overlap, all to be memorized. Professor Fountain assigned me three solos.

The morning we departed for the airport, my buddies showed up to see us off. Nobody could have prepared me for the banners and chanting as we boarded the bus and headed down College Street to Cleveland's airport. I realized that the college choir was considered a big winner at Oberlin, as important as any winning sports team. We were ambassadors going out into the world.

Flying was new to me, of course. The flight from Cleveland to Idlewild Airport—now known as John F. Kennedy International Airport—in New York was a total thrill. Jean-Pierre and I sat together with a couple of other singers. I asked about everything, not even bothering to pretend I knew anything about flying. I reveled in juvenile curiosity, pressing my nose to the window to watch like a child.

At the airport in Moscow, our surprise continued. The building was so drab and colorless that we'd have all dropped our luggage immediately and helped with a paint job if we hadn't been hurried through the customs process and onto a bus, pronto!

In the wee hours of Monday morning, March 2, 1964, we sleepily dismounted the frigid, crowded bus and stumbled with our luggage into the lobby of the Moskva Hotel in Leningrad (now called St. Petersburg). If anybody had any notions of the glamour of show business on the road, they had been totally disabused of the idea by now. The hotel seemed mammoth. What little I could see of the marble facade seemed to go on forever.

After the first night in Leningrad, we all remarked on the enormous size of the accommodations. For just two people per room, it didn't seem right. The living room alone was big enough for a full choir rehearsal. Even though the furniture was big and chunky, it barely filled the room. The only problem was that it was cold. I mean it was as cold as outside!

At night, I took extra blankets to my bed to snuggle into and sometimes wore all my clothes to sleep. It must have cost a fortune to heat that place.

There were sixty-seven members of the choir and only three of us were black—me and two women, Joy and Myrtle. Often, I felt that we, especially me, stuck out conspicuously.

Our concerts were usually in the evenings, so during the days we'd go sightseeing or visit the local conservatory to spend time with other music students. Joy and I usually attracted the largest crowds of students; we gave the interpreters a real workout with our questions and theirs. Questions weren't limited to music.

Students all over the U.S.S.R. wanted to know if I had ever been discriminated against and if I was treated equally in the choir. At first this shocked me, but I got used to the questions and found some responses that satisfied them. I wanted to tell the truth but felt this was not the venue to air our dirty laundry of slavery and discrimination. I was diplomatic and told them as much as I could, but none of them got the full story.

Being in Russia and hearing people ask pointed questions about *our* racial problems brought out in me a surprising sense of patriotism. There were many things I didn't like about the plight of black people in the United States, a country dominated by people of European background, but I wasn't going to cast them all to the devil while I was in Russia. There were social issues—school segregation, housing segregation, and more—but I felt they should be handled by leaders like Dr. Martin Luther King Jr. and groups such as the NAACP. I didn't want my photo on the front of some Russian newspaper condemning white Americans for the effects of decades of racism and discrimination. I was in Russia to sing and make friends, not complain. The truth could wait until I got back home. But for many of them, I was the first black American they had ever seen in person. Out on the street, they often stared at me and tried to touch and rub my skin. They didn't ask my permission to touch me; they just started reaching. I had to let them know—in some very descriptive English—that it was not acceptable. It was not a part of the diplomatic package. It was surprising that so many did not understand boundaries, or fully understand my humanity. In this way, they showed their naïveté and their version of racism that didn't see me as a person.

Over the next two months, we sang thirty-nine concerts in fourteen cities. We began in the conservatory in Leningrad and moved on to Moscow. Other cities included Kiev, Odessa, Yalta, Ryazan, Kishinev, Lviv, Minsk, and Bucharest. Full-capacity theaters and concert halls; rapt attention; loud, long, rhythmic applause; and people rushing the stage at the close of the performances: this was the case for each performance. The Russians couldn't get enough of us, nor could I get enough of performing.

Some of us choir members had made special arrangements to attend the orthodox services at Easter time in Odessa and Kiev. I was fascinated by the music and incense and loved the pageantry and robes. How could all this music, color, and fragrance be the seeds of such sin? I was one confused young man. I watched and experienced all of it with such profound ambivalence. I wanted so much of this to be good, inspiring, and right. But I kept running into a roadblock of puritan morality.

I realized that if I could just shut up my brain and refrain from judgment, I could still have a good time. We were treated like celebrities when we went shopping or walking in the streets, especially us three black choir members. Everywhere I went, I walked proudly as a black American and tolerated the stares, photographs, pointing, and indecipherable commentary. I got used to salespersons giving me presents just for walking into their stores. They gave me pieces of handmade jewelry, a fur hat, a balalaika, a harmonica, many postcards and buttons, a little toy soldier, and several shirts. I tried not to take advantage of the situation, but the temptation was great. I smiled, and they opened their hearts and coffers.

Jean-Pierre and I pushed ourselves to see as much as possible. The circuses were spectacular, as were the Bolshoi and Kirov ballets and operas. I began to feel that the things I had learned in Youngstown were applicable only in the context of that small

Ohio clan. Those strict moral and sociopolitical attitudes and be-
liefs were restrictive in the larger world arena, and they were the
cause of my culture shock and confusion. I wanted to make peace
with this Soviet culture. It simply wasn't what I had expected.
These were not mean-spirited, backward people. They were as
bright and clever as anybody I'd ever met and just as proud of
their communist Russian heritage as I was of being an American.
They were normal, and I was even more curious about them now
than I had been at the beginning of the tour.

After our Russian tour ended and we arrived back in New
York City for our Town Hall concert, I was a different person. I
lay in bed at night and compared my new self to my former self. I
began to realize that for the rest of my life I would define myself
by how I felt after I returned from Russia. I had felt appreciated in Russia. Sometimes in the United States I had felt deeply
underappreciated, unnecessary, and even rejected. I knew that
certain segments of American white society would just as soon
lynch all black people, regardless of their gifts, spirituality, inven-
tiveness, physical discipline, or artistic accomplishments.

But the Russians, in spite of my moral uncertainty about
them, showed me that I belonged. I was an artist. The experience
gave me confidence.

Back at school, even back among friends, I felt the letdown
of normalcy. Who wanted to be in classes after such an adven-
ture? It was hard to settle back into the rigors of academia. It just
didn't work for me, and I had to make plans to attend summer
school at Youngstown State University to make up a few classes.

Though I was less than thrilled to return to Ohio for the summer, settling back into the Logan household in Youngstown was
amazingly easy. I arranged through Ron to move in a keyboard,

so I could practice more at home. He offered to help me increase my repertoire, and I jumped at the opportunity.

Though I felt profoundly different after Russia, I got together almost every night with Elaine and several of my buddies who were back from college. We played some cards, drank a little, and listened to music just like we used to do before going away. They treated me just the same, but on the inside I was not.

It was this summer that I met Vicky and Michael Beechwood. One night, Mary Lou invited me to the Youngstown Playhouse to see a performance of Tennessee Williams's play *A Streetcar Named Desire*. After the show, I was introduced to the cast and crew. Vicky was one of the assistant directors of the play. She spoke with me and told me she'd like to work with me sometime in the future. We agreed that I would contact her when I could get some time off from Oberlin. That night I also met Vicky's younger brother, Michael, an intense young man with a huge heart. He too loved the theater; it was his first love. Music and literature were close seconds.

Michael decided he wanted to get to know me better, and it was arranged that Vicky would pick me up the following week for dinner at their parents' home.

When we pulled up to the Beechwoods' gated community, I began to gain a different understanding of this family. The seven-bedroom house was relatively new and obviously designed by someone with aesthetic originality. It sat on about ten acres of landscaped grass and trees with a five-car garage in the back. I later found out that Michael's father, Dr. Tom Beechwood, was a renowned cancer diagnostician and head of surgery at Northside Hospital, and the family had also inherited money from both sides. They lived quite comfortably by any standards.

Dr. Beechwood shared Michael and Vicky's love for theater, and he served as president of the board at the local playhouse. Michael's mother, Helen, was a Vassar graduate in art history. She volunteered at the local museum several days a week but did not have to work. She spent her time buying art and giving presentations at the local art museum, where she was president of the board.

Though I was a bit intimidated at first, I quickly learned just how warm and generous the Beechwoods were—we hit it off immediately.

I began spending more and more time at the Beechwoods', and I would spend the night occasionally. They treated me like another member of the family, and it was easy to embrace their love. Michael, in particular, wanted to spend as much time with me as possible. Eventually, I realized he wanted more from our friendship.

One night as we were preparing for bed, I heard a sweet soprano voice singing the aria from Puccini's *Gianni Schicchi*. At first, I thought it was a recording, but I discovered that it was Helen Beechwood; she had a terrific voice. Michael said that when she was young, she had wanted to be a singer but found success in art. At Vassar, she studied voice privately and still loved the opera. The whole family had traveled to Cleveland several times when the Metropolitan Opera was on tour. They even vacationed in Manhattan three years earlier to see performances at the Metropolitan Opera House. Tom and Helen loved Italian opera. The performance programs were displayed on a special shelf.

I longed for this experience and wanted to hear more. Michael shared everything he could remember about New York: the opera, the food, the sounds, the smells, and the experience of traveling with his parents. I was fascinated and couldn't get enough. He didn't know much about the singing but knew that he liked the music. And he loved my voice. He had tried to sing several times and had given up. Sadly, he couldn't even stay on pitch. I thought for a moment and concluded that life has a way of balancing these things, however subtle. The charming boy who had everything wanted to sing and couldn't.

I lost all sense of time as Michael's stream of consciousness descriptions about opera performances and New York City cast a magic spell over me. He had my rapt attention. As I lay there listening, dreaming, deciding to someday go to New York City to see and experience these sights for myself, he suddenly leaned over and kissed me full on the lips. My body leaped to attention, although I didn't move. Sleep was the last thing on my mind. A thousand dialogues raced through my brain as I froze in place. I wasn't afraid or repulsed, but I hadn't chosen, I hadn't agreed—yet.

Ever so carefully, I moved away and stood up. "I think it's time to go to bed," I said. "Good night, Michael!"

The mix of longing and regret on his face was clear. The pain in his eyes was melting my heart. He looked like he was going to cry. I had no intention to be mean to him, but I knew that I wasn't ready for such intimacy yet. I went into the bathroom and closed the door. When I returned, Michael was gone. I crawled into bed and slept. I didn't dream. I didn't agonize. I just slept.

At about four in the morning, I was aware of Michael crawling into bed with me. Without completely waking, I let my arms entwine him in an accepting embrace, just as easily as when my little sister, my human teddy bear, slept in my arms. I wasn't unaware or numb; I acknowledged that he was a boy with a purpose.

I was awakened by Helen's gentle tapping on my arm and shoulder. The look on her face was free of judgment or concern. As I awakened and began to stretch, she quietly left the room and closed the door. Michael never moved. I got up and prepared for school.

When I arrived in the kitchen, Helen had already set out bowls, silverware, milk, cereal, orange juice, and a multivitamin.

"I'm sure Michael will sleep for at least another hour," she said. "I'm going up to finish dressing. I hope you don't mind eating alone. Tom is already gone to the office. I'll be down in about twenty minutes to take you to the college on my way in to the museum." With that, she was off, and I was alone with breakfast.

Soon Helen was driving me to the college. "I hope Michael didn't toss and turn too much for you last night. When he was little, he used to kick and pull the covers when he would crawl into bed with me and Tom," she giggled. "He hates to sleep alone. He's mad about you. I wasn't surprised when I saw him all curled up with you this morning. You both looked so cute sleeping! I hated to wake you up."

I could barely look at her, I was so nervous. I had been trying to control it all through breakfast. I was trying to figure out how to disappear! I assumed the worst due to my experiences with my own family. Helen's acceptance was mind-boggling to me. Her nonchalance was so shocking to me that I almost became an observer to our conversation—it was like having an out-of-body experience.

"He was no trouble," I said calmly, as though it all were normal. "I used to sleep with my brother when I was young. He's away in the army now. After he left, my little sister used to sometimes sleep with me. She's almost six now."

My ears were hollow as I heard the words in the car, not sure that I was saying it, but yes, I *was* saying it: "Mrs. Beechwood, may I ask you how you feel about me and Michael sleeping together? I mean, *really* sleeping together? Like maybe boy and girl sleeping together? I don't mean to offend you, but he practically left me no choice and came in and crawled into my bed. I would like to be friends with him, but . . ."

"Oh, you dear child," responded Mrs. Beechwood. "You don't have to worry about us. We know more about Michael than you think. Our deepest wish is for Michael to be happy. You know, he doesn't really have any close friends. The only thing we ask is that if you really don't care for him, you should tell him and then leave him alone. Otherwise, you'll break his heart. Occasionally he has had attachments for other classmates, but none of it seems to have worked out. For all his brightness, he can't seem to make friends—until he met you. And now that's all he talks about—you."

"You mean you're not angry with me, and you're not going to throw me out?" I asked tentatively.

"Heavens, no!" she practically sang. "That's the last thing I would do. You may stay with us as long as you like. And I mean it."

All through class I thought about her words and the sensation of Michael's warm body next to mine. You mean I was actually being given permission? I was totally distracted. By noon I was glad to see Ron for a voice lesson. I needed to get my mind off Michael and concentrate.

Though I proceeded with caution, I continued spending some nights at the Beechwoods', and it was amazing how readily we fell into a routine.

According to my clan, though, I was on the verge of mortal

sin and casting my very soul into "eternal hellfire and damnation." But I had no intention of pushing Michael away. Everything I'd learned in my youth spoke against this seemingly natural intimacy: men were not supposed to "appreciate" one another in this manner. Had I lost my holy-self forever? Is this what sin felt like? I had a million questions and no answers. Sleeping was easy for me, but my waking hours were inundated with relentless questions. I'd have to find a way to let them go—to stop this internal inquisition—or I'd end up hating myself.

I spent my last few days of the summer before returning to Oberlin with the Logans. One evening as we were all having dinner, we heard a knock at the door. Nobody was more shocked than I was to see that it was my mother. She had stayed largely out of sight, and that had been fine by me. I heard her greet Mrs. Logan and tell her that she wanted to talk to me.

At the front door, I saw my stepfather peering over my mother's shoulder. She greeted me cordially enough. A dark cloud began to form in my mind. I sensed that no good could ever come of this meeting, yet I still blithely stepped out of the house onto the porch.

My mother began immediately to ask me what kind of people I was spending my time with these days when I was not with the Logans. And just what did I think I was up to living the way I was, making such commonality with sinners? I was aghast. I feigned and protested that I had absolutely no idea what she was talking about. But it was soon made crystal clear to me. She had somehow heard from someone else that I was living at Dr. Tom Beechwoods' house and sleeping with his son. It was simply surmised that I was up to all kinds of "sin."

I was stunned to be so publicly exposed. I was still sorting out my relationship with Michael and the Beechwoods; I hadn't discussed it with anybody. I was not prepared for this onslaught and was caught totally off guard. My mother tapped her determined finger into my chest as she exhorted me to "repent and come back to the straight and narrow." She said that I "needed to be with my Christian friends living for Jesus." She had already tried and convicted me!

As she continued her barrage, I actually began to feel that I had been doing something wrong. Right there on the porch, I became her child again. She ended by suggesting that the reason I was susceptible to the suggestion of sexual involvement with another boy was because I was still a virgin and hadn't been with a "real woman" yet. That's where my stepfather stepped in. He said that he recognized this was my problem all along. He had known that this was going to be difficult for me, he added, and had offered to "assist in my coming into manhood several years ago," but my mother had prevented it. Now he was prepared to follow through on his offer.

Mrs. Logan wondered what was going on in this otherwise calm summer evening. My stepfather assured her that I was not going to be harmed physically in any way and would be back within a couple of hours—safe and sound. My mother turned to her and suggested that they all go back inside to talk and "let the men tend to men's business."

Reluctantly, I allowed my stepfather to lead me off the porch to the car. I forgot all about my partially eaten dinner in the Logans' dining room. We hardly spoke during the short trip across town to the south side. My stomach was swirling like a Florida hurricane, and I was wringing my clammy hands over and over. As we entered the south side, I recognized the area we were riding through as being not far from the Beechwoods'. Soon we pulled up in front of a nondescript, rundown Victorian house on a quiet side street. He pulled the car up to the curb and indicated that we were supposed to get out here. There was no noise coming from inside, and the house seemed deserted. After my stepfather gave the door a couple of sharp raps, someone inside moved a curtain and asked in a menacing, aggressive tone, "Who dat? What you want?" I froze in my stepfather's shadow and hardly permitted myself a breath.

"This is Warren," my stepfather replied. "I'm here to see Miss Ella Belle. She know me. Tell her Warren is here."

"You just hold on. I'll tell her," came the response.

After what seemed like a very long time, the door cautiously cracked, and someone stuck her nose through the opening and yelled out, "Miss Ella Belle say what you want and who dat with you?"

"She know me. I'm Warren. Fatmeat's son. This boy here is Inez's son. I want her to do me a favor!"

The door closed for another very long time.

When it opened again, a middle-aged, unpretentious, no-nonsense, and very imposing woman stood blocking the doorway with her hands on her hips.

"What you want with me? Who dat chile you got wid you, boy? We don't want no trouble with no babies up in here. How old you, chile? Warren, you know better than to bring that young chile up in here!" She kept talking as though not expecting an answer.

"He won't be no trouble. He's Inez's son—my wife's boy." The second phrase he added quietly, and then he reluctantly began to whisper, "I need you to do me a favor till I get paid tomorrow."

The knowledge of what was happening finally hit me like a

brick in the center of my forehead! My feet were like lead weights on the wooden porch floor. I felt stunned and immobilized as I listened to my stepfather make all the arrangements for my *deflowering* at the hands of one of Miss Ella Belle's "girls." After much negotiating, my stepfather grabbed my elbow and pushed me ahead of him into the room. It was all dimmed lights, and I could barely see what was in front of me. Gradually, I became aware that there was music coming from across the room. The room reeked of perfume, body odors, cigarette smoke, and alcohol. I was overwhelmed by the heavy smells all around me. There were seven or eight sultry-looking women seated on couches and chairs around a living room in various stages of undress. Some wore high heels; some wore slippers. It was as though they all were just lounging around on a lazy summer evening waiting for the Easter Bunny to come along. All eyes were focused on me.

"You see something you want, boy?" one of them asked. I could sense and feel the snicker on the corners of her mouth. My stepfather never said a word. Miss Ella Belle conducted the whole affair.

"Well, let's go, boy. I done tol' you we ain't got all night. You up dere working on dat college degree and don't know how to ask for some pussy! Come here, Li'l Bit! You carry this tongue-tied filly-boy on upstairs and be gentle wid him. I declare, he just might be a virgin, chile!"

A young lady who looked like she could be my sister stepped casually forward and said, "Come on!" She looked like she was wearing a slip with nothing under it. I was as embarrassed as I had ever been in my life. As I mutely ascended the stairs behind Li'l Bit, I was acutely aware of the snickering and outright laughter following us up the stairs. It was humiliating!

I obediently followed Li'l Bit up the stairs and down the hall. When she entered a room on the left, I followed her. The room seemed to have only a big bed against one wall and several chairs on the side. The walls were painted a dull pea green.

"You can leave your clothes over there on the chair," said Li'l Bit. "What yoh name?"

My heart was pumping so loud I could hardly hear anything and could barely speak.

"Jonathan," I lied.

"Well, come on, baby. We ain't got all night," she nudged me to start in a slightly less hostile voice.

I sat down on the bed and tried to gather my thoughts.

"I need to go to the bathroom," I suddenly blurted out. I was shocked to hear my own voice.

"What?" Li'l Bit looked suspiciously at me. "Well, hurry up. It's down the hall on the right," she said as she stood rubbing her hips with one hand and pointing with the other.

I gathered myself together, stood up, and walked down the hall. Once in the bathroom, I closed the door firmly behind me. I noticed a little window with a fire escape leading back down to the side yard. I unlocked the window and opened it. I moved instinctively without consciously thinking. I climbed out and filled my lungs with the cool night air. At the bottom of the stairs, I had to jump another eight or ten feet to the ground. I landed squarely on my feet and instantly began to run as fast as I could. I could hear dogs barking in the yards on both sides of me as I ran. I was too afraid to even glance back for several blocks. I felt a twinge of regret for Miss Li'l Bit, running out on her like that, but this was far more than I was able to handle.

After about eight blocks, I recognized that I was near

Mahoning Avenue. I turned and walked rapidly west several blocks. It took me only a couple of minutes to get my bearings and realize that I was nearing the Beechwoods' neighborhood. I started running more slowly because I didn't want my step-father to catch me, but also didn't want people to look at me suspiciously. I stayed in the shadows and kept my head down. I kept going. After about twenty minutes, I got to the gate where the Beechwoods lived. I ran right past the confused guard, who was trying to say something to me. He ran after me for only a few seconds, gave up, and went back into his little guardhouse. I guess he must have telephoned the house because when I got there, the whole family was standing at the door waiting anxiously for me.

They were mortified when I told them the story as they tried to console me. Michael was my attentive personal nurse. I couldn't have imagined a more solicitous attendant. Every time I turned, I felt his eyes caressing and following me. I slept lightly for a few hours. Finally, I turned and let my eyes meet his. I wanted to reach out and help him to understand that my emotional wounds went deep. How could he understand how I felt? I know that he wanted to help, but could he understand? He had been born to loving parents, and I had inherited the parents from hell! I again realized to my everlasting disappointment that we were on the same page but writing in different languages. We were alike but from different worlds.

I spoke to Michael softly and sincerely: "Under no circumstances must you ever feel in any way to blame for what happened tonight. I certainly don't blame you. My parents believe very differently than I do, and I can't change that. Look into my eyes and know that I'll never fault you for all your kindness to me. When you feel bad for me, think of the good you have brought into my life. In every way, you have made me feel at home here. I never felt like this in my mother's home. I'm here now, and I'm safe. They didn't achieve what they intended, and I'm glad of that. I couldn't stand the idea. Let's ask your dad to call the Logans and let them know where I am. I think it's okay for him to explain to them what happened and that I'll call and talk to them tomorrow."

I felt vulnerable staying at the Logans' and knew that my mother would not stop until she got to me again. I was not going to make it easy for her.

The Beechwood family immediately came to my rescue, no questions asked. In fact, they had to persuade *me* to take them up on their generous offer to stay.

The Logans fully understood my reluctant decision to move. They didn't completely understand what had happened with me and my mother and stepfather that night, but they fully accepted the fact that I didn't want to be harassed by my parents anymore. Living with the Beechwoods was easy and guaranteed my protection. When it was time to return to school, everyone climbed into their Buick station wagon with some luggage fastened safely to the top and headed out to Oberlin. Once I was settled in my new single room, we went to the Oberlin Inn for an early dinner. Then they headed back to Youngstown. Although I was sorry to see them go, I was ready for some serious academics again.

✦

BECAUSE OF THE RUSSIAN TRIP, THE MEMBERS OF THE choir were more popular than ever. Even though we were learning new music and planning a spring tour, everyone wanted to hear the music from the Russian tour one last time. Consequently, a concert was planned in conjunction with the opening of the new conservatory building.

Oberlin, very good at showing off its prodigiously talented student body, planned a recital featuring young pianists, violinists, violists, cellists, flutists, clarinetists, trumpeters, trombonists, drummers, and singers as well. Through these recitals, I became aware of a young black baritone named Glover Parham, who was a year ahead of me. He was from Birmingham, Alabama, and was definitely one of a kind. There were many eccentric people in the Con, as we affectionately abbreviated the conservatory, but none of them had the uniquely compelling magnetic combination of personality, talent, looks, and brains that Glover possessed. His voice was one of the most beautiful and expressive I had ever heard.

Glover was tall and lithe with long expressive fingers, which he used well on the stage. When he looked at me, I always got the impression that he was reading my thoughts, not just listening to what I said. I immediately took a liking to him, and he started hanging out with a few of us occasionally.

Right from the beginning, he was not a good fit. He was too eccentric and noticeable, and I realized that he made some guys nervous. He didn't have a hostile bone in his body, but several of my buddies confided to me that his eyes made them uneasy. I soon discovered that Glover was gay and looked at some of the fellas in a very blatantly appraising way. He was giving them the "come on." They knew it and were nervous. He never said anything improper, but the vibe from him was intense. Sometimes it was funny. I was surprised at how many big, butch, straight-acting guys were afraid of this sensitive, assertive, gentle gay guy.

Several times, I actually invited him to sporting events on campus, which he informed me he would not otherwise have gone to, just to see how the jocks would treat him. It was always civilized and subtle, but I was aware of the uneasy truce going on among the objects of his gaze.

Although I was very close with Glover, I never discussed Michael Beechwood with him. When I was around him, I put a heavy filter on my thoughts and my mouth. I was not going to let anything slip. Glover had a sharp and perceptive intellect, and I was afraid that one day he'd know more about me than I'd ever want to reveal to him.

But he could tell, and one day he confronted me when I came to listen to records in his dorm room.

"What kind of music do you want to hear? Johnny Mathis or Teddy Pendergrass? I can close the curtains, turn the lights down low, and we can get comfortable. Why are you sitting on that chair looking all *starchified?*" he said.

"I'm not *starchified,*" I answered defensively. "I'm quite comfortable. Just turn on some Motown. We can listen awhile before I have to go."

"Is Smokey good enough for you, Mr. Starchified?" he said, still on his seduction tack.

"Yes," I answered, "and please don't start calling me 'starchified'! I love your company, GP, but I'm not going to sleep with you."

"So you want me to just stop and act like normal, like you're not feeling nothin'? I'm into you, Little Man, and I think you'd be into me if you weren't so scared you'd pee on yourself! Why don't you just come on out of that closet or let me in with you?" He lay there with his hands on his hips, challenging.

"I'm definitely not afraid," I answered. "Let's just get this over with. I want to be your friend, but I'm not going to sleep with you. That's all I'm thinking and feeling. Regardless of what you're thinking, I may one day find a good woman and get married. It's what everybody expects me to do. And—I want to have a family someday."

"Well, if that's how you feel, go right ahead, *Miss Thing*. If you ask me, I think it's a complete waste of time and a pox on some poor woman's life. Chile, why don't you just come on out as gay and be done with it? It's not the worst thing in the world, you know. And I'm sure there's somebody round here who'd give you some dick! You are truly one good-looking stalker. It's just a matter of time. You just wait and see. Don't say I didn't tell you so." With that he seemed to be satisfied. We listened to some music, and I headed over to Warner Hall to study and practice.

Glover had lived in the South all his life and had a brilliant, analytical mind. He knew far more about the subtleties of race relations than I ever could know. He could speak with authority about governors of southern states and the mayors of major southern cities and their racial attitudes. He raised my political awareness. I helped him organize the first protest rally in which I marched. He sent out the word, and the faithful and curious showed up.

He managed to secure three college vans for the event, and we filled them with students from the Midwest and beyond: Ohio, Indiana, Illinois, Pennsylvania, and New York. A few locals led by the local Baptist minister, Dr. Jones, joined us, and we began to feel like a community. While we fashioned signs in the church basement, we sang hymns with Dr. Jones leading. We sang and chatted all the way into downtown Cleveland. For most of us it was our first picket line. In Cleveland, we all unloaded in front of the big downtown Woolworth and went right into our rehearsed positions.

There were many curious onlookers, and Glover had prepared us—some people hooted at us. A few other stalwart souls joined right in with us on the spot and sang with us as we marched. Even though the Woolworth in Cleveland permitted blacks to sit at its counters, we were protesting Woolworth's national policy, which did not permit blacks to sit at the counter in southern states. We were adding to the other protests in northern cities to keep the pressure on to integrate in the South. Glover firmly believed that every little bit counted.

I observed Glover's leadership qualities and thought about him a lot. He was an enigma to me. I couldn't imagine that a gay person could be so politically astute and courageous. The people in my church had made me believe that essentially anyone who was gay was also stupid and a sissy. That's one of the reasons they'd convinced me that I *shouldn't* be gay—I was just too bright. But here was Glover—totally gay and totally brilliant.

I had never read about anybody except James Baldwin who was gay and politically astute. Now Glover introduced me to the writings and theories of Bayard Rustin. I had never even heard of him before. Glover not only knew a lot about him but had even met him on one of his trips to Birmingham. I was fascinated by the things Rustin had been doing since the late 1940s and early '50s. Where had I been? I listened with rapt attention as Glover informed me that he was openly gay and had been a loyal follower of Mahatma Gandhi. How could God have allowed someone gay to be so socially relevant and innovative? It just didn't fit what the Christians said. They had never told me about this.

I made up my mind that if I could ever meet Bayard Rustin or go to a march where he was, I would be there. I learned that a lot of what he did was kept out of the papers because powerful white people didn't approve of his demonstrations. He worked endlessly and humbly behind the scenes. I learned he was the mastermind and a foot soldier for the likes of Dr. Martin Luther King Jr., Rev. Ralph Abernathy, and A. Philip Randolph. There would have been no famous March on Washington without him. It took me a while to accept all this, but I began to read books, magazines, and newspapers. I educated myself about what was happening on the civil rights scene.

During this same time, there were auditions being held for a music department production of Donizetti's *The Elixir of Love*. At Miss Repp's urging, I listened to a recording and fell in love with the character Nemorino, the tenor lead. This was the perfect role for a lyric tenor, and I wanted to test whether I could learn and perform a full-stage opera. I had never once sung a full production of anything. I wanted to test my stamina and my memory as well as learn what is called the *Donizetti style* of singing. Up to that point, I had sung spirituals, gospel, and popular music the way I had wanted to. Ron Gould had worked with me on my audition pieces for Oberlin, and I had looked at a few songs apart from the Oberlin College Choir. I felt that I was ready to take on another challenge.

After the auditions, I could hardly wait until the names were posted on the bulletin board in the student lounge in the Con. When I found my name, I whooped for joy.

Learning this role was like sunlight and water to a rose for my voice. I flourished and grew under the discipline of regular voice lessons and coaching sessions. There were so many aspects of the role and the bel canto singing style that challenged me. I did research on the composer and performance traditions of the period. I couldn't get enough of the sweet melodies, divine harmonies, makeup, and costumes.

The production was a smashing success. I was speechless when I called "home" and the Beechwoods decided to drive up and attend one of the performances. I was deeply affected that for the first time my "family" was supportive of my artistic work. They gave me flowers, cards, and a special care package. As they congratulated me and hugged me, I realized it was as close as I had ever come to heaven on earth! It would be a long time before I allowed myself to fully absorb the fact that my mother and stepfather hadn't even been notified of the performances.

After *The Elixir of Love*, I buckled down on my regular coursework. I also started learning a variety of French songs by Henri Duparc. These beautiful, brooding, sensuous songs seemed to connect to my passionate southern migrant past. I'd sing them and wonder to myself what my Great-Grandmama Laura Mae and Granddaddy Saul would think of me now. Would they even consider what I was doing as right?

For an uptight, born-again Christian, Midwestern-Southern, church-singing, sharecropper's son, this was a stretch. The magnetism that drew me to this repertoire also repelled me. I began to practice and read about deep prayer and meditation. This practice helped me to stop feeling guilty and worried about everything. Did I really belong at Oberlin? Would I graduate? Did people like me as I was? When would I settle the question of my sexuality? Would I ever get married and have children? Would I . . . ? The questions went on and on. Meditation gave me the focus, relaxation, and confidence to take life one day at a time.

✦

AT THIS TIME, THE FAMOUS BARITONE ISAAC TOBIN
came to campus for the college recital series. He also conducted
a master class for voice majors. Several of us were selected to perform for him before the entire conservatory. Also, as an honor,
I was selected by the conservatory council to show Mr. Tobin
around campus and to share a meal with him, if he wanted the
company. He and I went to the student union and ate an unin-
terrupted simple meal. I had many questions for him and had to
continually remind myself that he had a performance that evening. He was gracious and smiled a lot.

As we walked back from the dining hall, he suddenly stepped
off the path into the shadows and pulled me to him. Just as in
the storybooks, he looked deep into my eyes and kissed me right
there, for what seemed like forever. He had the softest lips I'd
ever felt. He was wonderfully aggressive and daring, and his arms
held me strongly and gently. I was weak with acceptance and un-
expected passion. For the rest of the evening and all during the
concert, my mind lingered on that kiss.

Maestro Tobin sang exquisitely that evening, and the audience demanded several encores. He sang mostly French songs,
but I'd never heard Schubert sung more authentically and with
such mindfulness of the details. He was a masterful interpreter.
His charm was effusive and irresistible. At the reception afterward, I stood where I could always see him; he kept looking at me
from across the room and winking. His accompanist was the superb Steve Parker, who at one time had been a student at Oberlin. It was rumored that they were lovers. I could not reconcile
the kiss with Tobin's public image or the possibility that he and

Parker were living together as a couple. Did Miss Repp know? Did any of the faculty know? Did they *all* know?

I had overheard several conversations in the student lounge about Tobin and Parker, and it was speculated that people in Europe were far more tolerant of all sexual behavior than Americans. Because of Tobin's prominence, the public would tolerate his decision to live however he liked and not harass him. I couldn't imagine a great American pop star living an openly gay lifestyle. It could not happen. It made me want to go to Europe to learn more.

The next day at the master class, Maestro Tobin showed artful criticism and a wellspring of knowledge of the French, German, and Italian repertoire. All of us improved as he demonstrated a crescendo here, a delicate pause there, clarification of pronunciations, the importance of some of the rhythms—all of it dictated by the composer, or the music, or tradition. When it came my turn to sing, I was nervous, but I sang well. He was most complimentary. I felt that this was a beginning for me. I wanted to someday be known for my recital singing, and this repertoire was important.

After the master class, I kept hoping for a private audience, but it never happened. I never had the chance to ask him any of the questions that were still on my mind. He spoke to me briefly as he was preparing to go off to a faculty reception. He suggested that if I ever came to Paris, I should look him up.

◆

THE END OF THE YEAR WAS QUICKLY APPROACHING, AND that meant preparing for student recitals.

One day while I was rehearsing, I noticed someone lingering outside of the practice room, listening while I sang. This was not so unusual, and I paid it no mind at first. When I finished rehearsing, I went to the student lounge and sat for a bit to recover and think about what I was trying to say musically. As I sat there ruminating and relaxing, a handsome black student came over and asked if he could sit down next to me. He didn't wait for me to answer. He sat down and introduced himself as Charles Angus Solomon IV. It only took me a second to surmise that he was as arrogant as he was handsome—and he was very handsome. I was prepared to have a short conversation to be polite and move on. He smelled as though he had been smoking.

But before I knew it, an hour had passed. I had to return to class. I made my apologies for leaving so abruptly, and we promised to stay in touch. A few weeks later, I ran into him at a service at the local Baptist church. Afterward, Charles Angus suggested we go to a local diner instead of the regular college dining hall.

We were well into the bacon, eggs, toast, and coffee before I realized that he was flirting with me. He was talking to me just as I'd heard some of my friends talk to girlfriends in Youngstown. I sat there basking in his surprising pursuit and wondered how this conduct fit in with the sermon we had both just heard at Calvary Baptist Church. My delight was tinged with a little sadness: nothing risqué or overt had been said, yet already I was mentally pulling back.

But I kept listening and he kept talking. He liked my eyes, my lips, the way I talked, my nose, on and on and on. I couldn't help but listen. I was titillated to think that not another person in that little diner had any idea just what we were talking about. For the first time in my life, the forces pulling me toward something sexual with a man were stronger than the ones pulling me away. I let him walk me as far as the conservatory practice hall, where I feigned the need to practice for my upcoming student recital appearance. We would have embraced, but instead, we just said goodbye. To do more would have been much too aggressive and too public.

Two agonizing weeks later, he called and insisted on our getting together that weekend—no matter that I had made other plans. I compromised and agreed to meet after a basketball game at my dorm.

When I got back to my room, I turned off the overhead light, lit a candle and a low lamp, and turned on the stereo. Smokey Robinson could help me relax.

Even though I was poised and waiting, the gentle knock at the door shocked me. I tried to seem calm, and when I opened the door, there stood the object of all my daydreams and emotional wrangling of the past two weeks, in the flesh, smiling. My anxiety vanished.

The next day, as I lay in bed in the early morning sun, I was grateful that Charles Angus hadn't snored. Parts of my body were tired and other parts were rejoicing. I pushed away the last vestiges of Christian guilt and apology from my mind. If I couldn't enjoy this feeling, what could I enjoy?

◆

AS SOON AS I SAW THE LETTER IN MY MAILBOX WITH that handwriting, I knew something could happen and it wouldn't be good. I prepared myself, but I wasn't optimistic. I was still getting over the Miss Ella Belle incident and wasn't yet ready to deal with them again. I reluctantly opened the letter and immediately stood up in horror. My mother was coming to visit the next day after church! It was only a two-hour drive from Youngstown to Oberlin, and she was taking the Greyhound bus to spend the afternoon with me. After my sudden glowing encounter with Charles Angus, I was just as suddenly plunged into despair and stress. I ran into Jean-Pierre. When I told him what was happening, he leaped into action and invited all twelve of the guys from our section of the dorm to meet my mother and keep her distracted for the afternoon. It began to feel more and more like a mob—a civil, friendly mob—that was looking out for my interests. All my instincts told me that my mother never did something for nothing. She had a plan. I felt approaching doom. My only consolation was I was not alone.

When the bus pulled in the next day, I had a tough time staying put. The scared child in me wanted to run away and hide. I watched anxiously as passengers got off the bus before she appeared.

She was nearly the last person off. When I finally saw her, she was smartly dressed in a green pants suit. Her hair was dyed auburn, nicely cut and styled. She had on a new hat and matching shoes. She carried her purse and no luggage. We walked toward each other. She looked older and quieter, as though she was trying to be a professional, educated lady. She smiled and seemed deceptively gentle—she was trying to convince me that she had never wielded a knife. The guys stepped forward eagerly and introduced themselves. It took a while.

As we headed down the street, the guys gradually took over, and I deliberately moved to the rear of the pack. They seemed so mature and capable, and she seemed so loving and nonjudgmental.

I began to relax but remained alert. The consensus was we would take a leisurely walking tour of the town first and then hit the strategic points on the campus. My mother didn't seem to mind. I think she was intrigued by all the attention.

Eventually someone suggested that Jean-Pierre and I sing a little for my mother. I was shocked—I hadn't prepared myself at all. Jean-Pierre felt likewise, but we were carried away by the flood of general goodwill and, on my part, gratitude for their efforts. We each agreed to sing three songs.

My mother's presence made me nervous, but I didn't want to show it. I decided that I'd sing for the guys. *They* gave me strength and focus. I composed myself and launched into Beethoven's "Adelaide." My vocal production was lyrical and easy. I allowed the melody to sing itself. After everyone's applause and whoops, I centered myself for Faust's aria, *Salut, demeure chaste et pure.*

For my final selection I began softly, "Dere is a balm in Gilead to make the wounded whole." I wanted to keep it soft and intimate. I ended it on a breath, and I floated the high ending note forever. There was a palpable hush in the dorm lounge. Then applause! I called Jean-Pierre up to the piano. We acknowledged the accumulated audience that was packing the lounge and hall. It was a successful ad hoc concert. The guys helped me fill the rest of the afternoon, and before I knew it, it was time to put my mother back on the bus home.

The fellas were still making much ado about her and kept up the general commotion right up to the door of the bus! I hoped my mother had satisfied her curiosity about where I was—and could see that I would not be coming back soon. If she could truly see that I was at a great place and far better off than I would

have been had I gone to Youngstown State University or some
vocational school to learn about cooking or bricklaying, the day's
efforts would be well worth it.

The farewells progressed, and I was once again the last one
to awkwardly hug her. The doors closed, and the driver revved
up his motor. For a short time, we stood there silently watching
the disappearing bus. Finally, I let out a yell and started grabbing
my buddies and expressing deep thanks. The dancing, yelling,
and roughhousing went on all the way back to the dorm. We had
hatched and executed a plan to meet this emergency, and it had
been successful.

On the way home, Jean-Pierre handed me a letter. He said
that my mother wanted him to give it to me after she was gone. I
was shocked. I put on a brave front but inside I feared the worst.

When I got back to the dorm, I rushed to my room to read
the letter.

October 1, 1964

Dear Son,

First giving honor to God and praise to His
Son Jesus Christ. I was sitting quietly at home
last week when The Lord told me to go and find
my "lost sheep." I knew that He was talking
about you. I am responsible for you, and I am
asking you as a mother who loves you to come
back home. I feel that the occasion to sin is all
around you at Oberlin, and you have no one to
protect you and stand prayer-watch for your
soul. I know that you think you are grown and

you can do whatever you wish. But God sees you and knows your silent desire to sin. Singing well is not enough, son. You still must serve the Lord. I don't feel that you can do that so far away from your folks and home. You also need to get married and settle down and raise a family. No son of mine should be gay. It is the Devil's work for you to be thinking about men in that way that I know you do. I am praying for you every day. Your friend LaTanya Mae Sheridan from the church, and who you took to the prom, asks about you all the time and I told her I would tell you to call her. Her phone number is 749-3657. Call her, son, and get on with the Lord's work for your life. I have included some money for you to call her and get your ticket home to Youngstown. I will be waiting to hear from you.

I am always your mother.

All my love,
Inez Delois Boswell

My heart sank. I stared at the page for a long time. She wanted a macho, hetero son like my stepfather or brother. I'd never measure up. I wanted to tear up the letter and throw it away, but I couldn't. My mother's letter destroyed my sense of self and calm. She felt that I was evil and that the devil was the center of my life. I was no more interested in LaTanya Mae Sheridan than I was in eating barbed wire sandwiches. I had taken her to the senior prom because I needed a date. I had known her since the seventh grade. We frequently had interesting conversations because we were both interested in politics and black writers. She was a nice person, and I had positive feelings for her, but nothing more.

The phrase "No son of mine should be gay" kept repeating in my mind like a tormenting chorus. This was as close as my mother had ever come to giving me an ultimatum. I either had to conform to her way of living, or she seemed to imply that my life with her was over. Even though I had left home in my senior year of high school, I hadn't fully comprehended what life without my mother would mean for me. To leave home was one thing. To be shunned was another.

But whatever shame my mother managed to project onto me with her letter began to lessen and dissipate. I got my courage back. My shame all vanished in Charles Angus's steady, passionate presence. I resolved that I was prepared to rebuke my mother again, and I was not going to swallow her angry, poisonous letter anymore. I was not going to be her docile, obedient baby boy. I had a mind and a life of my own.

One night, Jean-Pierre and I were walking home after dinner. He had waited for me to finish washing the pots and pans in the kitchen. We had decided to hang out that evening and listen to some Renata Tebaldi and Leontyne Price recordings. We were opera fanatics by now and loved to just sit and listen to the greatest singers of the century for hours on end. But that evening on the way to the dorm he asked casually, "François, why don't you date any girls? Have you ever had a date since you came to Oberlin?"

I was caught unawares and couldn't answer right away. I dreaded where this conversation could go and was never entirely prepared for the outcome.

"Why should I date if I don't want to be with somebody? Should I do it just for the sake of show—to appear a certain way to everyone?" I answered, a little harshly. I was trying to buy some time and get a feeling for where this was going. But he was curious and didn't seem hostile.

He continued, "Well, I was just wondering. I've never seen you with any girls. Do you like girls?"

Well, there it was. Straight out! The direct question—no beating around the bush there.

I was prepared to finesse this one. It just wasn't the right time for me yet. I had no intentions of telling Jean-Pierre or anyone else that I was gay unless there was a confession to me first about them being gay. Then I'd think about it. I just couldn't take the risk yet.

"I know what you want to know. All right, for your information, I *am* seeing someone. I'm seeing someone from back home. She and I dated in high school, and I'm very close to her. I've avoided getting involved with anyone here because it would be like being unfaithful to her. She means a lot to me. I don't talk about her very much because I think that some things should be private. We talk sometimes and we write letters. She's an English major at Youngstown State University. Satisfied?"

He was quiet for so long that I wondered if he had heard me. "Why haven't you told me about her?" he asked, plain and simple.

"Because it's private. It's really nobody's business if I'm dating or not."

We walked quietly and slowly, still friends. I looked casually at my buddy and wondered just where this friendship would end up. I really didn't know from his questions just how he felt about having a best friend who might be gay.

It turned out that Glover Parham was the one person I could talk to about Charles Angus. How he perceived so much about us, I couldn't have known. But right from the beginning, he sensed our intimacy. One day, while I was saying goodbye to Charles Angus near my practice room in Robertson Hall, Glover happened by. As he rounded the corner, he saw us standing very close as we murmured last endearments before parting. I recognized his gait as he moved silently, almost floating, down the hall toward us and then suddenly stopped. Very dramatically and exaggeratedly he just turned and stared at us, seeming to look right through us. He put both hands on his hips and pulled up his chest and continued to stare. Glover looked us over, up and down, and all around. It was pure *Parham*. Charles Angus panicked and made a hasty retreat, not even finishing our goodbye. I stood there alone, enduring Glover's long, languid assessment. I felt like I had been struck by a hammer. I deeply resented this rude interruption. Before I had time to think or say anything, he proclaimed in a clear voice for all the world to hear:

"Honey, what y'all doin'?" He asked this very slowly and carefully, exaggerating his southern accent. Ordinarily he spoke very elegant English with the barest southern intonation. But now, he continued his resonant announcement in full southern: "Now, you know very well, I know what y'all been doin'!"

I screamed inside, *Please stop this nightmare!* I thought my heart would stop from fright. My mind raced a thousand miles a minute. I knew I could no longer conceal my heart's love. Reluctantly, I paused, gave a swooping mock bow, and smiled. Mustering as much charm as I could, I graciously invited Glover into my practice room. The alternative was his resounding baritone announcing my secret courtship to everyone.

Accepting my invitation, he moved in dramatically. He sat down at the piano, absorbing all the air around him. He sat high and regally erect, facing the door, like a queen taking her throne. I entered the practice room right behind him and quickly closed the door. I leaned against it, securing for the moment my privacy and my temporary prisoner. After a moment's pause, I tried to challenge him: "What are you talking about, chile?" I struggled to put on my most serene face.

"Don't 'chile' me, Miss Honey!" he shot back. "I know exactly what y'all been up to. This is not the first time I've seen what y'all doin'! Down home we call it *on the down low!*"

He stopped to let that sink in. I did not let on that this was the first time anyone had called me "Miss" anything. It had a strange feeling—not altogether objectionable, as though I were now in some exclusive club. Now I was officially gay. Miss Glover, the Queen of Oberlin, had proclaimed it.

"On the down low? What do you mean by that?" I really didn't know.

He jumped right in with the full explanation: "It's when somebody wants a whole lotta dick-suckin' and balls and maybe more, like some boy-pussy and male-lovin', but don't want nobody to know about it! Oh yes, Miss Honey, I know what I'm talkin' about; we have lots of *dem* down home! Sometimes we call it bein' in the closet." His attention seemed to focus even more on me. "You try to still be in the closet sometime, but I know ya! You nor Miss Solomon ain't foolin' me!" he said. He looked almost menacingly at me. I felt his gaze bore deeply into my chest and into my frantically pounding heart. I was stunned by all this— his oddly elegant southern crudity, his body language, and his completely accurate assessment of who I really was. I felt naked.

"I've never heard of any such thing," I stammered.

"Happens all the time, chile," he said with satisfaction. "I could tell you about lots of 'em, black and white. Has nothin' to do with race, honey."

The look on his face told me he was enjoying this conversation very much. I had stopped trying to conceal my surprise. I settled in to listen even more.

"Oh, yes, Miss Thing, sometimes it's the preacher, or the deacons, or the judge and the police chief. You name it! Whole lotta 'em wants some dick. Down home they were constantly pullin' after me once they knew that I was gay and not tryin' t'hide it. Chile, suitors came out of the woodwork! Well, you might as well go on and admit it. I know what I saw!"

"Well, yes," I managed weakly. "But Charles Angus doesn't want anyone to know. I really don't want anyone to know either. My mother will kill me. She's already down on me about getting married and all. I know what I've been doing, but I've never heard it called *the down low*."

"It don't matter what y'all call it or anybody else calls it, honey. He ain't right for you. You don't need to be *sneakin'* 'round with Charles Angus! Charles Angus is looking out for number one, himself, and dat *excludes* you. How is he in bed, Miss Honey? He looks like he could have some real meat, chile. How is it?"

"GP!'" I gasped. "He'd kill me if I told you that. It's personal."

"Either you tell me everything, or I'll tell *everybody* everything! Just watch me and see if I don't," he threatened, most convincingly.

What could I gain from fighting? He seemed to hold all the cards. It was as simple as that. Could GP keep a secret? I made my decision.

"Yes, dear, he has a nice dick, and so do I. I barely know him. We've been together just a few times." That was the best I could get out. I had to find a way to finish this conversation, clear out of there, and hold him to his promise.

He threw back his head and howled quadruple forte in response to my confession. He leaped to his feet and circled around the piano, dancing all around the room. He grabbed for me and tried to pull me into his celebration. I wasn't smiling. I wasn't dancing. I stood there glaring at him with my hands on my hips.

"Please relax, Miss Honey. Now listen, I'm not going to tell a soul about you and Miss Solomon, rest assured," he offered. "But now you have to tell me everything! I'm going to keep your secret and not tell a soul. But you're going to need some help with him because you're truly sweet and innocent, Miss Honey, and I just know he's not. He needs a queen like me to keep him in line. Chile, I will read him for filth if he even tries to look at someone else instead of you! He'd better not mess with you! Chile, now tell me how you two met. Who approached whom first, and where?" GP just kept digging.

I acquiesced. We huddled with our heads together for almost two hours. I told him nearly everything. He shared much with me about his family and his life with his mother and father and brother in Birmingham. He shared that his parents fully accepted who he was and, unlike my parents, never tried to make him deny whom he was or make over his sexual orientation. I found the concept wonderfully mind-boggling. I didn't tell him, but his explanation helped me to understand Michael Beechwood and his family much better.

He knew all about being on the down low. Back home in Alabama and even in Oberlin, he regularly had many exciting trysts with attractive married men of the community who would never openly admit to being gay. He even told me about a goodly number of single men with girlfriends with whom he'd had sex. They kept the whole thing clandestine. They communicated with one another through glancing eyes, vague hints, and anonymous networks, plus fake locations, theatrical or cryptic names, and occasional phone numbers. He met several of them in church, but he said that he just as frequently met men in the supermarket or at the movies. The movies were great, he said, because he could have sex right there in the back row in the dark. When he got older, he met men at cocktail parties, bars, and receptions. It didn't matter where he was. Through the afternoon, I learned that his imagination and daring were absolutely unlimited. I felt a little jealous at his freedom. I confessed to him that in many ways, I thought that I was in love. But Charles Angus was not. He thought that it was enough to have great sex and be great friends. I wanted a relationship with Charles Angus like all my buddies had with their girlfriends. I never really liked the surreptitious running around. Charles Angus's father was the most prominent black preacher in Pittsburgh, and Charles didn't want to do anything that would cast a bad shadow on his father and his legacy. Charles Angus was *very* much on the down low—he could never embrace me or acknowledge me publicly because his father was so important. It didn't matter how we both really felt. So, I was glad I could finally share my secret with someone. I knew that GP was more than an able ally.

When we finally parted several hours later and I headed back for the dorm, I realized that I was immensely relieved to have told someone about me and Charles Angus. I walked with a lighter step. I knew that I had unburdened all my guilt and problems on someone who could handle it. I couldn't be false to myself any longer, and I recognized that GP was a remarkable gay man. I would have felt very different about myself if I had had someone like him to talk with back in Youngstown. I was not going to let this angel get away.

✦

I HAD LEARNED EARLY ON THAT MANY MEN WERE SUS-ceptible to flattery and the genuine interest of their admirers. I studied sports and followed them in magazines and on television. I frequently impressed the guys with my knowledge and enthusiasm. Since coming to Oberlin, I had followed most of the athletic events—official and intramural. My interest was heightened because I knew guys on all the teams. In my naïveté, I flirted with them and smiled my way into their confidences. Once close to them, I learned that some of them permitted me certain insider's liberties: a relaxed acceptance that they didn't permit the general public. I was allowed into the locker room before the games, especially if I was singing the National Anthem, and I soon realized that many had a cavalier attitude about their bodies and were inattentive about the attention I paid them. It intrigued me to discover that others flirted right back with me! Some of them were charming, subtle, and disarmingly gentle, like I was a precious girl. Or they liked my voice, so they flirted right back with me, singing themes from popular love songs.

My voice gave me license! I even thought of myself sometimes as a singing mascot, an admired mascot, or even a sorcerer. The more the team won, the more status I seemed to have.

Maybe they saw something in me I wasn't fully aware of

myself. These guys seemed to instinctively know that I was more than just casually interested in them. I vaguely believed that there was something unconsciously symbiotic about our regular subtle exchanges. It gradually dawned on me that they looked forward to my presence as much as I looked forward to seeing them. Yes, the guys began to *look* for me.

I eventually became pretty good friends with one of the co-captains of the football team, Nicholas Gelosi. He was a rabble-rousing prep-school transplant from Pennsylvania that was six feet four with dark hair. He was serving as the second-string quarterback and first-string defensive guard. Everyone expected him to take on a major leadership role next year as a senior.

He was half Greek and half Italian, with bulging biceps, thighs, and an amazing butt. He had charisma. I became aware that his command of the English language was beyond that of most. He later confided to me that his first poems, several short stories, and two plays had been published while still in prep school. He usually talked loudly and forcefully for all the guys in the locker room to hear. In the evening, his rowdy conduct pushed the celebration envelope. Nobody tried to stop him.

Everyone seemed to know that he liked me. It was clear that he was the unofficial focus of the team, on and off the field. I had become accustomed to his dramatic arrivals and the company of his constant and surprisingly discordant jock entourage. He had fans.

One night after a game, we found ourselves alone in the locker room together after the rest of the team had left.

"The game was rough tonight," he said almost in a whisper, as though someone might overhear us. He had no trace of the crass enthusiasm he had displayed earlier in the company of his groupies. "I don't usually feel so whacked out and sore, but I really got in there on those suckers. I nailed a couple of them good. They'll be sorer than me tomorrow!"

With that he moved fully close to me. The touching felt good and natural. I kept telling myself to breathe deeply and try to relax. Involuntarily, I leaned on his powerful legs. The instinct was so deep that I was only half conscious as I raised my arms and tentatively returned his embrace, slowly, sensuously moving my hands around him. He moaned softly, squeezing me strongly and decisively.

I knew that I was lucid and fully awake. *This was no mere accident*, I thought. Even though I was getting exactly what I wanted, I felt ambushed by him and totally vulnerable. What if someone walked in and caught us? How much was I willing to risk? How would I explain this to the Oberlin Alumni Club of Youngstown?! How would he explain it to his family? I was relaxed and terrified at the same time. My old Christian panic was very close to the surface, ready to rush me out of the locker room.

✦

AS THE DAY FAST APPROACHED FOR MY SECOND RECITAL appearance, I went down the hall to the lounge to read and mouth the texts.

The three songs I was working on were *Chanson Triste* (*Sad Song*), *Phydilé*, and *Le manoir de Rosemonde* (*Rosemond's Manor*). For the time being, these songs were my life. Miss Repp encouraged me to read all about eighteenth century European culture to know how people dressed and behaved, what they ate, and their personal habits. It helped me to get even deeper into the messages the composers and librettists were trying to convey. I was living my music.

Although I loved this French music, I knew that it was not the music for the sexually conservative. It is totally secular. I was beginning to consider myself sexually liberated, or at least politically and culturally liberated because of my new independent college life and my new romantic experiences. I wanted so badly to be my own man—to leave the condemnation of the church behind and make my own decisions. One day I'd exorcise myself of all the demons I'd gotten from my mother and live a free, whole life. I fashioned an image of the future in which I was a successful singer, making plenty of money and sharing the wealth with those who had less. I had confidence that this was going to be my destiny.

I had been studying for about an hour when Nicky Gelosi strolled casually into the room wearing only a T-shirt and running shorts. He projected a healthy glow. He walked directly over and sat down very close to me on the couch. I quelled the instinct to move over. His body seemed at ease and totally at his command. He looked more tanned and sweaty than usual, and I remarked on it. There was no trace of the macho braggadocio he usually displayed in the locker room.

"What are you working on?" he asked, sincerely interested. His voice had a natural carrying power, and I found its timbre full and satisfying. If he had wanted to be a singer, he could have been. His tall, lean body and dark, handsome good looks would have made him a romantic lead in any theater production. I knew from talking with him that it was never even a consideration. He was fully committed to his poetry and other writings. His dad had understandably wanted Nicky to go to the University of

Michigan, where he had played quarterback for the Wolverines. He constantly pointed out that the athletic program there was even better now. His dad had dreamed that his gifted son would one day even play in the pros. But Nicky had rejected all that for the small liberal arts college and conservatory traditions of Oberlin. He preferred its reputation for political activism, with its history of involvement with the Underground Railroad and other social justice causes. Its balance of academics and athletics was, for him, a better fit. Nicky had set his mind on being a writer for as long as he could remember.

"Thanks for helping me out the other night," he said. "I was pretty sore and tired. Thanks to you, when I finally got home, man, I was nice and relaxed and had no trouble whatsoever falling asleep."

I admired his ease discussing our first sexual encounter. He didn't seem embarrassed or apologetic at all.

I chose my words very carefully. "No trouble, man. I found lots to like about getting to know you better. I never imagined that I'd get to know you so well."

"Neither did I, but you can get to know me as much as you want to," he offered. "I'm totally open to you. I sure know that I like me some François the Singer-Man, and I'd like to keep getting to know you, if you're willing. What d'ya say?"

Right to the point, I thought. I really liked that about him. But I was cautious. I had no reason to expect that a guy like Nicky Gelosi would take a relationship with me seriously. Besides, he had a girlfriend that he took around publicly—Alison. She was politically active on campus, and I genuinely liked her. I didn't feel good about sharing Nicky with her. Doubtless, she would feel the same way about me. I wasn't going to set myself up for heartbreak.

"What about Alison?" I asked. "I know she's your girl."

"What about Alison?" he said. "She's my girlfriend, yes, and we're very close, and I may one day marry her. But that has nothing to do with you and me." His eyes never left mine.

"What *does* it have to do with then?" I asked. "It would seem hypocritical to me to date both of us at the same time. I would like to think of you as a boyfriend. Is that silly?"

"It's not silly to me. It's rather flattering. I think that you're an artist of substance, and I value that. I don't care what you do in your private life, as long as you're tight with me. I'll treat you right regardless of who my girlfriend is. That's my promise to you. What is between us is between us, always." He leaned even closer to me, our lips almost touching. "I feel this need to be close to you, and I don't want to deny it. I think it's something special. You're someone special. I won't cheapen it or let anyone else cheapen it. If Alison finds out or someone tells her, I won't deny it. But I won't go around advertising it on billboards either. If that can work for you, then we're in, and I'm a happy camper. If not, no hard feelings. I'm still your friend."

At that moment, no was not in my vocabulary.

So, with that, we started our affair. Nicky came to my recital and after the last song, a carousing sound in the audience began to rise. This was more than the polite applause of students required to attend recitals. It was clear to me that the noise would continue. So I returned to the stage for another bow.

Nicky was standing and leading his entourage. They were a crowd, in full throttle, standing and cheering. I was a bit embarrassed and tried to soften their enthusiasm. They would not be placated. They urged me to sing another song. They started chanting, "François! François! François!" I motioned for them to sit down and relax. I'd gladly sing another song. After they quieted down, I began singing "There Is a Balm in Gilead" a cappella. When I finished, I accepted their still-thunderous applause and left the stage. Nicky was the first to get to me and congratulate me. His entourage followed. Before leaving, Nicky and Alison, hand-in-hand, presented me with flowers and a card, along with several hugs. I stammered my gratitude and said goodbye. It seemed surreal. The rest of the evening, I couldn't get Nicky out of my head. *So this is what it's going to be like: him with his girlfriend, me watching and behaving politely. Now I'm really on the down low,* I thought, *and he is too.* Not only that, but I was seeing both Nicky and Charles Angus at the same time. I knew that I had a lot of thinking to do when the year was over.

✦

THE WEEKS OF FINAL EXAMS CAME, AND I HUNG IN there. The recital was over, and I could hit the books hard now. At this point my nightlife came to a radical halt. Final exams were not playtime, and I took them seriously. I lived constantly with the fear that if I didn't make it at Oberlin I could wind up back in Youngstown, slaving away in the steel mills and automobile factories and not singing a note. So I got to work, and I did well.

After exams, many students were dying to get out of town. But there had been talk and speculation for weeks about who would give the commencement address. Finally, the *Oberlin Review*, the campus newspaper, announced that Dr. Martin Luther King Jr. was to be the speaker. A large audience was expected: people from all over the state, alumni, and families—they all wanted to see Dr. King and hear him speak! Kids who didn't have to be here for graduation were staying around just to see *him* too.

It was easy to wake up that morning. I washed and dressed quickly, grabbed my choir folder and robe, and went down the hall to look for Jean-Pierre. He was ready too. We headed for breakfast hardly letting our feet touch the ground. Excitement was in the air. When would we finally see him?! The dining hall was buzzing. After a quick breakfast, Jean-Pierre and I left immediately for the choir warm-up and rehearsal.

Everybody was on time. Even the choir director, Professor Fountain, seemed to move with more than his usual intention and purpose. He gave us fewer than expected directions during our warm-up. He said that he trusted that we would "come through just fine to honor the occasion." He communicated to all of us exactly what he thought of the man who was about to do this commencement address: his reverence was palpable. We already knew the music and had performed it many times on our California tour and in Russia. Our winding, humming human column slowly filed out of the choir room in Warner Hall and moved across the street to Tappan Square.

Jean-Pierre and I surveyed the setting. Flowers everywhere. The place was beautiful! We found the choir area. It was too soon to settle in, so we casually roamed here and there greeting friends and families all set on finding the best seat in full sight of a beloved soon-to-be-graduate.

Jean-Pierre and I kept hoping for a glimpse of *him*! Through the crowd, we became aware of another kind of buzz, an anxious anticipation. He had finally arrived, and we practically ran to where he was walking near the front of the room.

Amidst a buzzing, growing crowd, he looked calm and relaxed, smiling and nodding from time to time. The faculty and board of trustees flanked out informally in front, beside, and behind him. All were in full commencement regalia. He looked more vibrant and alive than in any of the photos I had seen. Some unseen cosmic magnet was steering me toward him. My heart thumped, and I felt faint. Jean-Pierre and I were standing side by side practically holding hands, we were so nervous. Then it happened! I have no idea how I had broken through the crowd or how I had introduced myself to Dr. King. All I knew was that I was suddenly standing in front of him and had his hand in mine and was looking deep into his eyes. His gentleness reminded me of Granddaddy Saul. My soul was dancing and singing!

I remember Jean-Pierre breathing at my side. Suddenly, without any warning, a well of joy and inspiration leaped out of me, and I flooded him with praise and introduction all in one breath. Dr. King's patience and wisdom encircled the whole experience. He never pulled away. I eventually slowed down. I still don't know if Jean-Pierre even got a word in. I was still holding Dr. King's hand and hearing the echoes of myself finding some sanity. Eventually, my dream state ended, and I remember him nodding and looking at us with infinite kindness.

I heard him say, "Well, just keep on keepin' on, young man. We, the Movement, need people like you. I'm grateful for your help and cooperation. I'll be listening for you in the choir."

Then he turned to his growing mass of admirers. I stood and watched his back and head as he calmly moved through the dense crowd. He kept nodding and taking a hand from time to time.

I had had my moment and was walking about six inches

off the ground. I felt a definite unfocused haze throughout the rest of the proceedings. I know it all went well because of the many congratulations and handshakes afterward. There were big smiles and hugs and kisses and long, tearful farewells. I knew that the Beechwoods would be looking for me, so I began to wander. Graduation was in the air, but it was mostly a hazy dream for me.

The next day, as I was packing up to leave for the summer, the telephone rang down the hall from my room. I took my time getting there to answer. When I got there, it was Charles Angus. He sounded uptight and abrupt, and as surprised to hear my voice as I was to hear his.

"Hey, can we talk? We need to talk."

"Well, yes," I answered. "What's up? You don't sound good."

"Well," he said. "I'm pretty upset. I was out with some friends, and I ran into Glover. He kept looking at me and smiling. He never looks at me or says anything to me. So, why now? I was very uncomfortable."

"Hey, come on, man. You can't stop people from looking at you. You're a good-looking guy, and GP can be pretty friendly when he wants to be," I hedged, trying to avoid where I thought this conversation was going.

"I don't need his admiration or his friendship. I'd rather that he just stay away from me. He makes me nervous."

"Hey, man, slow down. Why are you so upset? Did he say anything to you?"

"No, but that look of his—like he's looking through you. It gives me the willies."

I knew what he was talking about. Glover was known for that look.

"Anyway, I need to talk with you." He hesitated while I waited. Slowly he began, "Look, maybe we should stop seeing each other for a while. My parents are coming up to get me today, and I'd die if they ever found out how we feel about each other." He went on, "My dad's church would die if the congregation knew that his son was gay."

"That's not exactly my fault, now, is it?" I answered cynically and not very sympathetically. "Look, man, nobody made you come over to see me the first time. In fact, the way I remember it, you were the one insisting on coming over. I've never even been over to your dorm room." My voice rose steadily. "I don't know your room or your roommate!"

We were silent for a while. I was glad no one was around. I did not like this conversation.

He continued, "I don't want to hurt you or anything. I just know I can't handle anything so personal right now. Why don't we just stay in touch over the summer and talk in the fall when we get back."

The phone felt heavy in my hand. I was burning up but not from passion. My ears were ringing. "I'm not hurt, man," I lied. "It's not a problem. Look, man, just do your thing. I'll be fine. You know, I do have a life. I understand this thing with the parents. I have my own issues with mine. So don't mind me. I'll talk with you later. Have a great summer!" I ended the conversation abruptly.

Back in my room, Nicky kept flashing across my mind. I wondered if I was going to have one of these conversations with him next. I didn't have the experience to predict any of this.

◆

I SPENT THE REST OF THE SUMMER WITH THE BEECH-
woods, and our daily routine quickly became eerily normal.

Elaine and the Logans had left several messages. I planned
to spend some time with them before summer school began at
Youngstown State University. They had been a haven for me
during those last turbulent months of high school and my freshman year at Oberlin. I didn't want them to think I had forgotten
their generosity.

I allowed the joy of having finished the academic year at
Oberlin to settle in and began to accept the interest and questions of the Beechwoods and my high school friends. More than
anyone, Michael was intrigued by all aspects of my college life
and seemed to approve of everything I shared with him.

Toward the end of the first week back, I phoned Mrs. Logan and Elaine and suggested that Michael come along with me
to dinner—he was one of my best friends and the first person I
came out to. When I told Michael about it, he jumped on the idea.
It was settled. On the way to the Logans' house, my heart was
beating faster. I was excited about seeing them but recalled the
episode with my mother and stepfather the last time I was there.

Even though I felt very close to Elaine, we hadn't written or
communicated very much during my year away. I had never discussed with her my being gay, and I felt that in this Christian
environment, she just wasn't ready for that conversation. It was
sad but true that I avoided many people, not just her, who I felt
wouldn't understand that I was gay. Would I have to hide for the
rest of my life? Was there any real choice? Will I ever be able to
be myself totally? I wondered. My final thought as we parked
the car and climbed the stairs to the house was *Michael certainly
didn't have any trouble accepting my being gay!*

The house smelled great, and I couldn't wait to see what Mrs. Logan was preparing for dinner. When we got to the kitchen, we were not disappointed. Helping her were Prentiss and Malvina Louise. There was a flurry of kissing and hugging greetings. Somehow Michael got introduced.

"Be careful with those tops and that steam, y'all!" warned Mrs. Logan as we tried to peek under the lids. "That stove's red-hot, and I don't want anybody getting burned. Dinner will be ready in a few minutes. Y'all get cleaned up and ready to eat."

In the midst of all this familiar confusion, Elaine's voice broke through, "Well, pipe down, everybody. I've been trying to tell you that I invited LaTanya Mae to join us for dinner. We talked this afternoon and I said that it would be okay!"

Everything stopped. Slowly we turned and saw an attractive, black, Afroed coed of medium height standing next to Elaine. She was dressed in a light blue shirtwaist off-the-shoulder summer dress that hugged her frame modestly. Her eyes were smiling openly as she took in our confusion. LaTanya Mae Sheridan— my senior prom date and the girl my mother tried to push on me in her letter. She extended her hand and spoke before I had a chance to cover my awkwardness.

"Hi, François. How are you? Hi, everyone." She looked directly at me and spoke again. "Your mother told me that she had been up to Oberlin to see you and that you'd be calling me to say hello. Maybe we could get together sometime. I don't start summer school for a couple of weeks." She spoke so confidently that I was speechless for a moment.

Recovering, I extended my hand and introduced her to Michael. They spoke easily, and I began to relax. We all moved gradually toward the dining room table. Dinner was a huge success, and Michael and LaTanya hit it off immediately. They were ignoring everyone else as they discussed the virtues of Mozart as a child genius, as opposed to Beethoven who was a master scrubber. He was never satisfied with his final version of an overture or symphony and continued to rearrange different sections of a commission even after its premiere. I had no idea she knew so much about music or even cared!

As I caught up with the Logans, I realized that something was very off with Reverend Logan. During cleanup, Mrs. Logan called to me from the living room. I put down the potato salad I was wrapping and went to her. I smiled at Reverend Logan but got no response. Mrs. Logan was sitting on the couch with her hands folded and motioned me to join her. She took my hand and began very gently.

"I told Reverend that you were singing for the Oberlin Alumni Club in a couple of weeks, and he says that since he probably won't be able to come, would you be kind enough to sing something for him today? You know, I don't know if Elaine told you, but he had a massive stroke in March and hasn't been able to get around much without pain. His whole left side is paralyzed, and he can't feed himself. I have to help him get dressed and everything now."

"No, I didn't know," I said.

"Don't worry, sugar, it's not a problem. We all understand. It would mean a great deal to all of us if you would sing something for Reverend. He hasn't been to church since the stroke. I don't reckon on when he'll be able to go again," she murmured as she lovingly massaged my hand and arm. "You see, he can't talk much. I seem to be the only one who can understand what he's saying."

"Yes, ma'am," I offered. "I'd be happy to sing for him. I'll sing 'His Eye Is on the Sparrow.' I know he used to like that song."

She called everyone into the room and whispered to the reverend that I was going to sing. I swear it looked like he was smiling. At least his eyes looked like they were smiling. As the rest of the gang came in from the kitchen, and I began:

> *Why should I feel discouraged?*
> *Why should the shadows come?*
> *Why should my heart feel lonely?*
> *And long for heaven and home?*
> *When Jesus is my portion*
> *My constant friend is he.*
> *His eye is on the sparrow.*

When I finished, I looked at Reverend Logan, hoping for some obvious sign of approval.

Mrs. Logan's voice was choked with emotion. "It was beautiful, Franç!" She tried to smile as she stood and pulled me to her bosom for an embrace. As she pulled away, I could see the tears running down her cheeks. She tried to let her smile dominate. "I know he loved it. I can feel it. He might not say nothin', Franç, but I know what's in his heart and what he'd say if he could. He loved it! God bless you for being so sweet and kind to Reverend, Franç. You'll go a long way in life for being kind to those who are down and weak. I'll be prayin' for you, boy. You sure do have one beautiful voice!" Then she turned and helped the reverend gently to his feet. They headed upstairs.

The young folks then decided to go out and listen to some live music, which turned out to be a B. B. King concert. At the end of the evening, I offered to take LaTanya Mae home. Michael insisted that we all get together the following week.

At her house, we walked her to the side door. We had all liked one another and enjoyed a rare evening of intense sharing. Michael gave LaTanya Mae a gentle hug, and I followed up without hesitation. Back in the car, we danced around our unspoken thoughts.

I felt Michael's eyes on me. "She's crazy about you, you know," he finally said, almost to himself. "She. Likes. You. Like. I. Do," he said, halting between each word. "I know it. I can feel it. When you weren't paying us much attention, she practically said as much!"

"What are you talking about?" I protested. "She hardly knows me. We went to school together and dated a few times. That's all! I had to date someone in high school or the guys would make fun of me. So, I chose her. I could have chosen anyone. Besides, I'm *gay*," I added emphatically.

Searching my thoughts, I fumbled on, "I don't have anything against getting together again with her and going to see a movie or bowling or something like that. You can come along. In fact, I'm hoping that you will come along. You two seem to have a lot in common! She talked with you all night. I hardly said a word," I said, rolling my eyes.

"Hey, man, that's great. I'd love to come along. But she really wants to be with you. Alone. She practically told me so!" exclaimed Michael.

I was feeling tired. We headed upstairs arm in arm. I didn't resist when he joined me in my bedroom for the night. Kissing him had become a positive ritual, far from distasteful, but nothing at all like kissing Nicky.

"Is this the way you kissed LaTanya Mae?" he asked suddenly.

I eventually answered: "I never kissed her at all!"

✦

I AGREED TO ANOTHER CONCERT FOR THE OBERLIN
Alumni Club with Ron accompanying me, and the Beechwoods
and Logans came to hear me sing. When it was over, the applause
was long, loud, and intense. My heart filled and overflowed. Soon
there was a standing ovation. It felt as if I had the most supreme
gift possible from an appreciative audience. I kept blinking and
turning my head to keep from falling into an all-out cry. When
my high school principal, Mr. Tear, walked on stage to present
me with the flowers, I lost it. The tears took over, and he seemed
to fully understand. He gave me the flowers as he put his arms
around me in a warm, fatherly manner. My soul felt cleansed and
justified. Ron joined us, and the audience seemed to move closer
and closer as they continued their applause. Everything seemed
to flow right into the informal reception. People were talking
among themselves, gesturing and laughing. I felt pulled in all directions at once. I was happy so many of my high school buddies
had heard about the concert and showed up.

At the reception, I was shocked when my mother walked up
to me.

She didn't hug me or stand too close. She didn't mention how
well I sang or how good I looked in my new tux, or even that she
was proud of my accomplishment. No! She told me, "I spoke to
LaTanya Mae, son, and I'm glad you two are talking again. She
certainly is a lovely girl."

That was the sum of the evening for her. Her dutiful Christian son was playing the straight role again! She could hold her
head up high in the community and go to church on Sundays and
talk about her "answered prayers."

As much as I resented my mother's words, I did like LaTanya. As a good friend. And Michael adored her. One evening, Michael invited her to dinner at the Beechwoods' home, and as the night went on, it was clear that LaTanya was interested in me romantically. This made me deeply uncomfortable, but I thought we could keep things as they were if we didn't talk about it. I felt Michael was a safe buffer, although I didn't quite understand why he was encouraging the relationship between LaTanya and me in the first place. I would have thought that he would be jealous and possessive. Nothing made sense!

LaTanya kept up her pursuit, and I kept managing to evade her. Instead, I tried to lose myself in my new recording of Hector Berlioz's *Les nuits d'été* (Summer Nights) with soprano Eleanor Steber, and I was madly in love with it all: the song cycle, Berlioz, and Steber. That's what I could handle. Steber was the great American diva who had sung Mozart, Puccini, Strauss, and Verdi in all the European opera houses and come home to the Metropolitan Opera a national hero. She appeared often on the *The Bell Telephone Hour* and other seasonal TV variety shows that showcased operatic talent. I admired her for her mixture of grit and elegance. She sang exquisitely and yet cultivated her image of the girl next door.

I soon discovered that when I was working on an opera, I did the perfunctory work required to mimic the tenor role, but my soul was in the female roles. During rehearsals and performances, I was singing the female roles along with my colleagues. I had to work to squelch the urge in performances. Eventually, I could do it without moving my mouth, but my brain was busy!

It was in those moments that I truly felt like a woman. I felt tricked into my masculine body and existence. I wrestled with my sense of having been misplaced, misconfigured. What had gone wrong? I sang and agonized over this dilemma for years. I was struggling for an answer that I could live with. Who had mismatched me? God? If God was so perfect and so all-knowing, all-creating, and all-loving, well—what had gone wrong? I was stuck in this place. Nowhere did I feel that I had someone in authority—a champion, a mentor, a savior—to speak up for me.

✦

ADJUSTING BACK TO OBERLIN FOR MY JUNIOR YEAR WAS easy in some ways, very difficult in others. I was seeing Nicky at the time, but I needed some air, some time to breathe, and time to return singing to the center of my life. Everybody loved what I was doing, or what they thought I was doing. Everybody except me. I wasn't there. I was back to performing in absentia and trying to somehow please my mother and the Christian community in Youngstown. I would ask myself why it was so important. Why couldn't I just disappear into the mesh of my songs? I wanted to say to everyone, "Don't pay me any attention except when I'm singing." When I wasn't singing, I wanted to be Mr. Nobody and disappear into average, everyday life. This path I was on was going to drive me crazy!

I had been selected to be a junior counselor at one of the dorms for the incoming freshmen. It gave me some pocket money, but more importantly, it made me give up many of my own self-absorbed concerns. I had to see to it that most of my sixteen new guys got off to a good start at Oberlin. I had a single room and spent my time in my room listening to music and studying. In the past, I had usually studied with Jean Pierre or some of the conservatory guys.

The neediness of my new charges made me decide to stay close to them. I began to plan time just for them. It didn't take me long to realize that I am an instinctive nurturer—a natural mother. The guys could sense it too, and they brought all kinds of issues to me that they might have just sat on or taken to a professional. I heard many things that other junior counselors were probably spared. The boys shared their broken hearts, drunkenness, horniness, facial and skin acne, body odor, bad breath, bad hair, trouble with money, trouble with old friends back home, trouble with clinging girlfriends, clinging parents, absentee parents, sibling rivalry, the inability to eat the food, loneliness, insomnia, unrealistic academic expectations, what to wear, what not to wear, what music to listen to, confusion over their majors, indecision about what to major in, and—underlying it all— general homesickness. It was endless. I was amazed at how easily they let it spill out to me. I just had to listen, and I heard about everything that was important in a freshman's life at a small liberal arts college.

At this time, I also totally capitulated to my love of gospel music. When I wasn't listening to Leontyne Price and Maria Callas, I was listening to gospel greats like Albertina Walker and the Caravans, The Davis Sisters, James Cleveland, The Mighty Clouds of Joy, and the Barrett Sisters. Gospel! Gospel! Gospel!

Mahalia Jackson was at the top. I listened to her when I should have been doing my other studies. Somehow, I felt gospel music could save me from my sins. I felt the music intensely and never doubted its miraculous power to lift me up and transform me. I gave myself over to it even when I went to sleep. The passion of those singing ladies stopped my doubts about who and what I was and made me a son of God again. As I moved to the rhythm of their songs, I sweated and swooned and danced in that sea of sound that purified me and swept away my shame.

I mimicked the dustiness of Albertina Walker's voice to the extent that Miss Repp asked me, "What are you doing to your clear, sweet lyric tenor voice?" Didn't she know? Couldn't she figure out that that newfound huskiness was the evidence of my salvation?

I didn't know any adults who could empathize with my being gay. Sure, I had read about the Mattachine Society and people like Truman Capote, Walt Whitman, Oscar Wilde, and Gertrude Stein. They existed—but not in my world.

The Beechwoods were people I lived with, but I never talked to them. I knew that what I really wanted was to know whether the Beechwoods could protect me in the real world. That was the real test. They had certainly passed every other test locally. Some tests I hadn't the sophistication to even challenge them with. But to go out into the world and survive as gay and free. That was the *real* test.

And Michael—the sweetest friend on the planet. Why couldn't I be in love with him? I allowed myself to care about Michael and in my way to value him, but I never felt any passion for him.

✦

I began to work on Benjamin Britten's *Serenade for Tenor, Horn, and Strings*. Britten was such an enviable character to me. He was an esteemed composer who was not stigmatized for being gay. He was well off and unapologetically, openly gay. How'd that happen? Then I learned that the great tenor for whom Britten wrote all his music was his gay lover: Peter Pears. Hallelujah! Someone had escaped the dungeon. I wanted to know how.

Reading about his life didn't tell me a thing. Critics and theorists analyzed his music constantly and never once mentioned that he was gay. I got the information by word of mouth from some New York students who claimed to have empirical evidence. I wanted to know how guys like Britten could live an openly gay life and not feel condemned to hell, while a plain old guy like me couldn't do it in the United States. There were no answers.

As I drew back from most people, I discovered that time I spent with Nicky was actually energy-generating and rewarding, rather than an energy loss. His actions, his attitude, his language all spelled one thing: Victory! Success! I could do it and do it well. He wanted me to succeed as much as I did. I had an active, unabashed ally. He even came to a couple of rehearsals. He wasn't my boyfriend, but he was acting like one. We didn't walk around holding hands, we didn't kiss in public, but we looked into each other's eyes and communicated without speaking. We moved close to each other when we walked, with our shoulders touching from time to time; we danced more than just walked. We sat with our legs touching at games and concerts and dinner: it was intimacy without confession or exposure. It was the most active and intense non-relationship I'd ever had. He seemed to be daring anybody to say anything, to see anything. And nobody did.

Where was Alison during all this? I tried to avoid her. It was as though she hadn't noticed our intimacy, so frankly, I was reluctant to have any conversations with her.

Once when we were alone, he held my face in his strong hands and showered me with a thousand kisses and apologized profusely, having bought me flowers after he had accidentally called me Alison! Late at night he whispered, "I swear I know the difference!"

Would he have done all that if he had known how I felt—that I hadn't minded at all being called Alison. She had many qualities I secretly admired. Maybe I was even jealous. She could walk around campus in full public view holding his hand. She could openly sit on his lap in any dorm lounge regardless of what time it was or who was there. If she wanted to, she could walk down the aisle with him in any church and legally marry him. I could do none of that. I was always going to be that "extra" person, that invisible person who couldn't shine, couldn't sing, couldn't brag about my love. I couldn't even whisper about it. Even thinking about it made me feel guilty. I had to pretend that I was invisible to the person I loved the most. I, the quintessential extrovert, had to be quiet!

My mind wasn't the only thing in turmoil in those days. There were riots in Detroit, Watts, and Newark. I considered joining the Student Nonviolent Coordinating Committee (SNCC), the Congress of Racial Equality (CORE), the National Association for the Advancement of Colored People (NAACP), and the Black Panther Party. I finally settled on the Southern Christian Leadership Conference (SCLC), the organization that Dr. King was president of.

Dr. King was asking my kind of questions about the Vietnam War, and I hoped that someone in a position of responsibility—starting with President Johnson and Vice President Hubert Humphrey—would give us all some answers we could swallow.

There were more things happening in Vietnam than met the eye. We had a right to know more than the authorities and politicians were telling us.

I didn't want to go to war, but I knew that my time of reckoning was coming. I didn't want to learn to kill anybody. When I got the call from the draft board in Youngstown, I panicked.

After the draft board called, the Beechwoods stepped in. They seemed to know a lot about conscientious objector status. I discovered that historically there were lots of people who had not gone into the army, who were nonviolent like Dr. King. With the help of my family and friends and the people who were advising me at Oberlin, I did have some choice. However difficult, I was determined to play that option.

Glover and I talked about it. He hadn't been called up yet but was apprehensive. He knew his parents would support him if he decided not to go. Both of us had choices, but not very encouraging choices. Nobody walked around bragging about being a conscientious objector. People could even get violent. They made you feel like you were a coward for opting out of killing other people.

I could tell the army recruiters that I was gay and see how that went over. Then I'd have to deal with it for the rest of my life. I didn't know which option to fight for: gayness or conscientious objector status. Either way, I was going to be extremely unpopular with the "real men."

The Beechwoods would support wholeheartedly whatever decision I made. I didn't have to go if I didn't want to, and they'd do everything they could in Youngstown to get my 1-A status changed. I procrastinated and procrastinated until the day for my physical exam arrived. Dr. Tom was able to get it transferred to Cleveland.

About sixteen guys from Oberlin and the surrounding area were called up for induction. From the bus station, the army recruitment center was only a few blocks away. Some of the fellas carried duffle bags and small suitcases. If they passed the inspection today, some of them would leave Cleveland immediately for boot camp. I could have eaten and spit out nails, I was so angry.

The general inspection and health examination was singularly one of the most humiliating experiences I have endured in my entire life. The army recruiters acted as though you were already in the army and they owned your ass. I immediately resented their authority and arrogance.

We all stood in lines where a single letter on a sheet of paper corresponded to our last name. We stood there to fill out health forms, take shots, and talk with the interviewing physicians. It was all one big open space with guys in all stages of undress. I liked and hated it. I was curious and wanted to look around but didn't dare. I was in a state of heightened awareness. I felt like all eyes were on me as I undressed to my shorts.

When the interviewing army inspector started reading my form, I almost passed out. He read to me loudly as though I were fifty yards away, calling out my name and address. As I answered him, suddenly, my own voice boomed out. Even though I was trying to talk between him and me, it was impossible. My adrenalin overwhelmed my modesty, and I heard my voice being projected loudly.

"Yes, I have had homosexual feelings for men in the past," I checked with myself mentally and—bless God—it surely *was* me talking just that loudly! How I hated being in this situation, and I hated what I'd just said loudly for all to hear.

The sergeant stopped momentarily and looked up from his

paper. His passive face seemed to struggle to hold back his re-vulsion at having to deal with the likes of me. His disgust en-circled us. I was sure that duty kept him from reaching out and strangling me. He barked out of the corner of his mouth, "Boy! You need to talk to one of our shrinks. Go over there to the line marked GCOM (Gay, Conscientious-Objector, Medical) and wait there. Next!" He went right on to the next befuddled re-cruit. I was dismissed.

I moved to the line where he had pointed and waited with several other boys who had already arrived. The line was sepa-rated from the rest of the sea of milling manhood. I felt like an outcast. All of us had stumped the sergeants with our answer to the homosexual inquiry. We had all said yes.

It didn't take long to realize that our part of the arena was for psychological outcasts. No one spoke to us or looked our way. Each of us, individually and collectively, knew that somehow all traces of "manhood" had vanished from our section of the floor. We were marked as men who were not willing or fit to fight and die for our country. I would not soon forget my awareness of the disgust of many men. No words were spoken but the message was the same: You and all that you stand for are forevermore unmanly and unfit to be a part of this society. Get thee from our sight!

After that ordeal, I dressed and walked back to the station and took the next bus back to Oberlin. It was a long and lonely ride. I was granted the exempt status. I kept trying to pretend that I was all right and that everything was the same as yesterday, but I knew better. The actions of the sergeant and all the men in the arena told me that I was stained, unfit, and unacceptable.

There were the Inez Delois demons again. No matter how

I tried to rise above them, they caught me and dragged me back under my real self. Here I was about to graduate from Oberlin College, the first person in a long line of farmers and plain people, and I was haunted by my sexual nature, my pervasive and persistent love for men. I asked myself, *How long can you be gay and shunned?*

✦

EVERYTHING WAS HEADING STRAIGHT FOR GRADUA-tion. The long haul was nearly over. Nicky was going to the University of Chicago. Most of my other buddies were going to grad school too. They also seemed to have *time* for more schooling. I didn't feel like I had time on my side. I was in a hurry. I was eager to begin my career. I reluctantly began to think about graduate school, because everyone around me strongly felt that I wasn't quite ready for New York, and they said it in no uncertain terms. Miss Repp talked and talked against the idea: New York would eat up my young voice. "If you had just a little more time," she said, her voice full of frustration, "your voice could mature a bit more, and survival would be assured."

Begrudgingly, I listened. She was articulate, even quarrel-some for her cause. She knew my voice better than I did, so she pressed her points. I began to relent. Several of my other professors added their voices to what was becoming a din of dissent. I kept wondering how they could know so well. I loved the idea of New York and was determined to live and work there one day. But I finally conceded that it didn't make a difference if I waited a year or so.

I sent for the grad school applications and began to fill them

My father, Willie Son, Sr. (*Photograph courtesy of the author*)

Yearbook photo from The Rayen School in Youngstown, Ohio.
(*Photograph courtesy of the author*)

The Rayen School Boys' Octet. (*Photograph courtesy of the author*)

Rehearsal with Fred.
(*Photograph courtesy
of Janet Jordan*)

Fred Rogers with members of the Harlem Spiritual Ensemble.
(Photograph courtesy of Janet Jordan)

Mr. McFeely (David Newell) and I pose in the *Neighborhood of Make Believe*. *(Photograph courtesy of The Fred Rogers Company)*

Chatting with King Friday and Queen Sara.
(*Photograph courtesy of The Fred Rogers Company*)

At the keyboard with Mister Rogers and Mr. and Mrs. McFeely in
Mr. Clemmons' Studio. (*Photograph courtesy of The Fred Rogers Company*)

Betty Aberlin, Mr. McFeely (David Newell), and myself on set.
(*Photograph courtesy of The Fred Rogers Company*)

Dedication of Baby Grand Piano to Ross Commons by
Dr. François S. Clemmons, Middlebury College, 2004. The piano
originally belonged my dear friend Maestro Thurman Bailey.
I inherited it when he died in August 2001. Now it has a happy home
at Middlebury. It's interesting to imagine that long after I am gone,
a very special part of me and my friend Maestro Bailey will still
be here making folks happy! (*Photograph courtesy of the author*)

Paying homage to the late Dr. and Mrs. King at
the Martin Luther King, Jr. National Historical Park in
Atlanta, Georgia. (*Photograph courtesy of the author*)

Let it shine, let it shine.
(*Photograph courtesy
of the author*)

Receiving my honorary doctorate from Sewanee University of the
South in January 2019. (*Photograph courtesy of Sewanee University of the South*)

Accepting the 2019 Vermont Governor's Award for Excellence in
the Arts in the Concert Hall of Mahaney Center for the Arts at
Middlebury College, November 2019. (*Photograph courtesy of Todd Balfour*)

out. I aimed for the big ones: Juilliard in New York City; Eastman School of Music in Rochester, New York; University of Michigan in Ann Arbor, Michigan; Indiana University in Bloomington, Indiana; and Manhattan School of Music, in Harlem, New York. I wasn't sure how I would pay, but once the Beechwoods heard that I was seriously intending to pursue graduate school, they jumped on board and made it all possible for me. They sent me money with strict orders not to worry. They urged me to get busy filling out the applications. They didn't try to tell me where to go; they said, "just to do it." Time and love made it easier for me to accept their help.

Miss Repp was relieved at my decision and did all she could, short of singing for me, to help with the preparations. Together, we strategized and sorted out repertoire; we rehearsed and prepared tapes. I knew that she had been down this road time and time again and would guide the way for me. So now I was listening and cooperating. I perceived a gentle and subtle change in our relationship. I didn't make it difficult for her. I allowed her once again to be my champion and surrogate mother. I never regretted the decision.

The most significant event of my senior year was my senior recital in Warner Hall. I had worked toward this moment for the past four years; all performance majors had to do a senior recital. It was complicated by the presence of the Beechwood clan, LaTanya Mae, and Nicky all at the same concert! Luckily, Nicky was predictably understanding and made no demands on my time. Michael and LaTanya Mae had brought their own sleeping bags, and we all passed out immediately after the full evening. It was a relief when they left right after breakfast; they knew nothing about my relationship with Nicky, and I was trying to keep them separate. These were our last days together on campus, and I wanted to spend as much time with Nicky as possible.

In January, I entered the Metropolitan Opera National Council Auditions, a big deal among us singers. We talked about nothing else after the Christmas break. It was not unusual for ten or twelve singers from Oberlin to go each year, and as often as not, we won all three places.

I sang *"En fermant les yeux* (Dream Song)" from *Manon* and *"Il mio tesoro* (My Treasure)" from *Don Giovanni*. I felt optimistic that I had a good chance of winning. The judge liked me and spoke with me frankly afterward about singing and my career. She felt that I should go to grad school and take my time coming to New York City. She took the time to tell me examples of singers whose careers were ruined before they got off the ground by stepping out into the professional world before they were ready. Again, as with Miss Repp, I listened to her advice. She made sense. She gave me her card and made me promise that, when I was ready, I would be in touch with her. She said she would do what she could to help me launch my singing career. Her promise made the difference to me. Of course, I was very disappointed when I didn't win, but looking back, I know that I was too young. But I didn't understand it at time. I was simply not as developed of a singer.

The next contest I entered taught me the value of being a tenor. On a lark, Jean Pierre and I entered the contest for the Ohio National Association of Teachers of Singing (NATS) held at Baldwin Wallace University. The judge, mezzo-soprano Beatrice "Bea" Krebs, gave me first prize of five hundred dollars and asked to speak with me afterward. When she finished talking about my performance and how impressed she was, she explained to me all the special qualities of the graduate program she headed at Carnegie Mellon University in Pittsburgh. They had a great opera program with several performances each year. She made it clear that they could use a tenor like me. At the end of the day, Miss Krebs gave me her verbal promise of a full graduate fellowship and help in finding local work in the churches and community theaters. In two years, I could have my MFA and finally head for New York. I could go to graduate school and study in peace. I was glad when Jean Pierre shared with me that he felt the same way. We settled on going to Carnegie together.

Throughout my years at Oberlin, I had chronic bronchial infections and trouble with enlarged tonsils. During my senior year, this vulnerability became acute and caused me to spend too much time coughing, sputtering, sneezing, and visiting the college physicians. I had not taken care of the problems, but I knew I had to have my adenoids and tonsils taken out. And with my senior recital and several contests under my belt, I decided to have the operation. I always felt good about singing when I was well, but singing when I was not well felt like dancing in bare feet on a wooden floor with thumb tacks all over it. I couldn't continue to risk my career like this. Once again, Dr. Tom took charge and made the whole thing work smoothly. At his suggestion, I went back to Youngstown for a few days and had the operation. After the operation, I ate Jell-O and ice cream until my throat healed. That was one diet I could stay on long after its practical usefulness!

✦

AFTER RETURNING TO OBERLIN WELL RESTED, I SPENT a lot of time catching up on class reading, recreational reading, and listening to records. Having all this extra time allowed me to experiment with some other roles in the theater. I always loved musical comedies and had wanted to perform in one since high school. But as a black tenor, I soon learned that my fantasy was just that. I never got hired to do any romantic leads, even though some of the parts were perfect for my voice. After I saw and heard some of the lovely white boys who were hired for their looks and not their musical talents, I stopped auditioning. That message was clear.

Nicky knew of my love for musical comedy. We had listened to recordings of several of the shows together and sometimes we would walk around campus singing and horsing around while harmonizing on some of the tunes. He would sing the male parts, quite decently I might add, and I would hack the female lead part. Nicky loved to be on stage, whether for one person or for thousands.

One day when he came over to my dorm, Nicky suggested that both of us audition as dancers for Oberlin's production of *Finian's Rainbow*. At first, I laughed. I also shared with him my discouragement with the results of earlier auditions. He pointed out what a pleasant new experience it would be for both of us, and how much time we could spend together without having to worry about what anyone would say. I didn't need any more convincing.

At the audition I found out what a well-coordinated dancer he really was. He also informed me that he had danced in *Oklahoma!* in his freshman year. Within a day or so, we learned that both of us were cast in the male chorus of dancers. As a bonus, it included various featured spots. I was in dance heaven!

Dancing in this production gave me some insights into what

Alison might be feeling while studying with our guy most evenings. I soon found out that Nicky was purposeful and fun. He remembered his choreography, certainly as well as I did, and he often pitched in and helped some of the slower dancers. His leadership qualities were always present. He was always on time and frequently early to rehearsals. We were a fine team. We inspired and challenged each other, serving as the core leadership for all the dancers.

This was a different kind of fun from singing. Singing was competitive in an individual way. This dance chorus had a group mentality, and we cheered for one another all the time. We paid close attention to one another and tried to work together regardless of how challenging the choreography was. And it was difficult. I actually began to feel like a dancer. It was one of the most fun times in my entire life.

But much as I enjoyed it, I knew in every bone in my body that it wouldn't last. It would have been reckless of me not to get well and get back to my music. I had lofty singing goals, and I knew that was the space where I wanted to put all my time, energy, focus, and passion. All during my recuperation, Miss Repp did a thorough job of getting my vocal chords back into shape with special exercises and lots of breathing techniques. Several times she brought teas and vitamins to class. Gradually, my voice returned to its normal condition, maybe even better than before. I was happy to be singing again.

But by the time I finally graduated, I was glad to be done. Even though I was overjoyed to have my first college degree and appreciated all that it had meant, the ceremony felt hollow. I was walking through the paces to please the adults around me: Ron and Marsha Gould, Mary Lou Phillips, Mr. and Mrs. Miller, the

Logans, the Beechwoods, LaTanya Mae, Miss Repp, members of
the Oberlin Alumni Club of Youngstown, and my other professors. All I could think about was saying goodbye to Nicky. He
had become the central person in my life.

When I gently shared with Nicky my reticence about leaving
him, he refused to take me seriously. He refused to see our parting as anything more than temporary. He eagerly shared with me
his plans for graduate school in Chicago and gave me his word
that he'd be in Pittsburgh to visit. I was dubious, but I listened.
On our last night, he begged me to get up, get dressed, and meet
him behind one of the dorms. Reluctantly, I dressed quickly and
met him.

In the dark with the faint illumination of moonlight and
streetlights, I could see that he was carrying a bundle and wore
a backpack. Then I noticed that he was wearing short, gray-and-
green lederhosen exactly like Austrian-Swiss travel posters of
guys in native dress. He even had suspenders over an embroi-
dered shirt, plus the traditional cap. It looked like any minute he
might start yodeling. He was smiling, very pleased with himself.
I couldn't help smiling and shaking my head in disbelief.

"You might have told me to dress up," I said, feigning annoy-
ance as I got closer. "I didn't know we were going to a costume
party."

Without a word he set his bundle down and grabbed me by
the arms. He gently pulled me into the shadows and kissed me
full on the lips.

"Come on, I prepared a surprise for you. We're not going to a
costume party; we're going to a Midnight Picnic!"

He could have knocked me over with a feather. I looked into
his eyes; he wasn't kidding. He began to walk and pulled me after

him. We wound our way through the gentle undergrowth that grew loosely behind the dorms.

A bit farther down he took out a flashlight and we traveled easier. At last we came to a small clearing near some trees and a gently flowing stream. Then Nicky unloaded his bundle and an enormous amount of gear from his backpack.

He gave me the flashlight to hold as he spread out a large blanket and set up two dinner places. The plates and cups were from the dining hall. Next, he pulled out several aluminum-foil-wrapped parcels and laid them aside. Then a silver flask, a wine bottle, and a corkscrew appeared. He even had insect repellent! He paused, taking his time, and made me put some on both of us before we sat down.

Nicky had outdone himself, and Mother Nature was totally cooperating with us: it was warm and there was a gentle breeze. The moonlight was pale and dreamlike. The night birds and frogs serenaded us as I took in this perfect fantasyland. When we had finished eating, Nicky cleaned and packed everything into the backpack.

Next, he unrolled two sleeping bags and carefully zipped them together, laid them out, and invited me in. Inside, both of us swiftly undressed. I watched his body as he moved, more fluid shadow than concrete form: confident, virile, all male. When he turned back to me, I was practically levitating from the rush of desire. As we made love, I kept thinking, *Life is great. I have lots to be thankful for.* I couldn't hold his hand in public or sit on his lap in dorm lounges, but I could love him in private. Nobody could take this wonderful feeling from my heart. I lay down that night where I most wanted to be.

PART IV

There Are Many Ways to Say I Love You

"Love isn't a state of perfect caring. It is an active noun like 'struggle.' To love someone is to strive to accept that person exactly the way he or she is, right here and now."
—FRED ROGERS

A FTER FOUR HARD-FOUGHT YEARS AT OBERLIN College, I finally arrived in Pittsburgh in 1967, ready to go at Carnegie Tech (which later merged with the Mellon Institute) to pursue my MFA. I could never have anticipated how Pittsburgh would change my life.

Nicky was waiting for me with open arms. He and his parents lived in Penn Hills. Nicky knew his parents and assumed that they were neither curious nor suspicious about us. We set our own schedule, and they went about their own business. Until Nicky left for Chicago, I didn't sleep in my own bed and they didn't ask.

Nicky offered to show me Pittsburgh and drove me through the different ethnic neighborhoods, commenting on this and that, pointing out where he used to jog. I had no idea it was so diverse.

The racially ideal neighborhood I had imagined didn't exist here. Nevertheless, I was excited about all the possibilities. Nicky showed me Irish neighborhoods, where there were no blacks, and Homewood and the Hill Districts, which were practically all black. There were neighborhoods that were almost 100 percent Italian, and Squirrel Hill, which was 70 percent Jewish. Around the university, it was mostly white or Jewish with lots of public institutions like banks, restaurants, bookstores, WQED, the Catholic cathedral, and other churches and synagogues. There were some Latino, Greek, Polish, Lebanese, and other Middle Eastern communities, as well as the North Side neighborhood, which was close to downtown. The North Side was an ethnic melting pot full of second-generation Italian and Greek immigrants. They had historically worked in the mills and were still struggling.

This pattern of racial polarization continued in all the suburbs from Upper St. Clair and Mount Lebanon to Penn Hills and Wilkinsburg on the east side. The diversity was rich, but very separate. Despite this, I loved my sense of freedom and independence. I was dying to be on my own.

It was due to the insights of Nicky's mother that I eventually realized I needed to search the *Pittsburgh Courier*—the black newspaper—if I were to find an apartment anywhere near the campus that was decent. I had been searching through all the Oakland real estate listings to no avail. Everywhere I went, the apartments had already been rented, and indeed, I was growing very frustrated. True to my optimistic nature, I made a note that at least the rejections always had a smile.

I finally found a spot in Schenley Heights, on Clarissa Street. Once I was settled, there was plenty to keep me busy on campus, so I would rarely be home anyway. Nicky helped me shop for food and sundries, and later we put up a few posters of Leontyne Price, Joe Louis, and Dr. Martin Luther King Jr. Then we christened the bed! When it was finally time to say goodbye, it was easier than it had ever been. Somehow, I knew that Nicky would stay in touch and find a way for us to be together again.

✦

I LOVED ALL THE ACADEMIC NEW CHALLENGES AT CARnegie Mellon, especially the opera workshop under the direction of Rudi Fellner, also our coach and conductor, as well as the projects presented by the dean of the music department, Sidney Harth. We sang Massenet's *Manon* that semester, and since I was the only tenor in the entire music department, the lead romantic role of des Grieux fell to me. There were lots of wonderful new solo repertoires to explore, like Mozart's *Requiem*, Haydn's *The Creation*, and Benjamin Britten's *War Requiem*.

I immediately felt that I was being kicked up another notch from my Oberlin days. People would get to hear me sing and think of me not as a young student but as a noteworthy young professional on the brink of a major singing career.

Even though I had a full-ride scholarship, part of my challenge was finding a church job that would help pay for my living expenses while I was in school. Expenses added up for things like music scores, textbooks, performance clothes, and car maintenance. I found a position quickly at Mt. Lebanon Methodist Church, and the salary was enough to get by.

Lots of projects and good ideas happened by word of mouth in the student lounge, where my peers shared information about events that were happening on campus and around Pittsburgh. That's how we heard about job vacancies and when a conductor or organist was looking for a substitute or full-time singer.

At this particular time, there was lots of gossip going around the lounge about a certain organist named John Lively. It was said that John had fired his entire professional solo quartet in a wild rage several weeks earlier for showing up late to rehearsals and not singing as well as he expected. Word went out that he was looking for some good singers who were willing to work hard and not mess around. It all sounded a bit loose to me. But even though I already had a job out in Mt. Lebanon, one of the nicer suburbs, I wanted a job closer to campus that paid more. After chatting with a couple of my buddies, I decided to give him a call. He seemed nice enough, and we arranged an audition at the Third Presbyterian Church in Shadyside.

Frankly, it seemed too easy. I sang an aria from Mendelssohn's *Elijah* and was hired on the spot! John had fire in his personality, and he kidded me, which actually helped me to relax; we were on the same wavelength. I liked him right away and actually enjoyed our short time together. He also asked to hear a spiritual and I obliged him with my rendition of "Swing Low, Sweet Chariot." It was amazing—the man could follow me like a second skin, and he could improvise. The whole time I wondered, *What is all the fuss about?*

When I got back to Carnegie Mellon and shared with my buddies how the audition had gone, they couldn't believe it. They expected a nightmarish experience commiserate with the gossip they had been spouting. It never happened. I soon discovered that everyone in the music department knew that I had gotten the job. Several of the other tenors around town had auditioned too and had been turned down. Two of them were favorites of my voice teacher at the time, Bea Krebs. That didn't endear me to her anymore, but I knew that I didn't care. We had a rocky beginning, and I realized early on that we weren't a good fit in the classroom. We were like water and oil. I started out very much wanting to get along, indeed, to learn to sing better. But she had a brusque way of dealing with me that set me off. I often had to conceal and squash my temper. Essentially, I felt like an adult and fully expected to be treated like one. She had the wrong assumption that she could make decisions concerning my performances and repertoire without asking me. I totally balked. She always seemed to be challenging me instead of encouraging me. I listened very carefully to her words and watched her face, and often I perceived ridicule in them. Her bossiness rang jangling chords of resistance in me. This was not the way for me to sing. I needed some honey in my relationship with my voice teacher, and in this case, I had a shower of vinegar I couldn't avoid.

Despite my issues with Bea, I was becoming a known quantity around the music department, and I was beginning to like it. Because of the way this man ran that audition, I always adored and enjoyed working at Third Presbyterian Church. Years after I left Pittsburgh for Manhattan, I kept in touch with John and his family.

Singing in the choir at Third Presbyterian Church with John was as exciting as I had imagined! Not only was the music interesting, challenging, and frequently beautiful, but John planned several lovely parts for me and the other members of his quartet. It was highly invigorating, and I paid attention all the time. The other soloists seemed to have the same intention, and without going overboard, I know there were times we made great music together. Unlike any other choir that I had ever sung in, John lived up to his last name, and he kept us laughing for most of the rehearsals with his double entendres and fun-loving nature.

It was through this choir that I met Fred and Joanne Rogers. Joanne had a bubbly personality and a lovely smile. She could tell jokes with the best of them, and I loved listening. Her quick wit and humor were near legendary among the members of the Third Presbyterian Church Choir. I often sat close to her and the other altos at Thursday night rehearsal so I could hear what they were whispering and laughing about. Eventually I ended up sitting right next to her, and as we got to know each other, we frequently shared our own inside jokes and laughter when any opportunity presented itself. We were having so much fun that I insisted on wanting to know who exactly she was. John shared that she was Fred Rogers's wife. Since that didn't mean anything to me, John explained to me that Fred was a composer and arranger for the music on his own new television program, and he often came to support John's programs at the church. It was with Joanne's help and inspiration that Fred had started his work with children's programming and initiated the first community-sponsored television station in the country. John promised me that sometime soon he would introduce us and that he just knew we would get along.

✦

SOON AFTER I ARRIVED AT THIRD PRESBYTERIAN, I approached John about doing a special service of spirituals and Bible passages for Good Friday. I told him that I thought of this service like a black, Lenten "Lessons and Carols." It only took him a moment to consider. He totally fell for the idea and put it to the head pastor, Rev. Robert Daley, right away. He, too, loved the idea.

In no time, we set about choosing passages of the passion of Christ to match and augment some of the more powerful and simple American Negro spirituals I had in mind. "Were You There," "There Is a Balm in Gilead," and "He Never Said a Mumblin' Word," headed the list. It was fun working with John and Reverend Daley. We were like one mind singing and serving in harmony for our communal savior. As we sang through some of the numbers, I noted again that the acoustics in the church were great, and John was a master at creating subtle organ textures that did not overshadow the simplicity and direct impact of the spirituals. He was committed to making me sound good, and I poured all my ability into those ten simple songs.

Everyone, including Fred Rogers, came out that Good Friday noon. John said that in the fifteen years he had been there, he had never seen Third Presbyterian so packed for a Friday afternoon Lenten service. I was appropriately humbled. Along with John, I pulled out all the stops, and the audience responded approvingly. When it was over, they lingered and shared with one another how deeply touched they had been. Several people came over to John, and he encouraged them to meet me. I was gratified.

I spent a full thirty minutes listening to and shaking hands with my new parishioners. Fred was among them. Of course, I already knew who he was; his wife and John had made sure of that. He was still a mystery to me. There was nothing outward about Fred to call attention to him: not his physique, not his dress, not his voice. Nothing! *What is all the fuss about?* I asked myself. I'm glad I never said it aloud!

My clearest memory of that occasion was of Fred Rogers's sincerity and the deep look, bordering on passion, in his gentle blue eyes. He nailed me when he took my hand, turned his head slightly, and paused, as though he was waiting for me to say something. I waited too, because it was he who had come over to talk to me. He took his time and spoke of my lovely voice, my compelling interpretations, and the genuine effect the songs had had on him during the service. I smiled and returned his warmth and sincerity. It was easy to accept his praise. There was something serious yet comforting and disarming about him. His eyes hugged me without touching me.

I don't recall exactly what we said, but I came away from that conversation feeling that I had a real fan—someone who felt some of what I felt and didn't throw flowery words around for the sake of sound. He sincerely wanted to know where I was singing next and promised to be there. I took him at his word.

Just before he turned away, he looked at me, and in that gentle, bass-baritone voice with the light southern drawl, which I came to recognize as only his for the next thirty years, he invited me to lunch.

Without much fanfare or acknowledgement, I just turned to the next fan. When I looked back to see where he had been standing, he had disappeared into the crowd of well-wishers. I put the meeting out of my mind entirely. I didn't remember it again until John brought it up several weeks later after choir rehearsal.

"Have you called Fred yet?" asked John. "He says that he loved our Lenten concert and that he had invited you to lunch."

My silence and lack of response were too much for them, so John and Joanne took charge, and lunch was arranged for the four of us. After preliminary drinks and polite conversation, they made some excuse to leave me alone with Fred.

In just a matter of minutes, it suddenly felt like a strange dream cloak had been dropped over us. Everyone else disappeared. Fred listened, and I talked. He seemed to want to know everything about me, and I didn't hold back. We were sharing without him saying even a word. I was drawn into his easy manner, his unwavering attention. It was like I was hypnotized by his gentle stare and how he hung onto my every word. His focused attention told me how special I was, and I could have stayed there all afternoon. Fred never lost that gift.

After lunch, I wound up going to the station where *Mister*

Rogers' Neighborhood was filmed, just to be close to him. I stayed all afternoon. When I finally left the station, it was like coming back from a make-believe fantasy world and entering reality again. The cloak had been removed. The sun was so bright that it was mildly shocking—it actually took me seconds to readjust my eyes to the sunlight and to the passing automobiles rushing by me. None of it seemed to matter. I tried to prolong the sensation I had just had with Fred in the station. I wasn't ready to stop dreaming yet.

The truth was clanging inside me—that I had wanted to stay. I admitted to myself that few other places in my life allowed me to feel so loved and protected.

Still, there was this lingering hesitation about totally trusting a grown man who played with puppets. Where I came from, men gambled on street corners, drank cheap wine, got high on reefer, and shot up with heroin if they could afford it. They had all kinds of vices, which sometimes could be pretty violent and could include having guns and beating their wives. I knew strange men who dressed in women's clothing, and those who went to my church that people whispered about. I never had any proof, but there was a consensus among the members that they were gay. But with all that knowledge about how men behaved both in public and private, I never knew any men who played with puppets.

So here I was now, in graduate school in Pittsburgh, with a well-respected member of the community, who said very nice things about my singing, and who worked very hard in the television studio . . . and he played with puppets. But there was nothing childish or frivolous about this man, Fred Rogers. Indeed, the more I thought about him, the more I found him to be incredibly sympathetic and warm. I was learning a lot about this shy, soft-spoken, modestly dressed, introverted, but true giant of a man.

I started out as François Clemmons, the singer who was a friend of Mister Rogers. The first time I appeared on the show, I sang two spirituals. Fred and I had a simple dialogue—he would introduce me, we would exchange pleasantries, and he would ask me to sing.

Folks knew me and wanted to talk with me and be around me in the music department at Carnegie Mellon, and I was beginning to like it. Singing *Manon* and *War Requiem* had done a lot for my reputation. This Fred Rogers children's show was adding to that. People—even strangers—began to ask me about it.

Some people envied me, but some genuinely liked me and showed it. They also wanted to know some of the behind-the-scenes gossip of the show. I didn't know much and disappointed more than a few with my tight-lipped nonresponses. I didn't want to know anything. The gossip mill didn't interest me.

Nicky was exactly what I needed in the midst of all these challenging musical activities—in school and on the show. The invitations for singing gigs were coming in regularly, and I rarely had the presence of mind to decline. They were all great networking opportunities, and my voice teacher at the time, Lee Cass, encouraged me to sing at these events. He didn't have to tell me twice! I wanted to be the spontaneous life of all the parties—and I was. I took any opportunity to perform. Influential people were there, and when they heard me and liked me, it gave me additional opportunities. I needed the money and wanted the experience. Nicky's presence vanquished my anxieties. Whenever he came to town, he camped at my apartment. He brought what little luggage he had in from the car and just sat it down. When he turned to me his arms were strong and purposeful. Without speaking a word, we fell into a routine: one for the public, one for our private intimacy. It felt like we were married, like we were a couple. We just could never say it. He never said it. I thought about it all the time. Through my own self-observations, I knew I felt and was behaving like a combination of husband and wife with him.

With his arms around me, I felt taller and healthier. I breathed deeper. I couldn't have been happier. His presence was solid and focused. He said just enough to be totally genuine and always impressed on me his faith in my talents and eventual artistic success.

He was fascinated to know more about Fred Rogers, a man whose world I had just entered. I told him what it felt like to visit the studio for the first time. Nicky's attitude and interest made me feel a lot better about my new involvement at WQED and Fred's show. He made me promise to introduce him to Fred as soon as an occasion warranted it.

✦

THIS SHOW WAS TURNING OUT TO BE A FAR BIGGER feather in my cap than I could have ever imagined. I didn't want to tell anybody, but I had my sights set on the Metropolitan Opera, and I considered this just a minor stop along the way. But at least I had enough restraint to keep my thoughts and plans about branching out to myself. I didn't want to foul things up. Especially when I really hadn't begun my solo career yet, and I had no real idea of just how high *Mister Rogers' Neighborhood* would go!

Fred was his gracious, low-key self all through my growth period with him. I found him consistently encouraging and genuinely interested in what I was doing. I guess I could have taken my cue from the Lenten service, which had touched him deeply. During one of our conversations, he spoke of how unique he thought it was that I had created a special program for Good Friday that was like the American Negro spiritual version of the European lessons and carols. He wondered where I had gotten such an idea. After I explained to him how much I loved the music of black Americans and felt that it was my *anointment* to sing these spirituals, and indeed bring them to the world, he suggested that perhaps he'd mention it to a friend of his who was the pastor of another Presbyterian church. He asked if I'd be interested in doing such a program again. I jumped at the opportunity, and we made plans to follow up when the time came.

Fred being Fred, he said nothing more until one day his pastor friend from Allentown, Pennsylvania, Bill Barker, called and asked about the special Easter service I had done at Fred's church. Fred had indeed spoken to him. Bill really liked the idea and let me know he couldn't wait to hear it. In no time, all was arranged, and I wound up going out to Allentown to sing a program of American Negro spirituals for Rev. Bill Barker and his congregation. I thanked God for Fred's recommendation. I received several calls in this manner over the next years, and I always thanked Fred and tried to show my gratitude. He always refused any gift except a thank-you and a hug.

When I had a chance, I shared with Fred just how important those singing jobs were for my singing career—the work that I did while I was away from *The Neighborhood*. He knew! In private I had shared with him how often I knew I had been excluded from auditions in New York City and even in Pittsburgh because of my color. It was deeply humiliating because I wanted more than anything to work and share my artistry. This racial problem was proving to be far more insidious and impenetrable than I had ever imagined. Most of the time, I did not feel that it was a problem with my white peers, my white singing buddies. God knows they were the salt of the earth. But the conductors, arrangers, producers, presidents of boards, managers, casting directors, and sometimes theater directors had their idea of what opera was, and it didn't include a black romantic tenor regardless of how well he sang.

Even when I did go to some auditions, I was aware of typecasting and that many roles were already assigned before the auditions began. I heard the other singers talking. Sometimes I'd ask myself, *What is the purpose of my auditioning?*

Fred, of course, wouldn't leave it there. If he did, he would not have been our Fred. He made sure my voice was heard.

As he traveled around the country, making personal appearances for many of his ardent fans, he took me and several of the other Neighbors along. I loved it and spent a good amount of time just observing and thoroughly enjoying and learning! Once while we were in Indianapolis, the conductor requested that I return and sing as The Evangelist in *St. John Passion* by Johann Sebastian Bach. Lord, I was thrilled. I almost hugged Fred to death! Well, that was so successful that it became a habit, and I was invited to sing with some twenty or more orchestras after a *Mr. Rogers' Neighborhood* visit. Of course, it was all Fred, but he hardly wanted to talk about it.

"Only God knows how to make something out of nothing," I kept saying. I'd never have guessed. But there I was getting two for one—a gig with the *Mister Rogers'* crew and one alone with the orchestra as a tenor soloist. It reminded me of something I'd heard once: *There's more than one way to have a singing career.* With a little patience and some solid imagination, I was on my way.

As I got to know him, I was surprised to find out just how sensitive Fred was. Once he brought chicken soup over to my humble little apartment because I was sick with the flu. I was lying in bed agonizing over the fact that I was missing out on important, pivotal rehearsals, when my doorbell rang. I dragged myself to the door only to find that it was my new friend, standing there with a brown bag. He greeted me warmly and asked if he could come in. He said that he had heard I was sick and had brought me some chicken soup to help me get well. I was touched because he hardly knew me. I was twenty-four and had never had the experience of being cared for by a man, let alone a white man. At first, I was a bit hesitant. Through this loving gesture, and for the next few months, I would keep a watchful eye on him. I did not want to be caught unawares and get let down hard; I needed to see disappointment coming so I could protect myself. My experience up until that point was that some white people would never fully commit themselves to helping black people, while others would. I needed to know which kind Fred was.

Nevertheless, I began to trust him and stop by the station just to be *around* him and feel his warmth and approval. His door was always open to me, literally and figuratively. Soon we were discussing how I'd fit into a permanent role on the show. That's when *Officer Clemmons* was conceived, and he and I discussed it. We talked about how I viewed the policemen in the black ghetto and how young children should be able to turn to them for help in a crisis. Several of the other cast members were brought into the discussion: Mr. McFeely (David Newell) and Mrs. Frogg (Hedda Sharapan) and Dr. Bill Barker. I felt overwhelmed. I had no idea what I was getting into.

In my opinion, playing a police officer for a children's television program meant more than just putting on a uniform. From my earliest years, my relationship with uniformed policemen had been a complicated one, and I knew that they were not the best friends for a black American boy. All during junior high and high school, I had heard graphic stories of my black peers having traumatizing run-ins with uniformed policemen. These encounters almost never turned out positively, whether they were in the right or wrong.

As I shared these experiences with Fred, I wanted to make sure that he understood the difficulty of portraying a role of this seriousness all the time. It was like walking a tightrope without a safety net. It brought with it a burden that he, as an entitled white person, might not fully appreciate. Even though I was willing to take on the initial challenge, perhaps it would be even more important that I have other roles that I could portray from time to time to relieve the stress and tension inherent in the historical relationship of the policeman to the black community. A steady diet of acting as a police officer would present a monumental challenge for someone of my nature and background.

✦

ONE DAY, FRED ASKED TO SPEAK TO ME ABOUT RUMORS that I may have heard. He confided to me that a delegation from the drama and music departments of Carnegie Mellon had approached him and sought to have a different young actor, actress, or singer on the show on a regular basis, perhaps in my very role, or in another newly created slot that would showcase the many talents of the music and drama departments. Apparently, Bea Krebs had expressed her concerns about my abilities. She would have preferred another of her students to have a chance before the cameras, and her complaints were only stopped by a stern threat from Sidney Harth, dean of the music department. He felt that such contention was not good for the department or the school's reputation.

Ruth Topping, the accompanist for the department, confided to me that Sidney thought I was the right person for the job, and he was backed by Rudi Fellner, the conductor for the opera department, and Dr. Cass, my new voice teacher. Bea was simply outvoted! Ruth never did tell me where she stood on the matter, but it was fairly obvious from the way she shared the details of the faculty meeting.

I waited while Fred explained. He assured me that he wasn't having any part of it. It didn't fit in with his overall concept for the program. All along, he had resisted many opportunities to take his ideas to New York and Hollywood. His down-to-earth, laid-back style was perfect for the rich, life-sharing experiences he wanted to feature in his program as he reached out to his audiences across the United States. I listened to all of this without fully understanding what exactly was going on. I hadn't attended any meetings in the music or drama departments and was privy only to superficial gossip and hearsay. I told him so. This was my first official knowledge that something really was going on.

Fred had managed to make me feel very secure about my new role on the show, and that's what I wore for the public. He had chosen me. It was my truth. It was his truth. Others may talk, but Fred and I were walking the walk; I rested secure in that.

✦

Suddenly, though, I had a different focus. It happened around 5:45 p.m. in the afternoon in Memphis, Tennessee, on the balcony of the Lorraine Hotel. I heard the news on the radio. After a while, I turned the television on.

The assassination of Dr. Martin Luther King Jr. jolted my life like no other event before or after. Dr. King's words had forever rung in my heart after our encounter at Oberlin: "Keep on keepin' on, young man! We, the Movement, need people like you!" And now he was dead. I struggled to keep going and think positively. I worked harder. I wanted more than ever to be a credit to my race. So, I was more than surprised—I was mortified—when I heard on the radio that folks in the Hill District, not far from my home in Schenley Heights, Pennsylvania, were rioting! That surely was not honoring Dr. King or his legacy.

It's not possible to be prepared for this kind of tragedy, but the death of Dr. King stopped everything: wedding daydreams, rehearsals, voice lessons, academic assignments, flirting, casual meetings. I sat numb at home and watched the television and thought of death and the consequences of such a public, vulnerable life. I tried to put a cap on my rage and remember how wise he was.

I sat and scratched my head and called the Beechwoods. Everyone was glued to their television sets too. We all just sat. Nobody could think of anything to say. After I hung up, I called my friend Jimmy (affectionately known as Jimmyreen), and we couldn't think of anything to say either. We sat and listened to the radio together, finally hanging up not having said anything constructive or enriching.

I continued to sit and mope around the house. I wasn't going anywhere. At the time, I was living in a boarding house owned by the Lavelle family. I went downstairs, and the Lavelles were watching television and not talking much. They welcomed me, and I sat and said nothing. Even the baby was quiet. Frank Lavelle offered me a drink, and I took it. It went straight to my head—I hadn't had anything to eat, but I wasn't hungry. I sat in a chair and looked out of the window and then back at the television. It still wasn't sinking in that Dr. King was dead, and I felt lost.

By the time I went to bed, I was completely depressed. I woke up in the middle of the night crying. I had a massive headache. I tossed and turned, fitful and sweaty, with bitter dreams that bordered on nightmares. As I turned and cried and ground my teeth, I truly felt like my life was slipping away. I didn't know how to fight. How to fight this system—how to fight racists, how to fight murderers and assassins.

Since I couldn't sleep, I turned on the radio and lay there in the dark, staring into the void. I heard President Johnson call for a day of national mourning in honor of Dr. King. The tragic news was on every station, but I couldn't help myself. I listened as though the announcer's expression of grief and outrage were the last words I'd ever hear. I didn't want to be alone, but I was. I was grieving deeply, and nobody could make me feel better. For a moment I stopped, and I wondered how much worse it was for Mrs. King and her four children. Probably just like it was for Mrs. Kennedy when President Kennedy was killed. Now they were like sisters in grief and loss. Who could make them feel better? Dr. King, as with President Kennedy, belonged to everyone. Indeed, to the world. Was everyone as pained as I was? Were there people rejoicing? What kind of a bitter victory was this? We once had slaves in this country. I come from people who were slaves. So even in bitter grief, I wouldn't lie to myself. I knew full well that in America, Land of the Free, there would be madmen rejoicing in my sorrow. But I couldn't think about that now. Later I would be honest with myself and fully embrace the truth of the open wound that racism had left for this country. It was a pain that never seemed to totally go away regardless of how hard the good folks like Dr. King and those at the SCLC and the NAACP worked.

I put on some music. I needed to hear Mahalia Jackson sing "How I Got Over" . . . even though I hadn't gotten over. Dr. King hadn't gotten over either. But at that moment, I needed to feel like I was doing something successful. I needed to feel the power of the "keep on keepin on, young man," words Dr. King had spoken to me on the Oberlin campus. Mahalia's powerful voice could make that dream a reality. I drifted off to sleep vowing to try again tomorrow.

The phone rang early. It was my friend Gregory, and he offered to come by later and just hang out. I accepted. Then Jimmyreen called and decided to join us.

The next call was from Fred and John Lively. After inquiring about how I was doing, John asked, "Will you sing 'Steal Away' and 'There Is a Balm in Gilead' for our Sunday service? We talked about it, and if you're willing, we think it could have enormous healing potential for many of us who feel the loss of Dr. King."

I agreed. It was a good idea. They were concerned that I was alone. When I told them that friends were coming over later, they relaxed and told me to call them if there was anything they could do.

It was a tedious few days. I stayed at home and didn't go by the campus. I simply wasn't ready for a public show of any kind. I heard from a friend that many scheduled events and classes simply stopped. Some went on unattended and half empty. Other friends of mine came to the house. We just sat and listened to the news broadcasts and looked at one another.

It felt like something was in the air. I felt like I was suffocating, like I was holding my breath for hours. The riots began that night. There were reports of fires and shootings. The news flashes were disheartening. People were getting killed right down the street from me. That surely was not honoring Dr. King or his legacy.

We went out on the back porch, and I swear we could smell the smoke, see the embers, like scorched butterflies dancing among the stars and off into the air. Flames were eating up buildings and businesses in the Hill District.

The logic of folks burning and looting the Hill District and Homewood areas totally eluded me. Why destroy your own home, your own people in your rage and frustration? It was suicidal. I wanted to do something dramatic and shocking, but not sacrifice mom-and-pop stores and loyal businesses that had served the black community for years.

Now, I knew who the snipers and looters and flame-throwers were. They were black and young and married and single and sometimes middle-aged. But they all had one thing in common: they were tired of a system they couldn't seem to beat, a system they couldn't translate or get around, a system that had denied them what they sensed I had—an education and opportunities. They had grabbed for the first opportunity to lash out and hurt someone, even though that someone in almost every case was black and perhaps just as disadvantaged and frustrated as they were.

Eventually Frank Lavelle called Greg, Jimmyreen, and me to the front porch to join his family. He said he was going over to the Hill District to look after his office, and he asked us to keep an eye on his wife and child. I knew that he was serious because I could see what looked like a gun under his light jacket. For the first time since it had all begun, I was truly frightened. If Frank got hurt, his wife and child would really suffer. We all sat on the porch for a while, and I tried to play with the baby. He was such a cute crawling child. He knew me and came right into my arms. He started sucking his thumb and promptly fell asleep. The night felt so serious that I couldn't relax and just enjoy the sweet moment—I felt as helpless as a baby.

Back upstairs later, we listened to the radio as Governor Raymond Shafer and Mayor Joseph M. Barr declared a state of emergency and called in the National Guard. That meant tanks and guns in the streets. We were really curious and wanted badly to go look at what was going on just a few blocks down the street from us, but it seemed too dangerous.

Instead, we had a perfunctory dinner and stayed glued to the news. We kept wondering just how close the destruction was going to come to our home. In the middle of the night, I woke up to realize that I was sandwiched between Jimmyreen and Greg, like three brothers. It reminded me of the comfort of sleeping with my older brother as a child and how sibling-intimate we were.

All of us slept in the next morning. Frank had returned

home, and I was curious to go up into the Hill District, but the no-travel curfew was still on.

Fred called again. He insisted on having me come to dinner and told me to pack a bag. First, I tried to ignore him, then to argue with him. He spoke with such gentle authority that I allowed myself to be persuaded to stay over a few days until the danger passed. My friends also wanted to go, so it was decided.

When Fred drove up in his old gray BMW, we were ready. As we got settled, Fred said, "Joanne and I have invited John and his wife to join us for dinner. We're all concerned about you, Franç, so close to the burning and violence. None of us want anything to happen to you. We want you to know that you can stay with us as long as needed for this violence to subside. No one wants you to be at risk." That was the first time he had called me Franç, and I recognized it as an endearing nickname. He never called me François again.

I was curious as to what Fred's house would look like, what he was like at home, and what was his family was like—this man who was showing such kindness and interest in me.

We drove up Hastings Street just off Fifth Avenue to a three-story, part-stone house that looked as understated as Fred. It was large but not flashy in any way. It reflected the personality he conveyed in the studio.

Joanne and their two preteen boys, Jamie and Johnny, greeted us. Dinner was surprisingly pleasant despite the Hill District events. Jamie and Johnny appeared a bit oblivious to what was really going on. Fred didn't talk very much, but his warm, paternal presence was calming. I appreciated and noted the quiet tone of dinner and was able to hear all the various conversations going on at once.

The meal was prepared and served by Miss Ella Harris, a

fortyish-looking woman of average height. She was an efficient and decent cook. Her face had my general coloring with heavy pierced earrings that looked like they were dragging her ears down to her shoulders. As she went back and forth from the kitchen carrying hot serving plates, I caught her eye several times, and she attempted a smile. I hoped I'd get to know her better over the next couple of days that I would be there.

The place was immaculate, spacious, and sparsely furnished. Everything looked antique, but I had no idea from what period. Although Fred had family photos and paintings of relatives on the walls, the house had a bare look. It was as though they abhorred anything too frilly or ornamental.

Nobody wanted dessert or coffee. Just as everyone had done up on Clarissa Street, after dinner we crowded around the television set in the living room, and everyone got quiet. There was more rioting, looting, and burning in the Hill District. My headache returned. I slipped out of the room and went back up to the third floor to sit in my room and think, but before I knew it, I had fallen asleep.

I woke up an hour later when Greg knocked on my door and asked to be let in. His face was flushed, and he was carrying a drink. He offered it to me, and we sipped in silence. It was Drambuie. Jimmyreen soon followed. He fell in with his drink and sat down. The three of us were making conversation about the happenings up in the Hill District when Fred came into the room carrying a book. He had a collection of some of Dr. King's speeches and writings. He sat down and started reading. Dr. King's powerful words were a balm to my fractured soul. Fred's smooth voice seemed just right. We stayed that way for over an hour, listening. Then Fred hugged us all and said he had to turn in and would see us sometime in the morning after he returned from swimming. He laid the book on the dressing table near my bed.

The next day Jimmyreen and Greg made plans to go home; I decided to stay on Hastings Street until the end of the five-day curfew. Fred encouraged me to relax and find my focus again. Later that day, as we sat near the piano where I had tried to practice, I attempted to tell Fred what Dr. King had meant to me. In my opinion, he too was a gentle man like Fred. In many cases he appeared to be a fiery orator who could stir the masses to a near frenzy. However, it was important to note that his outreach didn't diminish his sincerity and effectiveness. Millions of us fed on his words, and his philosophy of nonviolent and civil disobedience.

I shared the details of my brief encounter with him at our Oberlin graduation. Since then, Dr. King had been my beacon of hope and inspiration. And now he was gone.

Then Fred turned to me and looked deep into my heart.

"You're not alone, Franç. I meant what I said. You are now a member of our family, and we care about you very much. Your life is not going to be easy, Franç. Nobody's really is. Take heart in knowing that as long as I live, you will always have someone who will reach out to you and show you love. Dr. King is gone, but I'm here with you. And that's what's important for you right now."

At that instant, his words breached the wall of emotion and feelings in my heart. Like a shattered dam, it snapped, and I loosed a flood of grateful tears. Those tears were strengthening and healing to me. "I want so much to believe, Fred," I said.

"Then watch me. I'll do all I can to be there for you, Franç. You have my word on it."

As I sat with his arm around my shoulders and my tears subsided, I felt myself becoming a new son. My loss of Dr. King had helped me to find a new, worthy father figure who had said all the right things about trust and commitment. I decided to give him every benefit of the doubt and give myself a break to get over this devastating experience.

Fred woke me up the next morning to get ready for church. He had already swum, and he looked alert. I took a quick shower and rushed downstairs to join the family. After a quick and almost haphazard breakfast, we piled into the BMW and headed for Third Presbyterian. It seemed like everyone showed up to bolster our sense of community and to pray for peace and calm in the Hill District. Despite my anger and frustration, I felt genuine love and appreciation coming from the congregation that day as I sang.

It didn't take much for me to realize that I was probably the only black person in the church that day. It was hard to be the token black when all I wanted to do was go home and sulk. I couldn't tell anyone at a time how awful I felt—it was better to say almost nothing. Fred finally rescued me, and we headed out the side door and then home.

After a light lunch of sandwiches and soup, we watched the funeral proceedings on television. There were more than 300,000 mourners with Dr. King's procession through the streets of Atlanta. We watched in silence—Fred and I did not make any specific references to our confessions the night before.

I had only one witness to my resurrection: Fred. For now, that was enough. Parts of me were wondering when he might say something to undermine his promise. I kept asking myself, *Did he mean it?* When would I learn to trust again? I slowly began to accept the words he had spoken the day before.

In a couple of days, I returned to Clarissa Street and set

about pulling my life back together. I knew it would be hard to ignore what had just happened, so I didn't try. Often, I yielded to the persistent void in my ears and was aware that I was staring at nothing, sometimes even while people were talking to me. Everyone at school seemed emotionally drained. We were all struggling to end the semester. I finished with Bea Krebs and said goodbye. In my mind, I said, *Good riddance!* I had already spoken to my new teacher, Dr. Cass, and would begin my lessons with him sometime in the summer. I was grateful that he was willing to begin before the school year began in September. I wanted to get a head start on my master's recital and be ready for the National Council Auditions in January.

Happily, he was full of some good suggestions at our first meeting. He agreed that I could and should sing some American Negro spirituals for the recital. We were off to a great start. I already liked this man. Secondly, I decided to concentrate primarily on only a couple of languages and not try to sing the five or six that I had dabbled in. I chose English, Italian, and German. We could always change our minds as we worked on the repertoire. He suggested that I turn in a recital program proposal as early as possible, so we could move pieces around as we heard how they went together and how they fit in my voice. Lastly, I liked that he was leaving the selection and date of the recital up to me. I could take charge of my own graduation process. Bea Krebs would never have allowed that. I went home and got busy listening and thinking. It was a good start.

Unsurprisingly, returning to singing and my regular routine was exactly what I needed to help heal myself during this trying time. And replaying the conversation with Fred was a balm for my soul.

✦

THE METROPOLITAN OPERA AUDITIONS WERE FINALLY
upon me. The first round took place in Pittsburgh—and I won.
That permitted me to go on to the regional auditions in Cleveland. After my performance in Cleveland, many folks applauded
for me as though I had already won Regionals. I thought so, too.
However, when my name was announced as the third-place winner, there were resounding boos. It was a minute before decorum
was restored and the event continued with the announcement
of second-place and first-place winners. From that moment until I left, there was a disquiet rumbling in the auditorium, and
afterward, complete strangers came up to me to express their
disappointment that I had not won the competition. I accepted
graciously and decided to say nothing publicly.

You see, everyone felt that the Metropolitan Opera auditions
were fixed! We all talked about it, but had no proof.

The attendant who was supervising the competition motioned to me that Maestro Ignace Strasfogel, who was a highly
respected conductor and coach at the Metropolitan Opera,
wanted a word with me before I left. She escorted me to the room
where he was settled. We shook hands, and he motioned for me
to sit down.

Once in private, he got down to business. He shared with me
how much he had wanted to grant me the first prize in the competition. But circumstances beyond his control did not permit it.
He had instructions from higher up before he left New York. He
could only really award the third prize. I sat there in shock. Who
would have thought? He didn't beat around the bush.

"I know this has not been the easiest last hour or so for you,

Mr. Clemmons. So, let's have a little talk, young man—just you and me. I can tell that you're disappointed at your third-place ranking in today's competition. I can only say so much to you. One must be very delicate when speaking of these matters. But please, hear me out completely. You sang quite excellently, and I wish very much that I could have given you the first place today. But I say this to you: there's more than one way to win this competition. If you will cheer up and accept your assignment graciously, you will find that I shall be most useful to you as you pursue your career in New York. I know from your file that you won the competition in Pittsburgh. I'd be willing to say that Pittsburgh, if it hasn't already, is fast proving to be a bit limiting for someone with your talents and ambitions." He paused, waiting for me to respond.

"Yes, I am disappointed," I began tentatively, "and I'm grateful for all that you have said. I don't know what to do. I've never been in this position before."

"Count your lucky stars, my good man, that you have learned such an important lesson early on: All is not always what it seems on the surface. Certainly not in this business."

I was silent.

He continued, "If you would permit me, I would like to give you the name of a cherished colleague of mine. His name is John Gutman. He is not a conductor, but functions as assistant manager of the 'big house.' In this capacity, he runs the Metropolitan Opera Studio. It is a fine professional company for young opera singers like you."

He handed me a small piece of paper with the name and address already written in a clean, elegant script.

"I feel confident in saying that I think he would be most

interested in your abilities as a tenor," the maestro continued. "Would you do me the favor of contacting him and coming to New York and singing for him? Rest assured that I shall be contacting him on your behalf soon. We will pay your way to New York and put you up in a hotel of your choice. If you present yourself to him as you have to me today, I can practically assure you of the outcome. I think that you are indeed ready for New York, and New York is always ready for talent such as yours. What do you say, Mr. Clemmons?"

He wasn't really asking, but his genteel manner was getting through all my defenses. I wanted so much to like and trust him. Again, I was reminded of some of my recent conversations with Fred. I asked for his card, and he reached into one of his inner vest pockets and pulled out a shining black leather wallet. He removed from it a monogrammed business card and handed it to me, smiling politely. I glanced at it and back at him; it seemed to seal the new relationship between us. He continued to smile and extended his hand. I shook it, even though I was still skeptical. With that, he stood up, signaling the end of our little meeting.

Suffice it to say, he and John Gutman were true to their word, and I was offered a spot with the company after I completed my degree!

✦

With all this going on, it was sometimes difficult to settle down and keep my mind focused on classes and getting my master's degree. It was easy to have a full social life. There were lots of activities on campus, and we had the whole city at our disposal. But finishing out the year well was a big thing for me. I didn't have any illusions about making the honor roll. I simply wanted to do well and be proud of my graduate school experience. I was enjoying my second-semester Shakespeare course and eighteenth-century counterpoint, much to my surprise. Work with Rudi Fellner and Ruth Topping proved to be enjoyable and refreshing. Both of them encouraged me to keep on working after the opera performance.

One day after a rough music exam, I stopped by WQED just to clear the air and think about something else. I truly felt blessed because they always seemed happy to see me. I saw that Fred was in his office and decided to see if he was busy. Out of the blue Fred asked me, "When are you leaving for New York?"

Even though I had been thinking a lot about the Metropolitan Opera auditions and the pros and cons of a future singing career in New York, I wasn't ready to discuss it out loud. Everything in my mind was up in the air. I guess I took too long to answer.

"You are still going, aren't you?" he asked.

"Well, yes," I managed to stammer. "It's just that there are so many basic questions I still need to answer. What about housing? Everyone says it's so expensive. I don't know my way around very well; I'll need a good vocal coach, and several have been recommended, and I'll be looking for a new voice teacher . . . it all costs money, and the Metropolitan Opera Orchestra is threatening a strike. If that happens, I'll be out of work right from the beginning. Sometimes I think I might as well stay here."

"Or you could put it off for a year. It'll still be there in another year!" he said.

"It's just too much information," I said jokingly and somewhat to myself.

"On the other hand, if you're still planning on going, I have a wonderful friend who sings at the Metropolitan Opera I could introduce you to."

This time I really didn't have anything negative to say. "Boy, that's terrific. He might have some good advice for me!"

"Sure," said Fred. "I'll give him a call and introduce you two. He's been there for a number of years now and could show you around."

John Reardon, baritone extraordinaire, turned out to be everything I could have asked for—friend, guide, advisor, language coach—and to top it off, he was very intelligent and tall and handsome. Lord, the man had every gift. Fred was the glue that melded a warm friendship right from the beginning. He was never too busy to see me and answer whatever questions I had about life, or career, or the Metropolitan. He had been singing there a number of years already and was only too happy to impart some advice on the many things he had learned over the years.

✦

AS A BOY, IT DIDN'T TAKE ME LONG TO FULLY REALIZE that underneath the public veneer, everyone in my family was angry. *Why?* I thought. I soon learned that women were angry because they were always afraid they'd lose their husbands at an early age and would be left alone to struggle and raise the children. The men were angry because they knew they could go at any time and for any or no reason at all—and nobody would really miss them. Black men had been lynched by white mobs, mostly the KKK, for as long as I was aware of myself and even before I was born. I never said anything, but I had heard them, the grown-ups, talking about distant relatives—cousins, and boys from across the fields who had to flee their homes in the middle of the night. I don't know where they went, but they never came back. I promised myself to keep my eyes down when I was talked to by white cops and to not open my mouth. I didn't want my mother to worry about me.

So, it seemed that I got the *sermon for survival* from everyone: be humble and don't irritate or make a white man angry, especially a policeman. "Keep your eyes down low, boy. And keep your mouth shut! They could shoot you and kill you for no reason at all and never go to jail."

My mother was so serious that I wouldn't even look at her when she talked like that to me. All during these sermons I'd ask myself, *Well, what have I done that was so wrong that I have to be afraid of a white cop?* It never made sense to me, but I was smart enough to be afraid.

One day I was walking from the playground with my cousin Johnny Mae, who was five years older than me, and I decided to ask her. When I asked her why everybody was afraid of the white police, she stopped walking and just stood there looking at me. "Why do I have to be afraid if I haven't done nothing wrong?"

"Buttercup, listen here, let me tell you," she began. "You ain't havta do nothin' wrong. You black, ain't ya? Ya a boy, ain't ya? Well, it's like jes being up dere in that cop's face and being black! Well, das all. You ain't havta do nothin' wrong. Being black at the wrong time, at the wrong place is wrong. It'll get you killed." She turned, and we kept walking.

"You don't have to be mad," I said.

"I ain't mad; I'm jes tellin' the truth!"

These are the memories I carried into my bourgeoning

liberated lifestyle. I fashioned myself a liberal democrat and felt that the system as it was constituted had to be seriously broken down and changed. I objected to the way our nation had gotten into the Vietnam War, how some politicians voted against programs for the poor and elderly, and the fact that gay folks were not protected under our civil rights laws. Therefore, I vowed to myself not to ever become lax and uncaring about our basic liberties. Over the years, I volunteered to work for several politicians and even campaigned for Shirley Chisholm when she ran for president. One of the true highlights of my life was meeting her at her office in Washington, D.C., and singing for her.

But just when things are going along smoothly, and you think you're in sync with the rhythm of your life, some major event intrudes and makes you realize that you're not in control. In many cases, you are not only out of control, but you're the victim. I felt this way when President John F. Kennedy was assassinated, and when Dr. King, Malcolm X, and Medgar Evers were murdered.

I was becoming more and more politically aware and frustrated, and I wondered if anything that "we liberals" did could really change this ancient, stagnant society. Our leaders were being killed left and right—all over the place!

Then, on June 6, 1968, Senator Bobby Kennedy was assassinated by Sirhan Sirhan. It pounded an already stunned constituency. The Vietnam War had caused a serious breach in the fabric of the American culture. I had become very active politically since my Oberlin days, and it continued all through graduate school. My views grew and became more intense as movements that supported civil rights, gay rights, and antiwar sentiments became more and more strident. I had no intentions of sitting on the sidelines as I watched our society change.

I admired Fred very much for tackling, on the show, such a difficult and painful subject as assassination. I doubt the youngest among us really understand the anger and frustration that go into such an act. But I do think they can share in the feeling of loss. They can also empathize if an adult near to them seems hurt and vulnerable by such actions. Perhaps the child could understand this based on the loss of a pet or favorite stuffed animal. It should be handled on a case-by-case basis, depending on the child's need to know.

During 1968, sometime over the summer months, I realized that I was feeling very vulnerable on many levels. It seemed to have been triggered by the untimely assassinations of Dr. Martin Luther King Jr. and Robert Kennedy. I began to question the Second Amendment and what happens to folks who have easy access to guns. Violence within our culture was becoming an issue we were going to have to deal with on a regular basis. Important folks, members of the clergy, politicians, and even innocent bystanders were being killed almost every day.

I was *angry*, and I was helpless. The thought of carrying a gun never entered my mind. So, what could I do? My only serious defense was awareness. I couldn't afford to become lackadaisical. The price I would have to pay for the rest of my life would be incredible vigilance. I could never really relax again.

As I would go about my daily business, the thought would come to me: Anger and vigilance were not a good marriage. I understood better what I was feeling, but I did not have a solution. It was totally unrealistic to think that I could go around angry all the time.

I thought about isolation. But being withdrawn, meditative, and internal . . . it'd drive me crazy. No people. No life. No sanity. I quickly moved on from that idea. *There must be another solution*, I thought. I spent many hours thinking about if a "peace pill" existed! But even if it did, how could you force folks to take it every morning like a vitamin? My deeper mind said it would be pretty difficult to make the hardened hunter take it, and what about those among us who forgot and became violent again? Would that be looked upon as an accident, or a disease?

✦

I CHOSE TO STAY IN PITTSBURGH DURING THE SUMMER months to film those early *Mister Rogers' Neighborhood* programs and to work at Carlow College where I had a job working with Upward Bound. During the spring after my Good Friday concert, I had mentioned to John Lively that I wanted to remain in Pittsburgh and would be looking for a job. I asked if he needed some singing. He suggested I speak with Sister Mary Margaret, the nun who was in charge of the Upward Bound program where he taught music. Sister Mary Margaret was a musician also and taught in the music department at Carlow College. She accepted my interview, and I was hired for the summer. I supervised some twenty young, junior high–age children during the day for several months and showed them around town. The nuns gave us a budget and provided advice when I needed it.

These were underprivileged youngsters from the surrounding area in Oakland. It was a great opportunity to take them over to my voice teacher's studio at Carnegie Mellon and to WQED to see the *Neighborhood* studio. Boy, were they ever impressed! I also personally took advantage of some of the nightlife during my off time.

I had begun to get closer to my buddy Jimmyreen. Every-thing about Jimmy told me that he was gay: the way he wrote letters and signed his name, the way he picked up and carried his notebooks and sketch pads, the gentle glow of his face and eyes, and the soft pursing of his lips when he was just about to smile. His rhythm and flow was gentle and harmonious to me. I trusted my instincts. Yes, I certainly felt that I was right. To me, he was gay; but when I brought it up, he denied it and wanted to change the subject. I didn't persist, but I began to say things to him and indirectly treat him like a "sister." He didn't seem to mind and that carried us for a while.

I invited him over, and he began to stay overnight sometimes. It was all platonic for my part, but I began to feel that Jimmy was attracted to me. Our times together were casual and fun. We'd shop and cook dinner together at my place and listen to mu-sic. Sometimes I'd practice singing, and he'd work on a sketch. Jimmy was handsome, but I wasn't sexually attracted to him. I didn't know why.

One day, I decided to ask him out to one of the local gay bars. At first he was reluctant, but I promised to pay the cover and do all the driving. Finally, he relented. We chose The Playpen, an understated dance bar in the warehouse district.

The crowd was mostly fresh and upwardly mobile blue-collar folks between eighteen and thirty. Everybody was a college boy or pretended to be. The jukebox was like a rock band, and the crowd danced until they nearly fell out. I loved it right away. It raised my spirits to see gay men and lesbians dancing together and having a good time in a relaxed place. It didn't take long for Jimmy and me to start talking and acting like sisters. He hadn't said he was gay, but our dancing was intimate. I loved matching him on the dance floor. He had great rhythm and style, but it still didn't add up to sex for me. I finally told him how I felt as I held him close. I could feel his body tense and then totally relax. When I looked at him, he was crying. I held him closer and just waited. He didn't say anything, so I continued.

"Mr. Jimmyreen, you know you're very special to me. That's what I've been trying to say to you all along. I want to be your friend. We have so much in common, and I feel that we can help each other, maybe just not to be so lonely. I've always wanted a great buddy like you, someone I could share everything with. There's so much that I just keep to myself. I wanna tell someone. Don't you feel the same way? Please let's be best friends." I paused and waited.

I finally realized that the music had stopped, and we were the only couple left on the dance floor. People were starting to look, expecting something to happen. Awkwardly, I grabbed Jimmy, and we headed back for our table. Both of us were mildly embarrassed getting caught standing on the dance floor having a serious conversation after the music stopped. Everyone else had gone back to their tables or to the bar. We smiled and sat close. Talk was easier now.

"I know what you mean, and I haven't been totally fair with you," Jimmy began. "Yes, I'm gay, and I didn't want to come out until I was sure you were too, and you wouldn't rat on me at CMU. They don't know. I don't feel comfortable coming out on campus. I've always been gay, and I've always known it. I still feel that I want to get married, and I hoped . . . that you and I could get something going on the side," he added thoughtfully. "You don't always seem gay, and you're great on stage. Don't you want to get married too? Our wives wouldn't ever have to know." I was taken aback, but he said it like it was nothing, so I didn't make a big deal of it either. I knew that gay men married all the time.

"Yes, I do, but I'm not making any predictions at this point. I am actually seeing someone, a woman, who I know wants to marry me. She's in Youngstown now and may come up for a visit in a couple of weeks."

"Same here. You'll see. Her name's Regina and she lives here. You'll meet her."

"Well, I'm glad that's finally over. You really almost had me fooled the first time I asked you. But as you can see, I don't give up easily." I paused and reflected. "You're going to meet Michael too. He's the first guy I ever had sex with. Maybe one day you'll meet Nicky. He's another case altogether. I'll have to ask him. He's definitely on the down low. We've never ever had a third party to our affair. That's the way he wants it."

"How do you want it?" Jimmyreen interjected.

"I want Nicky," I stated flatly. "He means the world to me. I see him when I can. So far, it's worked pretty well. He's in graduate school in Chicago. I can wait. Nobody knows about him or us."

It wasn't long before I paid for my appearances and familiarity with Pittsburgh's nightlife. One evening, I got a call from Fred Rogers asking me to make an appointment with his secretary and right-hand woman, Elaine Lynch, at his office as soon as possible. He didn't say what it was about. Several days later, I arrived at his office, not suspecting a thing. I imagined the meeting would pertain to my role on the show and how I'd fit it into my busy academic and performing schedule. When I arrived at the television station, Elaine pointed me to the room where we were to meet, and when I got there Fred introduced me to his manager, George Bacon, and closed the door.

"Franç, we've come to love you here on the *Neighborhood*," Fred said. "You have talents and gifts that set you apart and above the crowd, and we want to ensure your future place with us. You're a proud person, and you have every reason to be. We all agree that your singing has set a high mark around here, and we want to be an active part of your exciting career."

His demeanor was what I'd come to expect from him. It was as though George wasn't in the same room with us. Fred spoke quietly and totally to me. He was *in his gift* with me. It was like a secret that no one else in the whole world was privy to. If my daddy had ever been a true father and had spoken to me, I imagine that he would have looked at me and sounded like Fred. I couldn't help myself. I inhabited the role of a son, and I even listened to his breathing as he began again.

"Someone, we're not able to say who, has informed us that you were seen at the local gay bar downtown with a friend from school. Now I want you to know, Franç, that if you're gay, it doesn't matter to me at all. Whatever you say and do is fine with me, but if you're going to be on the show as an important member of the *Neighborhood*, you can't be out as gay. People must not know. What you feel must be your own personal business. Many of the wrong people will get the worst idea, and we don't want them thinking and talking about you like that."

I was stunned. *Who told him?* I wanted to know. As he spoke so gently, every sane, rational part of me shriveled up and disappeared. I wanted to be invisible so as not to die right there in front of him. Space and time were lost to me as I struggled silently. I heard his words clearly, but I was disengaged from what was going on. The hollow in my ears was expanding and pounding to my heart's pulse. I didn't move for fear that he'd think he'd have to call for an ambulance. I was struggling for my life while choking on his words that took my breath away and seemed to cut my heart out.

After a while—I don't know how long—I finally realized that he was waiting for me to respond. Every word he had spoken had stabbed me in my soul, and now I was expected to carry on and function like there were no wounds, no pain. I thought, *I had almost allowed myself to love this man.* He had so many things that I needed. Fatherly things that I hungered for. The flood of tears that rushed to my eyes felt endless. I cried for all those years I missed my daddy, for all those years my stepfather yelled at me and lashed me with his tongue and his belt. I cried for the things I couldn't have—my mother's love, my own gay marriage. I cried to be taken care of, to be understood, to be vulnerable, to be gay and black and weak and still be loveable. I cried so that he would know I was hurt. I was hurting and had no recourse. I cried because I felt so bad, I wanted to die. I cried because I knew that I needed his love and was willing to cry for it.

When he came around the desk and took me into his arms to comfort me, I heard the door to his office close as George left the room. I cried even harder. His arms were my cradle of despair. Little Buttercup, my baby nickname, was sitting on that chair now, and my Great-Grandmama Laura May was clucking her tongue and patting me and telling me "don't cry, everything will be all right." Her kisses and patting were so healing and miraculous, just as, strangely, Fred's presence was now.

He took out his handkerchief and offered it to me. I was still very much aware of him, even though I wasn't able to look at him directly yet. I knew he wouldn't rush me, so I just sat and wondered about us and about my future. Fred was my perfect comfort, just as he had become my perfect pain. He was giving me inspiration and stardom but telling me now that there was a cost.

Lord knows if I had known what to do, I would have done it then. Fred seemed to understand what his words had released there in his office, and he was prepared to wait while I searched for the pieces of myself I could use to survive. I needed to breathe again and think. Surely, in time, I could be put back together and function like new, like nothing had ever happened. I finally looked at him for a long, sad time.

"So that's how it's gotta be around here?" I finally managed. "And I thought that we were off to such a fine beginning. Little did I know how fragile our new relationship could be. What Bea Krebs and the CMU drama department couldn't do with all their efforts and pull, I did all by my little self." I sighed; my words reeked of angry irony.

"Now just a minute, young man. Who says that our relationship has to come to an end? You need to decide just what it is you want in life, Franç. I wish it were different, but you can't have it both ways. Not now anyway. Talent can give you so much in this life, but that sexuality thing can take it all away. Faster than you could ever imagine. The world doesn't really want to know who you're sleeping with—especially if it's a man. You can have it all if you can keep that part out of the limelight."

His manner still reminded me of that day I sat and talked with him in the restaurant and visited the studio. I remembered how he led without forcing, how he listened without prodding. From the beginning, I felt that he could see right into me. Then why had he not seen this? Surely he knew then that I was gay. Now it all seemed to be going up in smoke.

Then he said, "Have you ever thought of getting married? People do make some compromises in life. Only you can decide. How badly do you want a career?"

His gentle question seared into my soul, but now I was practicing survival. I covered it all up and tried to rise above the pain and humiliation. I had to get along with this career, with my life. If being gay could cause that much damage to everything that I wanted, then by sheer will and determination, I wasn't going to be gay. And if marriage to a woman was the only safe alternative, then I needed to start thinking about it very seriously. My plans for my future would have to change.

When I left his office, I had made up my mind to marry LaTanya Mae Sheridan. I never told a soul about that meeting in Fred's office, and the decision I felt that I had to make, but I knew my fate was sealed. I called home that evening and made arrangements for Michael and LaTanya Mae to visit.

Through the long, lonely hours in the days and weeks to follow, I watched myself as though somehow removed from myself, as someone who had never been through pain before. I forced myself to get reacquainted with the person I wanted to be, the person that I must present to the world—the boy who had survived Youngstown.

I always knew that the parts I had put aside weren't dead. But in this life, they were definitely not needed. I exiled the most passionate, the most loving, and the most sensitive parts of myself. I wanted a career more than I wanted those essential parts of me.

Fred had made it clear to me that an openly gay man couldn't have a major career on American television, and *definitely* not on a children's educational program. Regardless of what he could accept, of what he believed, he was the messenger of what was true in society. I was making the difficult adjustment to that fact. Coming to terms with that decision was part of my own survival package. If I didn't survive, what would the millions of young, impressionable black children caught up in America's television wasteland do for a positive self-image? I felt a sense of obligation and responsibility to them. I couldn't fail them.

When I proposed, I was astounded to see LaTanya Mae come alive at the moment she realized I was serious. Once she was over her disbelief, she became silly. Silly with joy? She squealed, jumped on me, and kissed me. I knew that she was in love with me, but I had been naïve not to realize how much. Michael was very happy too. He was right in the middle of everything. It was no secret that he and LaTanya Mae shared a deep love for each other. And that was okay with me. Even when he told her how much he loved me, nothing changed between them. They whispered, giggled, and shared secrets. They talked endlessly on the phone when not together. I knew the exact day that she had given him a key to her apartment up on King Street. I knew about it and approved. It gave me a buffer that allowed me to relate to both of them.

We called The Beechwoods and LaTanya Mae's parents and announced the "good news." I gave in to LaTanya Mae, who wanted a big church wedding. I secretly wished for a quiet non-ceremony in Pittsburgh, but I knew that that wasn't going to happen. She and our families launched into the planning as though I weren't there. She had a large family in Youngstown and felt she owed it to them to include them in all the goings-on. Michael sided with her. I grew silent as their plans mushroomed.

Michael was my obvious best man and would have been the maid of honor for LaTanya Mae too if everyone would have let him. He was excited; I was not. Things had to pick up for me somewhere. I couldn't stay down in the dumps forever, so I just decided to adopt a better, more positive attitude in life. I had to think and act successful. I made an actual decision not to be sad anymore. I fooled everyone, and after a while, I was glad. I began to take real pleasure in simple things again. I could still sing. I was still on the show.

For weeks, I had wrestled with telling Nicky about the upcoming wedding. I had no idea how he'd respond, but I knew that I had to tell him at some point. There was never going to be a perfect time. I just had to make the leap. But I never got the chance. Late one April evening, he called me himself.

"So, when were you going to tell me about the wedding?"

I almost dropped the receiver. When I didn't answer, he continued, "I know you're wondering how I found out, so I'll tell you. Your boy Gregory told his cousin Earl that he was going to be in a black wedding. He mentioned your name. And Earl, being one of my Oberlin boys, mentioned it to me. He assumed that I knew about it already, and I faked that I did. But I still don't know. And I don't like that. So why don't you tell me? Just what is it I should know about a wedding?"

"It's true, Nicky," I finally managed. "I'm going to get married in September to LaTanya Mae Sheridan, a girl whom I went to school with in Youngstown. For weeks, I've been going back and forth on how to tell you. It happened rather suddenly. I didn't know how you'd react."

"I don't know why you're agonizing about it. You knew that someday you'd make this decision. It was only a matter of time, and with whom, and where. I'll always be happy for you. It doesn't change a damn thing for me as to how I feel about you, and that I want to be with you as often as we can. In fact, I already told Alison that if she and I get married, I want you to sing at our wedding. I also want you to be *in* my wedding," he said with emphasis.

"How would you like to be one of my ushers, Nicky?" I asked. "I need two more."

"I'll be there for you," he said. "Just let me know where and when." He paused. "I may even bring Alison along. You let me handle that. I think it might serve us well later for her to see us together and you getting married."

He went on. "I want you to know that I had only one problem with your wedding. And I want you to listen to me carefully. That's the kind of thing I want to hear from your lips and not someone else's. Not even one of my boys. Whatever is happening to you personally, what you're doing or where you're going, I want to hear it from you personally. I've never put you off, and I never will. I want the same from you. I'm going to tell you something I may never say again. So hear me out: I love you, François, black and as sweet as you are. And it may not be possible for us to get married and live together, but for as long as you live, I want you to be my baby. I'm committed to you forever. Whether you marry one time or ten times, it doesn't matter to me. Nothing will ever change between us until you say so. You'll have to find the words to tell me to get lost. And then I'll get lost. Until then, I only know one thing: what's between us. There, now I've said it. You heard it. Let's move on and plan this damn wedding."

He loved me—I wanted to digest that forever. I had finally heard what I needed to hear, and he was many miles away. I wanted to get my hands on him so badly.

"I want to say one thing. I'm marrying LaTanya Mae, but I'm

yours forever. No man or woman will ever mean as much to me as you do."

Compared to all the build-up and planning that everyone was doing, the wedding was a sleepwalk. Like a zombie, I let them lead me into position, and I waited for the bride to come down the aisle. The music was joyfully somber. It all seemed to fit. I stayed in my dream world and just existed. Next thing I knew, I was hearing the words "Do you take this woman to be your lawfully wedded wife?" In my semi-catatonic state, they were some of the strangest words I'd ever heard. I knew I was supposed to say yes, but every fiber of my body was saying no. I didn't want to be married to any woman. I felt like one of those Ken dolls with all kinds of interchangeable clothes and accessories. This was my new outfit for my new role in life. It wasn't the real me.

The reception seemed to go on forever. At some point, Mama Inez and her little army of church ladies approached. She looked trimmer than before. She had on her Easter hat with the colored flowers and a pale yellow-and-green summer knit suit. She kept trying to give me a hug. I concentrated on my sisters and succeeded in moving away from her altogether. I know she felt that she deserved credit for my marriage, but in reality, she had almost nothing to do with it. Throughout the entire planning ordeal, I had managed to avoid her and refused to return her phone calls.

Later that afternoon, Fred and Joanne and John and Janet Lively approached us and gave us warm, congratulatory hugs. I had given them invitations, but I wasn't sure they'd make it. It felt like we were sealing some kind of secret bargain.

✦

ONCE I MARRIED LATANYA MAE, ALMOST UNCONsciously I became guarded about what I thought and said. I lost that natural, razor-edged sensibility I had always taken for granted and became awkwardly introverted. My outgoing self crept away to hide. I didn't wake up to myself until it was done. Without ever saying a word, I moved to an internal space, private and well removed from my public self. I returned to my place of secrets, as in my childhood when Granddaddy Saul and I used to talk. I became determined to succeed in my straight transformation.

I felt there must be a prescribed way that straight, married men were supposed to act. But I had to learn it. I secretly watched straight men, just to see how they behaved: which colognes they wore, how they walked, and how they dressed. If I could discern some unique way of looking at life the straight way, I would eventually be able to imitate straight behavior. I didn't want anyone else to suspect that I was gay—that part of me was to be tightly sealed away.

On weekends, I washed my car by hand, went to the hardware store, and bought a whole set of tools to make repairs around the house. I began to drink beer and participate in jokes about married men and women. I went to the neighborhood pub and sat at the bar. I began to run my eyes over women as they walked; I actively began to imagine how I'd feel if I were sexually attracted to them.

Toward the end of September 1968, I got a call from Fred. I had received several scripts in the mail, and we needed to schedule a time in the studio to film my sections. After we made the appointment, Fred wondered what LaTanya Mae was doing and suggested that if she was interested, she should stop by the office and consider working for him. Elaine would show her around and get her settled.

After spending a few hours at WQED, LaTanya Mae came home excited. She had found something in the studio she considered meaningful, and it paid decent money. On the other hand, because I was a student and a freelance singer, I had no idea how much money I'd be earning. She could easily make more money than I did, and I made it clear that I didn't have any problem with that.

She also discovered the Pittsburgh Poetry Forum while exploring the University of Pittsburgh's campus. There was a community-outreach poetry-writing program she became involved in. It gave her an even stronger focus for her poetry, and she was finding what she needed in Pittsburgh outside of me.

✦

IN THE SPRING OF 1969, I RECEIVED MY MFA WITH A major in music from Carnegie Mellon University. In the meantime, I continued to sing at Third Presbyterian Church as tenor soloist and film *Mister Rogers' Neighborhood*. It was finally time to take my place in the Metropolitan Opera Studio, and in August 1969, LaTanya Mae and I moved to New York. In September, the Metropolitan Opera went on strike. The money I had saved from the past two summers was soon gone. Instead of flying from audition to audition, rehearsal to rehearsal, I crawled around the city moping with existential questions, cursing taxi drivers and counting quarters. I was at the mercy of every friend and acquaintance who would listen to my tale of woe and despair. I had no voice teacher, no coach, no hangout, and no artistic point of reference. It pointed out how little I knew about the city: Those questioning eyes in the shadow of subway cars. Its bodegas, hiding its secrets. Its legendary opaqueness. How to woo its heart?

But my circumstances constrained me. The pressures of my career and my marriage kept me silent and obedient. And there wasn't even a hint of success about me. How had I gotten here?

On the other hand, during my frequent trips back to Pittsburgh to film episodes of *The Neighborhood*, I was finding my balance in a whole new world. My first impression of walking around the set was like being in a magic fantasyland. Nothing seemed real, but everyone, staff and Neighbors alike, talked about the puppets as though they were real people with feelings and goals and independent lives. That took some getting used to. I don't think I ever did learn what criteria Fred used to establish who was a Neighbor, but I got to know the different people who inhabited the Neighborhood of Make-Believe.

I had my favorites; at the head of the list was Lady Aberlin. She had gone to Bennington College, and we were about the same age. She was one of the prettiest women I'd ever met. She wore light makeup and plain, simply cut, and attractive dresses. Her articulation was natural, and her little, high voice suited her perfectly. Between breaks, her humor kept us on the floor of the studio laughing out loud.

On the show, she was called Niece Aberlin or Lady Aberlin and had a special relationship with the puppets King Friday and Lady Sara Saturday, who later married the king and became Queen Sara Saturday. I never got tired of how Lady Aberlin talked with the puppets like real people. She moved softly and quietly, keeping her feet together and her steps short. Deftly, she moved from one *Neighborhood* "house" to another to speak with or offer refuge to a struggling Neighbor.

Her relationship with Daniel Striped Tiger was sublimely tender. More than once, their encounters left me a little teary-eyed. He was such a sensitive character and seemed to need her encouragement and gentleness time and again. I began to think that Daniel was some special and vulnerable part of Fred's personality.

Ultimately, I also fell in love with the feisty and totally unpredictable spinster, Lady Elaine Fairchilde. Lady Fairchilde lived in the Museum-Go-Round, and in addition to coming up with some great ideas for festivals and plays for the Neighborhood, she often employed her magic boomerang, using the words "boomerang-toomerang-soomerang" to get around or to capriciously get even with someone in the Neighborhood who did something she didn't like. It could be as simple as children playing at the wrong place, or me singing too loudly, in her opinion. I was surprised the first time she turned me upside down with that boomerang while I was still singing. She aimed it at me, waved it around while singing a simple incantation, and through the magic of television, I was suddenly singing upside down! Of course, I continued singing normally, but the television audience saw me flip over. After I had finished singing, I expressed my "outrage," and with a little coaxing and threats to summon the king and queen, Lady Fairchilde waved the magic boomerang again, repeated her incantation, and magically I was turned back right side up. She also often starred in wonderfully goofy, made-up operas that Fred wrote and produced for the Neighborhood. Her ungainly, screechy voice—which was Fred's own falsetto—was a wonder I never wanted to hear twice.

While working with Fred, I began to understand that essentially all the puppets were aspects of his personality. When I thought about it that way, they began to make sense. He could hide behind the mask of the puppets and say all manner of things that were perhaps difficult for him to say as his *normal* self. This was an amazing revelation for me. Armed with this understanding, I could relate to each puppet ultimately as Fred. This made things much smoother for me, because after several years, I was still not totally comfortable with a grown man behind the sets playing with puppets. While I appreciated what Fred and the other Neighbors were doing, it was difficult for me to play pretend and handle any of the puppets myself. I felt clumsy and didn't want to ruin any of the filming. But I knew that wasn't the *real* reason. My reticence went deeper than that, and I wasn't quite sure why. Fred was patient to a fault and would have taken the time to teach me. But I was reluctant and never asked him.

I saw not just the public side of Fred, but also the private, vulnerable side. In public, he seemed all-powerful and creative, a mover and shaker in the Pittsburgh community. He had the creativity and foresight to start a community-based educational television station and to pioneer children's programming at a time when everybody else felt that it was an inconsequential, local task. I certainly did feel that way at the start. Yet, I knew that, privately, Fred harbored doubts about his ability to sincerely and continually communicate with the vast number of youngsters who came to his special afternoon haven at 4:00 p.m. on PBS.

Fred was shy, which gave him additional hesitation and feelings of inadequacy. He felt insecure even though people adored him. But he still carried incredible shyness and apologia for being who he was. Fred felt a connection to kids' souls as well their minds. But he also recognized that this was a tremendous responsibility, and he was very careful not to abuse his privilege. Sometimes he would speak of the "awesome responsibility" he felt. At the time, I didn't have a clue as to what he was talking about, but now I think of it as Fred possessing a soul key. He knew kids were vulnerable and impressionable, and he had to be very careful with their emotions.

I listened respectfully and went back to my singing and observations. For me, this whole thing was, at best, a career-filler, just something to do until the "real thing" came along. I was living and auditioning in New York, waiting for my Big Break in opera while flying back to Pittsburgh to film the show. As much as I enjoyed it, I didn't fully understand the show and felt I had little invested in it. I figured I would politely move on when my operatic career took off. It was just a matter of time.

Still, there were things to learn. I watched Fred intently, closely, both on and off camera, observing his every move and gesture to better understand just how this understated soul wove his way into the hearts and psyche of the American home and family. They knew that he was there just for them, all the time. I kept a mental account of the situations in the Neighborhood. I concluded that Fred sincerely gave the impression that he really wanted to help everyone. He looked out for the underdog, the lonely kid, the abandoned pet. Nobody was insignificant or unimportant; Fred Rogers had time for everyone.

During my observations, the refrain that he added toward the end of each episode rang in my head: "You've made this day a special day, by just your being you. There's no person in the whole world like you, and I like you, just the way you are." At that point, he would exchange his sweater for a suit jacket, leave his sneakers in the closet, change into his street shoes, and exit the set singing "It's Such a Good Feeling." Then he would quietly walk around to where we were standing and wait for Johnny Costa to finish playing his lovely music over the credits.

I realized that the elusive and mysterious magic formula that I was searching for was right in front of me—all the time. It was Fred's simplicity and sincerity. It was almost too obvious to be believed. Nobody else could say those hokey, sentimental things without eliciting some sarcastic reaction from people in general. But time and time again, I had watched the Neighbors, staff, friends, and observers—all of us, especially me—just standing there, listening and thinking, soaking it all in.

As I got to know more Neighbors, I started paying more attention. In my own quiet way, I would search within the experience of each to see what it was I thought Fred was looking for or, indeed, had found in the way they performed or sang. It became an obsession. I didn't always agree with his evaluation and choice. Sometimes I felt that the Neighbor or guest was a bummer—no stage personality, no good looks, and no sex appeal. Sometimes they didn't perform particularly well either. I didn't have Fred's patience or interest in many of those who trooped through Studio A to film and leave their mark on the *Neighborhood*.

Then I'd see the film while it was being edited in the special booth just across the hall from the studio. The footage didn't resemble what I had seen and felt in the studio at all! My youthful judgment had been too harsh, too cold, too quick. The scenes seemed somehow softened, intensified, meaningful. They often remained simple, even what I'd call babyish, but they had a core of care and intimacy that had eluded me in my initial watching. I got into the habit of watching the program at home every afternoon and between classes when I could. After three years, the show was finally growing on me.

I watched the episodes to see more of this transformation. I tried to analyze the way Fred might be thinking and why he looked at the camera the way he did. There was a part of me that was genuinely curious about what he was doing. I wanted to be able to do that on stage and in my solo singing.

One day, I asked him how he was able to look straight into the camera and speak so simply and lovingly to millions of strange children. He told me very earnestly that he considered the space between himself and the camera lens—which was essentially the individual child—to be a sacred space. It was so sacred to him that he would never do anything to violate that commission and responsibility that he felt came directly from God. I never forgot that.

From that moment on, I watched him even more closely. I vowed to accomplish the same simplicity and directness in my work on stage. It was a powerful tool, and I intended to practice until I felt that I had it. Along with this intensive communication, there was another quality about him that I tried to emulate. It was his quality of being serious, focused, and single-minded. He was about real business. Although he had a great sense of humor and often made himself the butt of his silly studio jokes, he could be absolutely serious about the children's issues that he presented before the camera. That, I valued in him very much.

As I practiced and sang my arias, I began to focus the way Fred did. It meant spending even more time understanding and analyzing the words and entire musical scenes in order to put the character into context and know exactly what I was saying and to whom. I was making a lot more work for myself, but in the end,

I felt that if I could come anywhere near what Fred was doing, it would be worth it. I kept at it.

The whole experience reminded me of an afternoon when I had dropped by the studio just to observe what was going on in the *Neighborhood*. Fred was on set, talking to the children and sharing with them that he had just gone to some factory that perhaps made crayons, or chocolate—something that he felt the children would be interested in. As he was leaving the stage, he took off his sweater, opened the closet door, and grabbed his sports jacket, as he did after each program. But this time, it seemed as if he was focused in on me, carefully standing in the shadows so as not be seen by any camera. As he changed his costume to put on his street clothes, his gaze became even more penetrating, and unmistakably riveted on me, as he said the lines he ended every show with: "You make every day a special day just by being you, and I like you just the way you are."

As he left the set, I began to move around the edges, closer and closer to him as though being drawn by some invisible magnet. Sure enough, when the beautiful music stopped and the director yelled, "Cut!" we were standing next to each other, as though hypnotized. I was the first to speak. "Fred, were you talking to *me?*"

He answered quietly and calmly, "Yes, I was. I have been talking to you for years. You finally heard me today."

◆

MY FIRST CHILDREN'S CONCERT WAS IN SCARSDALE, New York, with my accompanist, Nancy Roth. It was in 1970 at St. James The Less Episcopal Church and Hoff-Barthelson

Music School. It was so successful that I began to do some concerts for free at various daycare centers in my Upper West Side neighborhood. Friends of mine heard about it and suggested that I consult with John Gutman, who was second to Rudolf Bing, the general manager of the Metropolitan Opera. In addition, it was suggested that I contact Maestro Leonard De Paur, the famed black conductor who had toured with the Army Chorus all over the world for almost twenty years under the dual-management of Columbia Artists and the United States Army. He had settled down now as a community affairs officer for Lincoln Center and was busy bringing minority performers from uptown Harlem and the five boroughs to Lincoln Center. I was perfect for his program. He and John Gutman worked well together, and all manner of folks got on board to make this series of concerts, to be presented at Lincoln Center Library, a success.

As it turned out, I went on to have a long, very fruitful relationship with Maestro De Paur and was invited back to Lincoln Center several times to perform children's concerts and Christmas carols on his Community Holiday Concert Series. In later years, my group, the Harlem Spiritual Ensemble, would perform outside during their famous summer series in Damrosch Park at Lincoln Center.

Our first children's concert at Lincoln Center set a very high mark for all of us involved. During the singing of "Won't You Be My Neighbor," Fred walked into the entranceway and sang with me. My surprise was beyond monumental! Still, I had the presence of mind to keep singing, and we made it a duet; for a few minutes, pandemonium broke out among the children and their parents. I wound up welcoming Fred and then stepped graciously aside while his quiet charm reigned supreme! To everyone it looked as though it had been planned, and that was fine with me.

Word traveled quickly around the Metropolitan Opera House about the concert series. And after that spectacular show with Fred, I was hailed everywhere I went. Fred buoyed my efforts, and when he returned to Pittsburgh from Manhattan, he called and suggested that I prepare for him a one-page description of these children's concerts, aimed specifically for minority neighborhoods. Ultimately, he bought my suggestion and hired a black publicity firm, D. Parke Gibson, and together we fashioned a national tour that was the envy of any rock group or Motown act! I sang in inner city community centers, YMCAs, NAACP centers, Urban Coalitions, you name it. We went to Philadelphia, Baltimore, Delaware, Newark, D.C., Boston, Buffalo, Syracuse, Springfield, Albany, New York, Hartford, New Haven, Cleveland, Toledo, Columbus, Dayton, Detroit, Milwaukee, Chicago, Kansas, Memphis, Richmond, Atlanta, Nashville, Birmingham, Montgomery, Baton Rouge, New Orleans, and all over Texas. Subsequent tours took us to the West Coast and farther.

My personal goal was to eventually cover the country. So, if there were scheduling difficulties, or awkward travel arrangements, I suffered them silently and never complained. I sang for adults as often as for children, featuring *Porgy and Bess*. Because of my own deep, spiritual feelings, we never passed up a chance to attend a local church service or nondenominational gathering where I could talk about Fred and the show but also sing an American Negro spiritual. This undertaking felt more like a calling than a job. It was my original idea, and I really wanted it to succeed.

✦

IT'S IMPORTANT FOR ME TO SHARE THAT, FOR ALL THOSE years I spent on *Mister Rogers' Neighborhood*, I was never allowed to stop thinking about race. It's important for me to establish that I don't think Fred had a racist bone in his body. But neither of us lived in a vacuum. And the ultimate truth is *Mister Rogers' Neighborhood* was a reflection of the society in which we lived. If our program was a racial paradise, there would not have been any need to go on those tours to Atlanta, Nashville, Memphis, Detroit, Chicago, Los Angeles, or Cincinnati to encourage minority communities to support our program. Despite Fred's best efforts, I often found myself in the role of diversity officer. That was one of the reasons I urged him to bring the *Neighborhood* cameras to Spanish Harlem and other minority communities in the United States. He embraced the idea and came to my neighborhood twice to film. The folks in my community spoke about it for many years afterward. I think they enjoyed seeing themselves on television later as much as they enjoyed the actual day of filming.

In cooperation, the NYC park officials turned it into a "playstreet," roped it off from car traffic, put up a truncated basketball court, and set up tables for dominoes, checkers, jump ropes and jacks for the kids, as well as roller skates and two tether ball stands. Mother Nature worked with us and the sun shone brilliantly until late in the evening. The gathering crowd made it seem at times like the entire population from West 96th Street up to Columbia University stopped by to partake of the festivities. I don't think my feet touched the ground the whole time. I felt like I was an angelic hummingbird—darting this way, chatting with that one, listening to Fred speak with perfect strangers who were my neighbors, and recording it all . . . making a mental note that would last forever.

There were many fine black performers who appeared on the show as guests from time to time, and I frequently got to meet some of them, most notably Mabel Mercer, Wynton Marsalis, and Mary Lou Williams. However, the overriding impression was that it was a white show set in suburban America. A lasting impression that has stayed with me for many years are the private conversations I had with educators, social workers, administrators, supervisors, business men and women, and performers in minority communities of the various cities we visited. Nearly all the contacts that Dr. Mary Murray—my escort/host/ road manager—and I made agreed to put every effort toward the success of the program in their communities. However, the constant refrain they shared with me was that the show was *so white*. Could there be more black people, or could I appear more often on the show? They often compared us to *Sesame Street* and *The Electric Company*.

I knew that I didn't have the answer, so my goal was to share with them the fantastic ideals that I felt were unique to *Mister Rogers' Neighborhood* and why I should be on this program. Caring for your neighbor, showing love and consideration, understanding childhood fears, dealing with parents who get divorced, combating bullying, and being lonely are experiences that all human beings have.

In all my efforts, I urged my compatriots to look beyond color and to give us their full consideration for the unique and extraordinary work in which we were all engaged. I shared with them honestly that as difficult as this work was sometimes, I did not feel like the Invisible Man, but I did feel translucent. That was more due to some of the people who surrounded Fred Rogers rather than *his* attitude or ethos.

Through Dr. Murray's diligence, we often stayed in touch with these pacesetters and community leaders across the United States, and I know that our efforts and their outreach paid off by the correspondence that she shared with me. It would be too simplistic to say that they merely enjoyed my personality and my singing, and occasionally it was demonstrated in profound ways: In later years, when I toured these same cities as the founder/ director of the Harlem Spiritual Ensemble. Many of them were proud to say that this was their second time coming to hear me sing. Then they'd recount the occasion I had visited their fair city or concert hall as Officer Clemmons, and they'd spent the evening with me.

But throughout these tours, questionable things happened. The vast majority of the employees and attendants at the PBS stations really wanted Fred Rogers to personally come to visit, without me or other members of the cast. Some of that could be expected, but some of their attitudes were disappointing and downright rude. It would show itself by station employees not arranging a parking place for us in areas where parking was difficult, not greeting us in their offices or offering a seat or anything to drink, or even forgetting to warn security that we were coming. Sometimes only an intern took the time to welcome us. Other times folks who had planned to meet us were in meetings and couldn't get away, or they were caught in traffic and still driving to work! I still recall that several times our contacts made us wait for up to a half hour before seeing us. It was my observation that this happened far too often to be accidental. I was also aware of how seldom we were invited to dinner or lunch. Sometimes it was our schedule; other times it was our host's lack of planning.

Putting all this together over a period of time, it was obvious that some folks just didn't give a damn about Officer Clemmons coming to their station or town. So, we decided that if things appeared the least bit suspect, when possible we'd go directly to the black gathering center or black college. There, we always received a warm welcome and an invitation to return. Under those circumstances, we would try to connect with our contact and call the PBS station later. Then we'd play it by ear as to whether it was appropriate to visit in person or not. I think that that gesture on our part took some of the pressure off the local representative to be with us if, indeed, they had some place else they'd rather be. It is important to remember that all kinds of publicity material and calendars were sent and checked well before our proposed arrival. Frequently, I was in the offices of D. Parke Gibson myself and heard all the arrangements being made!

Looking back, even though I knew I had to hold on to my participation on *Mister Rogers' Neighborhood*, the role of Officer Clemmons was not a natural one for me. I'll probably always carry some measure of resistance to that role, considering how I, and many black folks, felt about police officers. But I was quickly learning that having a regular role on practically any television show, children or otherwise, had its advantages. Folks in New York knew about Fred and spoke liberally and often to me about what a plum role I had managed to land. I never volunteered any serious details except to share with them what a wonderful boss he was and that I was enjoying my little stint as a jet-setter flying back and forth from New York to Pittsburgh on Allegheny

Airlines to film from time to time! Despite what Fred had said to me earlier about how secure my position with him was, there was always a fear that someone might try to take the job away from me. The folks at Carnegie Mellon, led by my ex voice teacher Beatrice Krebs, had already tried that and failed. Who knew when someone else might try again?

Things were finally picking back up at the Metropolitan Opera Studio, and they ending up stamping me as being a prodigy from the Midwest—Ohio, to be more specific—even though I was born in Birmingham. Nevertheless, everyone at the Metropolitan Opera Studio thought of me as being from Ohio. So, I was their natural choice to go back to my home state and integrate the Cincinnati Opera. I had eagerly accepted the assignment for a chance to see some choice home folks from Youngstown, make some money, and perhaps continue to build my career. It was a natural move for a young singer.

On the day of my departure that June morning, the sun was up bright and early, and so was I. But it wasn't long before I realized that it was all a facade. Something deep and serious was going on inside me. As hard as I tried, I just couldn't shake it. I realized that I was afraid. I was afraid of all the unknowns that could happen to me while I was in Cincinnati, making my debut in Carlisle Floyd's opera, *Of Mice and Men*. The company was under court order to desegregate immediately. All my instincts said that as positive as I was going to act, the administration was not going to be glad to see me. Racists are never happy when they are forced to integrate. Token black person: Beware!

I called Fred. Dutifully, he listened and offered some sound advice. I had every intention of calling him as often as I needed to on this trip. I just knew I couldn't do this one alone. I'm an extrovert and being alone for prolonged periods of time is not good for me. I had learned that a long time ago.

Upon arrival in Cincinnati, there was no one to meet me at the airport, and I had to get to the hotel downtown from Lexington, Kentucky, on my own. At the hotel, there was a note from the opera company that said to call when I got in. Nothing more. There were no fancy flowers in my room and no bowl of fruit. This was no LA tour! So, I shrugged and called. They said simply to stop by the office before they closed at 5:00 p.m. and hung up. No ceremony there either. "That must be the special way the folks in Cincinnati have to welcome strangers," I murmured to myself. "No need to go out of your way for me!"

Civil society had spoiled me; normal folks had spoiled me; Fred had spoiled me. Everywhere we went as an ensemble, we were welcomed and eagerly met and showed around. I was disabused of that notion right from the beginning in Cincinnati. I unpacked, grabbed a sandwich and soda, and headed over to the opera company office a few blocks away. I made sure that I kept smiling. I entered, and no one, not the middle-aged receptionist or anyone else, paid me the least bit of attention. The receptionist handed me my rehearsal portfolio and kept right on working without lifting her head or uttering a word. Cold. I took the packet and stood there a bit, awkwardly waiting for her—or anyone—to make eye contact or say something. It took a minute before I knew she wasn't going to look up or say anything, let alone smile, so I simply turned slowly and left.

After I got outside, I took note of how nice the weather was and found my smile again. There was definitely an unmistakable air of gloom in that office, and I had a feeling I brought it in! That hadn't been my intention, but that was the truth. I made a note to myself that the next time I would smile harder and keep smiling regardless of how gloomy they were. Cincinnati was not going to take my smile away!

For the next couple of hours, I walked around aimlessly, checking out the ordinary store windows and sights of this new city and ratcheting up my determination to focus in on the good feelings I had brought with me from Manhattan. The next morning, I got up, ate a good breakfast, and planned to arrive at the rehearsal studio early so I could look around and meet and greet some of the cast as well as the director and the conductor. I got there in plenty of time, but no one spoke to me! *No one.* I said hello and not one person said hello back to me. Before I realized it, my smile was gone, and I stood there in utter confusion.

Later, I learned that the administration had instructed all the performers, crew, and other instrumentalists not to speak to me under any circumstances. In a flash I thought, *This is what it feels like to be shunned.* You don't have to do anything really wrong, but everyone has to agree that you're bad in some way and simply stop talking and communicating with you. Done! You can't explain yourself back into their good graces because they can't, or won't, talk to you. So, there I was with my music, my professionalism, and no one to sit with or communicate with.

Now, my role in the opera wasn't very involved or long, but I wanted to feel a part of the company. I even knew some of the singers by reputation. Julian Patrick was a well-known baritone in New York, and I had heard him sing at the NYC Opera. Carole Farley was also a very well-known singer around New York City. Grayson Hirst was one of the up-and-coming tenors at City Center. Indeed, he was dating a black soprano who was a close friend of mine. Being ignored by him was incredibly awkward and unbelievable. We had gone bowling together several times in New York and had a wonderful time! My brain was on warp speed backward. How had this happened? The questions kept coming, and I was past confused.

I forgot about smiling. I forgot about singing. I was trying to survive. I struggled to calm myself and breathe deeply. I could literally die just standing there looking at everyone not saying a word to me.

I vaguely remember muttering something to nobody in particular about having to go to the bathroom and turning and stumbling out of the rehearsal studio. I could hear them in the distance beginning to sing as though I'd never even been there. I went into the bathroom, found an empty stall, and just sat there. I don't know how long I sat, but eventually I began to return to some semblance of normalcy. I knew I had to go back to that rehearsal room again if it killed me. But what would I say? What would I do?

I had to be professional. I had to pull myself together, and when my turn came, I needed to be able to do my part, however small . . . however unimportant. I was not going to let them defeat me without uttering a note.

Going by the schedule, I wasn't expected to sing until later in the afternoon. I had a short arietta that would close the first act. Since I was officially abandoned, I had no trouble sitting quietly, waiting until my cue finally came. As they got closer to my cue, I rose, went to the assumed backstage area, and, at the appropriate time, began to sing. It went well, and the imaginary curtain was properly drawn. The act ended, and the rest of the cast all gathered around the conductor, Emerson Buckley, and the fast-talking director for critiques. I stood waiting: Not a word was said to me, so I assumed that I did okay. If I hadn't, I was sure they'd have said something to me. *Someone* would have said something to me.

I sat quietly for the rest of the rehearsal. On some signal I hadn't been apprised of, they all began to gather their belongings and leave the room. No one said "rehearsal's over" or "goodbye" or "see you tonight" or "see you tomorrow" or . . . anything. One minute they were there, singing away, and in a few minutes, they were all gone. I sat for a moment thinking about the day. I asked myself why in the world I took this job? Did I really need it? I could still quit! But in that same deep place, I knew that wasn't really an option. The die was cast, perhaps for all of us.

Slowly, I gathered my music and my painful rejected inner parts and headed back for the hotel. It was going to be a long, slow evening at this rate. I had lost my smile; I was angry. Occasionally I trembled with the rage I was desperately trying to control. I felt chills, but they were because of the destruction I knew I was capable of. I absolutely couldn't allow myself to go down that road. It had Dead End marked all over it!

At the first chance I got that evening, I called Fred. I thanked God he was home and had time to listen to my tormented tale. When I had finished, he answered patiently, "You did the right thing, Franç. You can't run away from these bad experiences. People like that would love to see you defeated and humiliated. Stay strong and know that your friends and your family here in Pittsburgh will be praying for you. You can call whenever you need to, and when this is over, and it won't last forever, you can shake the dust from your sandals and come here where your family loves you. You deserve our love and support."

So, I stayed. And eventually, I discovered that several

community members knew of my arrival and had given me a few days to settle in before they contacted me. When they called, they were like a breath of fresh air. I eagerly accepted their invitations to dinner, and the cloud of gloom began to lift. Members of the local NAACP and other civic groups asked how I was doing and if there was anything they could do to make my stay more comfortable. I told them, "How about a night out to show me around town and some common conversation?" Something an extrovert would welcome.

They understood, and from then on, I spent less time in my hotel room and wandering around downtown alone.

Surprisingly one other thing happened. One of the cast members, Julian Patrick, a tall, strapping, wholesome-looking man who spoke with a deep voice and was singing the baritone lead in the opera, approached me toward the end of the first week and asked me to lunch. You can imagine I viewed his offer with much hesitation. I asked him why he was extending an invitation now when he hadn't spoken to me all week! He said he'd explain at lunch. I reluctantly agreed.

Well, I got the surprise of my life. He told me that there had been several meetings before my arrival in Cincinnati and afterward. The cast had been informed of the court order that the opera company was under and therefore had been instructed not to speak to me. The management deeply resented this legal intrusion into their schedule of activities and would do everything it could to see to it that this order was not successful. That meant seeing to it that I had a horrible time.

At first, silently, the performers had gone along. They didn't want to be blackballed! But the decision had begun to haunt them. As I said, I knew some of them from Manhattan.

Previously, we had had some good times together. That's part of what made their silence so painful.

Several days after my arrival, they decided among themselves to have a private meeting without management present. It was agreed unanimously that I was owed an apology and the business of shunning me should come to an end immediately.

The sincerity of his words touched me deeply. I could hardly respond, and I listened to him through tears. The truth was that their silence had broken my heart. He knew it. I was thinking, *What do you do with the mad that you feel?*—a great Fred Rogers song.

What do you do when good people are silent in the face of such brazen racism?

I wish I could say that things got better right away. Not so. The management continued to shun me and, if possible, ignored me more and spoke even less to me. Nevertheless, one by one the rest of the cast members found their way to me, apologized, and made their peace. Without exception, they began to speak with me on a regular basis.

To make matters worse, or better, depending on your perspective, the eminent American composer Carlisle Floyd arrived and was eager to meet me. There were members of his family who knew me, and he had watched the program with them often. He loved *Mister Rogers' Neighborhood* and asked for my autograph! I was only too happy to oblige.

Well, this was perhaps the most awkward moment for the management. In his naïveté, Carlisle insisted that I come to dinner with him. I had no intentions of saying no. We arranged dinner, and I resumed rehearsing.

At dinner, Carlisle and I had a deep meeting of the minds. He too apologized for the behavior of the management even though he had had nothing to do with it. He wanted to do something to make up for it. He was living in Florida at the time and invited me to come visit him to perform a concert of American Negro spirituals, which he would sponsor. He also recommended me to do other productions of his opera.

The opera performances went very well, and the production received the fine reception it deserved both by press and audiences. I was happy for Carlisle and felt that because of him, the cast, and local citizens I did not suffer a defeat. My sponsors from the local civic organizations came to the performances and made sure I had the support that a visiting artist should have. I was grateful for their cards, flowers, hospitality, and the meaningful party afterward.

✦

IT WAS JUST MY LUCK TO RETURN TO CINCINNATI A FEW years later with a nucleus performing group of characters from the *Neighborhood* to appear with the Cincinnati Symphony Orchestra in a series of children's concerts. Various PBS television stations, community groups, children organizations, educational organizations, schools, research institutions, universities, and colleges were constantly requesting that Fred come and lecture or perform in one fashion or another. Because of our personal and professional relationship, he very often took me with him. On many of these occasions, I sang various arrangements of his songs to Johnny Costa's brilliant accompaniment. It was most fun when Mr. McFeely and Lady Aberlin also came along. I never let the opportunity go by to inform the Metropolitan Opera folks that I was singing at Yale,

Berkeley, the University of Illinois, Rollins College, or some other fine institution. They were just as impressed and happy to brag as if they had gotten me the gig themselves.

Per usual, I was up bright and early preparing myself for this wonderful new concert hall only recently dedicated for the Cincinnati Symphony as a gift from the Corbett Foundation. As I entered, it was hard not to notice that it was dazzling, with fabulous acoustics and great behind-the-scenes accouterments for visiting artists. Everything was worthy of the finest orchestra halls found anywhere in the world! I felt lucky and blessed.

In just a matter of minutes, I found my dressing room and put on my Officer Clemmons uniform and began to vocalize. I slowly made my way to the main auditorium, where several orchestra members were warming up, and said a quick hello as I passed them and headed for the stage. There was good noise all around me like it used to be at Oberlin College and in the practice rooms in grad school. I daresay this place was beginning to feel like home!

One of my best friends used to say that I always carried the air of innocence about me. Even at thirty, I seemed much younger, like a perpetual teenager. I always challenged him and went on about my business. But on this occasion, I knew he was right.

Even though I was standing in the wings of the stage, I was caught off guard when it seemed as though nearly everyone was motioning one way or another at me. The conductor asked in a not-so-friendly tone, "What are you doing there? What do you want?" as though I had invaded some sacred territory. I instinctively knew I was making him angry by being there.

I could scarcely answer; his tone was so cutting and harsh!

I stood stock still as he continued to stare at me, waiting for an answer. I finally realized that I was stuttering my name: "Officer Clemmons."

"Officer what? Why are you here? Please will you get off my stage!" he shouted.

I hadn't realized that I had started taking small baby steps toward him in my effort to be heard better! I just knew that this was all a mistake. It just had to be.

The sound of his voice was both deafening and pounding in my head. I was humiliated. I turned and stumbled off the stage and headed back down to my dressing room. *Good Lord*, I thought, *what is it about Cincinnati?*

I went into my dressing room and slammed the door. In a second, Mr. and Mrs. McFeely (Betty Seamans) were barging in, followed by Johnny Costa. They spoke at once, trying to apologize for the colossal bad manners of the young conductor. It was the very instant that I was putting on my coat to leave that Fred appeared at the door, looking totally confused. Everyone turned to him and again started explaining all at once. I stood there not saying a word but feeling their pain for me. My eyes locked on Fred's. He, too, was silent, but he knew perhaps better than all of us that something awful had befallen his son.

With a gently raised hand, some calm was restored and Johnny began to speak. Haltingly, he recounted the episode that had just unfolded on stage. I, too, stood silent, my rage not able to stem the tears streaming down my face. Betty and David each gave some version of the disaster on stage and Fred listened silently, as did I. Fred put his arm around me in a comforting, protective manner as any parent probably would have done.

He spoke softly but with final authority. He told me to take my coat off and come back to the stage with him. We all needed to speak with the conductor. We moved as one with no noise, only one united purpose.

It was amazing how casually Fred seemed to disregard the generous applause from the orchestra members and all those scattered around the stage as we entered the area where the orchestra was seated. They had been rehearsing for about half an hour by now. A tentative path had been set for the *Neighbors* to enter and leave the stage during the performance. We entered led by Fred. Even if I hadn't known Fred, I'd have suspected that something was wrong by the ashen, strained look on his face.

The conductor saw us and stepped forward, trying to greet Fred warmly. Fred was having none of it. When the commotion died down, he spoke calmly but with intent.

"I understand you had a few words with our Officer Clemmons this morning when he came here to rehearse with you. He says you said some very unpleasant things to him. In our neighborhood, we don't talk like that and especially to one of our Neighbors. We have come here today to have a pleasant visit with our many friends from Cincinnati, and we're sorry that this has happened. But we don't think we can carry on unless you apologize to Officer Clemmons. Unless there is something that he said or did to you, you owe him an apology right now or we are not going to work with you."

All around us the silence was thunderous! I stood there, a thousand thoughts going through my mind. I'll always remember this as my *John Brown Moment*. I had studied history but had only heard of one white man, an abolitionist named John Brown, who gave his life to end slavery in the United States. Of course, during our Civil War, many white soldiers of the Union cavalry gave their lives to end slavery, but John Brown stands out as the first.

The apology was awkward to say the least. With everyone watching, I was bound by Fred's word and protection . . . or this guy was due for a punch! I was not totally nonviolent, as I was sure Fred was. But in spite of the conductor's words, there was no peace between us. He had clearly shown me who he was, and I believed him. My passions run high, and I know the enemy when I stand face-to-face with him. Fred's presence had established a temporary truce, but I knew that people like him don't change just because of a few hollow words he had been forced to speak under pressure. Because of folks like him this battle would have to be fought again and again, as it has been lo these 150 years since our Civil War. I was not so naïve as to think it would end here because of the benevolent words of my hero, Fred Rogers. Fred might feel that way, but my experience had taught me differently.

I put my best smile on and allowed my professionalism to take charge just as I had years ago when the folks in charge of the Cincinnati Opera had shunned me. Outwardly, I was compliant. But I knew that if I was to survive this invisible racist army that lurked everywhere, I needed to always be vigilant and ready to do battle. Otherwise, I'd be bloodied and humiliated at any moment by a hypocritical and deceptive enemy that refused to change and accept me as an equal and deserving member of the human race.

After the performance, I was exhausted emotionally from the incident with the conductor as well as the experience of so many anxious, expectant faces singing and waving to us. It always took its toll. It was wonderful, but it was tiring. I had finally been able to retire to my dressing room to sit a moment before looking for the car to take us back to our hotel to relax before dinner and a good night's rest. Suddenly, the door opened without a knock, and it was Fred.

"Oh, Franç," he said all cheery, "your heated limousine is here whenever you're ready to go back to the hotel." He dashed out the door to the car before I could compose myself from laughing so much. Outside it was almost 80 degrees!

In these moments, his humor saved us all. I marveled that I could laugh so deeply and honestly after the ugly encounter with the racist conductor. But I also knew that if I stayed in that gloomy place, he would have won the day. Thanks to Fred, my efforts to rise up were going to be successful. Once again, I was able to leave Cincinnati with a smile on my face!

✦

MEANWHILE, MY MARRIAGE WASN'T GOING WELL. I became increasingly guarded about what I thought and said around LaTanya Mae.

I even felt a growing reserve with Michael. He was the person most responsible for my coming out, for my sexual self-discovery. I felt I had to watch my mouth and my behavior out of fear they would give away my secret passion, the life of my soul: my love of only men and my love for Nicky.

But LaTanya Mae proved to be far less demanding than I had suspected. After the wedding, she immediately set about changing the furniture in the apartment and settling in. I really didn't care one way or the other, so she had control. I helped when and where I could and generally stayed out of the way. I made constant excuses to go to campus to practice. I felt guilt spending more time with my friends than I did with her, but she never made me feel bad about it. Any other spare time I spent listening to gospel music or daydreaming about Nicky. Not once did I blame LaTanya Mae for what was happening. I knew better; I was gay, plain and simple. I just didn't need her in that way.

One night, after eating the dinner she'd prepared in silence, she called me on my attitude.

"So why aren't you talking? Cat got your tongue?" she asked.

"I was thinking about my fall schedule," I replied. "Classes begin next week, and I want to be ready."

In actuality, I was thinking about Nicky. How do you tell your wife you're thinking about your male lover? Privately, I was obsessed with Nicky and his distance from me. He had decided to leave the University of Chicago and go to the University of Michigan in Ann Arbor to finish up his PhD in literature. I wanted to see him, feel him, smell him, play with him. But I knew that was impossible. Still, I couldn't shut him out of my mind. No, the cat didn't have my tongue. Just the thought of Nicky. I never told LaTanya Mae how difficult it was trying to make love to her while I was thinking of Nicky. It stimulated me and made me very sad at the same time.

This pit of self-loathing and self-rejection is the loneliest feeling in the whole world. When you are down there, it feels as though there is nothing living or dead worth crawling out for. I wanted to stay there, to lie there, and just die there.

But life had a way of eventually pulling me out of that pit, and for that I was grateful. Michael played a role in my recovery. He called and proposed another visit to Pittsburgh. I was always game for that. LaTanya Mae was as glad as I was to see him. He began visiting us now regularly, once or twice a month, and we loved it. LaTanya Mae simply assumed that I was bisexual. She believed that I loved her romantically despite also being attracted to Michael, and I did not correct her.

But Michael and I knew that he was a balm for my non-relationship with LaTanya Mae. The only time we were intimate now was when he came to visit or when we went to Youngstown. LaTanya Mae and I were married and living in the same apartment, but we were shadow lovers: not touching, not interacting, not without Michael.

I was always a bit in awe of the way they related and was thankful that Michael took the energy and attention from her that I would have gotten otherwise. I didn't want a sexual relationship with LaTanya Mae, but I had access to all of her; Michael wanted her—wanted both of us—but she seemed to only be interested in a fraternal friendship with him. They could never be sexual partners without me in the middle. And there would never have been a reasonable sexual relationship between LaTanya Mae and me without Michael.

The American Dream was not the kind of life I could expect if I was going to continue to love Nicky. Fred Rogers and the show had made that clear to me. But still, I allowed myself to entertain the idea of what it would be like to live an openly gay life with a real and open partner. There were other guys doing it, but I didn't know of anyone with a public persona who was. American public figures—politicians, singers, entertainers, athletes—were subject to all kinds of intense scrutiny. No part of my private life would be off-limits. I couldn't stand that kind of attention. I'd have to find another career. What else could I do? Teach? Write? Maybe we could live in Europe. Everyone said that Europeans were more tolerant of sexuality than Americans.

By 1970, it became clear to both of us that, after two years, our marriage was simply not working, despite Michael's presence. So, LaTanya Mae decided to move out of our apartment. However, we decided to legally stay married for another four years.

When we did finally divorce, it was because she met someone and wanted to remarry. It was all amicable enough. We met in her lawyer's office, which was a bit awkward, as I hadn't seen her since she left our shared apartment. We'd only spoken briefly on the phone up until that point. I wasn't making much money yet, so we each paid our own lawyers and settled. I received my divorce papers and was again a free man. When I told Nicky about the divorce, he told me he respected any decision I made. He only asked that I wouldn't marry or live in a sexual relationship with another man. I never did. Michael took the divorce the hardest. Though he was upset, he kept in touch with both of us, equally, until his death in 1992. He respected that LaTanya Mae had finally met her soul mate.

◆

Through the years, I have learned better and better to turn my analytical lens on myself to improve my performance and to judge whether I'm achieving a desired effect in my work. Frequently, a performer will employ coaches, choreographers, and directors for new acts or new song cycles that require a dramatic component. We also will perform tryouts in out-of-mainstream theaters and venues to get the metal of our progress. I've used all these techniques, but none is as effective for me as a very quiet period of isolated, meditative self-evaluation. I prefer to be alone and have absolutely no one around, not even an accompanist. In many cases, I've taken a tape recorder with the material laid out in such a fashion that I can manage many repeats without interruption. I've also learned that it keeps other folks from going crazy!

One of my first aha moments came in the late 1970s when I was very busy building my operatic career while filming *Mister Rogers' Neighborhood*. Despite my many legitimate complaints about the racism openly practiced by operatic personnel, there was measurable progress in my career. At that point, I knew that I would probably never sing at the Metropolitan Opera, but I did have a manager, and more frequently than I would have imagined, I was either winning auditions and competitions or being hired on the spot, as with the Springfield Symphony or the Quebec City Orchestra. I was encouraged by these results.

During this period, I also won the prestigious Sullivan Foundation Award. Afterward, the very famous choral director Hugh Ross asked to chat with me. I had learned early on that these chats could be very meaningful, so I was optimistic. He informed me that along with the stipend of ten thousand dollars, the Foundation would act as agent if I were to decide to go to Europe. He encouraged me to suggest to anyone I knew who wanted to contribute to my career to contribute to the Foundation and it would be tax-exempt. Also, he guaranteed me that all of it would be used for my benefit.

I thought about it and told everyone in casual and every other kind of conversation and communication imaginable. I decided to go on a campaign. I was surprised at how many folks responded positively, and we collected a goodly sum of money I hadn't expected! Perhaps most surprising, Fred gave me a substantial contribution. I was surprised because black singers, along with many very talented black creative artists, painters, dancers, writers, directors, choreographers, conductors, etc., had been going to Europe to express their artistry since the 1920s Harlem Renaissance and frequently didn't come home for many years. Some took up permanent residency. Of course, there were many more classical singers, conductors, directors, writers, and painters who I knew had worthy careers in Europe teaching classes in singing, dancing, or even English language to earn a living.

Fred knew all of this as well; he approached me once and said, "Franç, we want you to come home when you're finished auditioning in Europe. We'll do all we can to help you, and you'll probably get a few good jobs, but please promise me you'll come home."

". . . Why would I not come home?" I asked.

"It's been tough for you here. Many fine artists have found great appreciation in Europe and decided to stay for the sense of purpose and accomplishment. Europeans feel very different about the support of the arts than most Americans. You'll be able to see it firsthand. I've been over there several times and I know."

I hadn't inquired more about Fred's trips to Europe before, but now I took full advantage of all he was willing to share with me. As I listened, I eased into the full realization that Fred had been mentoring me for years. He was more than just a patron of the arts—a few dollars here, a few dollars there. A mentor took responsibility for the person's artistic and professional development. He took me home in his heart. He considered me a protégé and wanted to keep me close to home until I was ready to fly away. All the special, caring, insightful things he had been doing for me right from the beginning went *click!*

I assured him not to worry, that I wouldn't forget his words, and I made a quick exit. I needed to be alone. When I arrived at home and settled down, I kept repeating the word: *Mentor.* It came to me: Mozart! Bach! Haydn! Schubert! Many of the greatest musicians whom I admired deeply had mentors. But how had I been operating so long *with* one and not known it?

It was the nature of race in our country. I found it hard to believe that a white man would make that kind of deep commitment to a black man like myself. It was like a lifetime commitment to me. Not something you did casually or on the spur of the moment and then, at some unspoken moment of boredom, just moved on. Mentorship was for life in my humble opinion, and that was Fred.

✦

SEVERAL YEARS AFTER THAT INITIAL LUNCH WITH Fred at Stouffer's Restaurant, I knew we'd have many important conversations based primarily on the fact that he was a great listener. An extrovert like me loves nothing more than a sincere listener. It's like air to life, or water to thirst. I soon found that I could tell him anything in absolute privacy and trust, and he wasn't going to be shocked by my personal revelations.

After my very conservative religious upbringing, it was a great gift to find an adult like Fred who could listen to me without moral judgment, in spite of the fact that he was a committed student at the Pittsburgh Theological Seminary. In many ways, he was a blessed continuation of the Beechwood family who had taken me in. It seemed so easy for us to talk about things that I felt awkward discussing with other folks.

After we survived the difficult issue of my being gay and

everything that came after it, I decided to risk sharing with him one of my most sacred feelings. Since the *Neighborhood* talked so much about feelings, and about the importance of the inner person—how each one of us is unique and special—I felt that I could risk telling him something that I had never dared tell anyone ever before: I wanted to "mother" a child. I wanted to hold, nurture, and love a child the way a woman did. I thought he'd be repulsed and shocked by this revelation, but instead he encouraged me to think about my feelings, so I could be as clear as possible in how I voiced this heartfelt emotion. He told me that he knew by the way I spoke to him how important it was to me. That was a part of his uniqueness, his gift.

Fred shared that he felt a deep sense of nurturance for his family, for his beloved wife, for the many close friends in his life, and for those whom he ministered to on television. As we chatted, I shared with him that I was very happy with my biological destiny of being a male, but somehow, I wanted to nurture children in a specifically maternal way. It all seemed impossible. And I seriously questioned many times just what the heck I was talking about. But his serious responses to me gave me courage to continue probing deep within myself to find the answer.

We talked about adoption. It seemed like such a clear answer, but I didn't feel that I was ready for a full-time commitment to anyone, even to an older child. I was on the road performing too much, and I didn't have a partner who wanted to stay at home and take care of the child. In my heart and in my mind, it was proving to be quite a dilemma!

One day, about a year after the adoption conversation, I heard a scratching at my apartment door that sounded strange but wouldn't go away. I finally got up and went to see who or what it was. I looked through the peephole and saw no one, but the scratching continued. Finally, I opened the door. There, on the threshold, sitting on the floor, was a young child of about three years old with a yellow sippy cup in his hand, pointing it at me. It seemed like he was asking for some milk. He was only partly dressed and was looking most expectantly at me. I looked around to see who might be with him, and even walked a few steps in two directions to see if I could ascertain just where he might have come from. I tried to talk to him. He wasn't clear about his name or where his apartment was, so I called out to nobody in particular. Eventually a black woman stumbled out to the hall several doors down and inquired if I had seen her child, Ishmael.

I pointed to the child and told her he had asked for some milk. If she'd wait just a moment, I'd get him some. She waited. He drank it all down right away. Then they left. She hadn't said hello, thank you, or goodbye!

On the surface, it was not a big deal; I like children, and he seemed likable enough! However, hours later, I found myself going through my routine and thinking about this child in the strangest way. It greatly concerned me that I could tell that the mother was under the influence of some kind, of drugs or alcohol, or both. I wasn't sure. She was one of my neighbors in this big building that even after twenty years I hadn't bothered to get to know. They had probably moved in while I was away singing. But it was her little son, Ishmael, who was on my mind. I felt deep compassion for this child, having to live with a mother who permitted him to leave their apartment half-dressed, seemingly hungry, and not particularly clean. He deserved better.

From then on, I always kept milk in the refrigerator. When I heard the familiar scratching at the door, I knew the routine and

we fell into a lovely pattern. He talked, and I began to understand his speech. In no time, I bought a few books to read to him
and a few toys I thought he'd enjoy playing with. His visits began
to last longer and longer. I changed my television-watching pattern to suit his needs, took him to the children's library, amended
my grocery list to include more fruits and vegetables, bought less
sugary cookies and desserts, and promised myself to curse less.
That's what "mothering" was doing to me! I continued to sing
and travel, but that mysterious place inside of me was contented
beyond measure.

But because of my busy touring schedule, I never formally
adopted any children. As I got to know folks better in my New
York City neighborhood, I discovered that there were many children in need of care and simple attention who were neglected
either by their parents or the system. Because of my extended
relationship with their families and Lolly, a social worker friend
who lived in my building, I was able to informally assist some
of them in getting the medical and home care they needed. For
the time being, I could serve as an advocate as my schedule allowed. Sometimes it was difficult for me because I could see
clearly that too many of the parents neglected their children to
get high. The children oftentimes just needed someone to go
with them to a doctor's appointment or make sure someone was
there on a particular day to bring them home from daycare or
school. Simple things to me, especially if one cared about the
child, but difficult if a parent was in jail or struggling with his or
her own substance abuse. Through the understanding cooperation of Lolly, we began to put some of the pieces together, and I
found a balance that matched my sometimes-hectic performing
schedule.

I was not a formal part of any program, but I did what I could to help inspire kids by talking and listening to them and taking them on field trips, like to the zoo, the balloon inflation for the Macy's Day Parade, and to meals at diners. I wanted to help children in similar ways that Mary Lou Phillips inspired me and gave me valuable life experiences. I wanted to show these kids that there was another life they could have.

I also started reading to kids at the Frederick Douglass Houses—they had a community space on the first floor that Lolly set up as a family room. Kids could read and study in relative quiet. I volunteered my time there quite often. Lolly and I encouraged parents to come downstairs and participate. The project was only about a block away from where I lived, so I spent a lot of time there.

Lolly was very dynamic and really excelled at her job. She lived in a community that was also her professional territory, so she knew the residents of the Frederick Douglass Houses very well. The space at Fredrick Douglass was such a success that two or three other buildings in the neighborhood started doing the same thing.

Furthermore, I sang at an Episcopal church and a Lutheran church in Harlem, and I would invite the kids and their families I'd met through the community spaces to come listen to the music. Many of the kids were Catholic, so at first there was hesitation, but eventually I had quite a few, along with their mothers, who would come to hear me sing. I started to become a leader and a sort of minister in my community: my goal was to embrace, uplift, motivate, and inspire.

✦

WITHOUT A DOUBT THE HARLEM SPIRITUAL ENSEMBLE
was my musical dream come true: a professional group of singers who dedicated themselves full-time to the promulgation and
promotion of the American Negro spiritual! It took me a while
to realize that this was what my deep, inner musical self was crying out for, but I eventually got there and embraced it totally. The
seed was first planted around 1970 when I went to Italy with the
New York City impresario Emory Taylor and his partner Jeannie
Faulkner. They put together a quintet, sextet, septet, octet, or
larger ensemble of various numbers that sang arrangements of
spirituals and other American folk music and toured Spain, Italy, and other tourist-filled islands of the Mediterranean Sea. I
was the tenor soloist. I toured with them between other engagements, more than a dozen times during the early 1970s. I was so
impressed with the group. For years, the *bravissimis* and rhythmic applause rang in my ears and in my heart. I used to dream
of this spontaneous, enrapturing applause embracing the whole
audience in unity. I'd see the many smiling faces and feel the vi-
brating pleasure of the audience. I wanted to sing these concerts
of American Negro spirituals again and again.

During this part of my career, I was basically a freelancer
and took jobs wherever I could secure a contract. My main jobs
were with the Metropolitan Opera Studio and *Mister Rogers'
Neighborhood*. As I traveled around the United States with Fred
and the Neighbors, making personal appearances, I noticed
that there were never any professional musical organizations
dedicated to the performance of the American Negro spiritual,
which happens to be my favorite form of singing and America's
first, original classical music. It came straight off the plantations. Numerous colleges and glee clubs made quite a reputation

for themselves by preserving this American tradition, such as Morehouse, Fisk, Tuskegee, Yale, Oberlin, Morgan, and Spelman. But something was missing. I asked every professional musician I could about it, and none of them had an answer that satisfied me.

The second part of this manifestation of the Harlem Spiritual Ensemble came during a life-changing trip a buddy of mine and I took to Machu Picchu in 1978. During that visit, in addition to enjoying the scenery and archeological wonders, seekers like us often had a session with a psychic. Folks shared the unusual power of these specialists to see into the future and sometimes to chat with deceased relatives. I was at least curious and decided to visit one. My buddy and I casually laughed it off when he said, "One day, you will be the director of a world-famous singing group that will tour the globe singing the sacred music of your people."

I had always thought of myself as a soloist and didn't— couldn't—take information like this to heart. It was even funnier when he tried to duplicate the music and sounded more like a Native American chanting ritual than a spiritual. I couldn't understand anything he was singing and chalked it up to spending vacation money for fun.

Nevertheless, that very night I had a captivating dream in dazzling Technicolor: I heard nine elderly gentlemen sitting in a burned-out railroad car, singing just as the psychic had, but this time, I recognized the song and its harmonies. The railroad car was sitting still, and all the elders were gazing far off into the sky. It appeared as though they were singing to me even though I wasn't there. I woke up crying tears of joy and singing that song. It's the only song I've ever composed.

When I got back home, I called a friend and she came over and we wrote the unforgettable song down. It's called "Till Dat Time" and it's now in my collection of arrangements entitled *Songs for Today,* published by Strube Verlag out of Munich, Germany. My Harlem Spiritual Ensemble sang it all over the world just as the psychic at Machu Picchu had foretold:

Verse I
Till dat time Lord, I been prayin'
Till dat time Lord, I been prayin'
Till dat time Lord, I been prayin'
Till duh Lord, He done done what He said He would!

Verse II
Till dat time Lord, I been singin'
Till dat time Lord, I been singin'
Till dat time Lord, I been singin'
Till duh Lord, He done done what He said He would!

Verse III
Till dat time Lord, I been tryin'
Till dat time Lord, I been tryin'
Till dat time Lord, I been tryin'
Till duh Lord, He done done what He said He would!

The group was officially born in 1980, and we dedicated ourselves to preserving, sustaining, and commissioning new and traditional arrangements of American Negro spirituals for future generations. In the beginning, a lot of our singers had part-time jobs. Gigs were sporadic, maybe once every month or so. But eventually, everyone was able to sing with the Harlem Spiritual Ensemble full-time, especially when we gained international recognition. This was the ultimate goal: I wanted the group to travel the world and share our unique history.

We first started singing for colleges and universities across the United States. I was ultimately introduced to John Folin at a music expo in New York, which ended up being a wonderful connection for the group. John ran Allied Concert Services in Minnesota, whose mission was (and is) to bring world-class artists and attractions to communities outside of major metropolitan areas in the central United States. At the time, the members were mostly comprised of older white men who just wanted to hear classical music. They never had singers and *never* had black folks! John agreed to hear the Harlem Spiritual Ensemble, and we sang the walls down for him! His heart and soul were touched, and he ultimately asked us to come to Minnesota to perform. He would pay for our travel expenses, but he wanted us to do more than just spirituals. We agreed to do some songs from Gershwin's *Porgy and Bess* as well. It was a *huge* hit, and it paved the way for us to start touring around the country, singing that repertoire.

Once the group had been singing together for about three years, we set about finding an agent. I advertised through *Musical America* magazine, and we held an MLK Jr. vigil concert. The auditorium was filled! However, only one agent showed up—Thea Dispeker. Luckily for us, she offered her services and represented the Harlem Spiritual Ensemble for nearly a decade until she died. Afterward, the group ended up partnering with another wonderful Dispeker agent who started her own agency—Michal Schmidt.

Fred took a special interest in everything the Ensemble did. I'll always remember how he gave us one of our first grants when we formed our 501(c)(3), the American Negro Spiritual Research Foundation, to support our educational work in schools, our commissioning of new arrangements of American Negro spirituals, and a grant for younger artists to include spirituals in their recital programs. Those few hundred dollars that we awarded those singers worked like magic. We were mentioned in folks' programs, and we used the recognition to book even more shows and events.

The Ensemble spent a lot of time teaching, rehearsing, and performing at our unofficial home, the Harlem School of the Arts. In those days, it was run by a rather well-known, over-the-top mezzo-soprano named Betty Allen, who happened to come from Youngstown. She could be seen quite often at various church and community functions, as well as at concerts and civic events on college campuses and concert halls uptown and downtown. We performed for four or five years domestically before we started touring overseas. Around 1985, we had our first real trip abroad, to Italy, and we were gone for about a month.

The first week of fall, October 1986, shall always remain dear to my heart. We were busy planning and coordinating the first New England tour for the Ensemble and had worked very hard to make it work financially. We drove across Lake Champlain toward Middlebury College in Middlebury, Vermont. The leaves were at peak rainbow color, the sun was out, and everyone had cameras; we stopped frequently to admire the foliage and take photographs.

Everyone we met was so nice to us. They helped take informal photos of the Ensemble and made sure we were on the right road when we asked. We found a lovely roadside inn with hearty country food and plenty of room to relax as we shared our joy for such a beautiful fall day.

Along the way, there were also the ubiquitous milk farms with picturesque cows and horses; open valleys leading up to the Green Mountains; old, worn-out barns; rusted cars; and antique shops that compelled us to stop several times where we *oohed* and *aahed* at furniture we could never use in our tiny Manhattan apartments.

As soon as we got to Middlebury, I couldn't help but feel that there was an energy on the campus. We checked into the Middlebury Inn and made ourselves comfortable for several hours before the concert. For a short time, I sat in the little park across from the Inn. Then I decided to walk to Mead Chapel, where we were going to perform later. This was Fall Family Weekend, and all the activities buzzed along Main Street in the stores around me. Folks said hello. They weren't like Manhattanites at all. I asked directions once, and a kind young man named Joseph offered to walk with me. I told him I was a guest artist who was going to perform that evening, and he shared with me that his parents were here from Ohio and all of them were looking forward to the concert.

We found Mead Chapel empty, and I decided to warm up and test the acoustics. Joseph asked if he could stay. He seemed to be enjoying this little treat. Suddenly, parents and visitors began to fill the hall out of curiosity. They came right up to me, and some very politely sat down while others began to ask a few questions. All of them were super-excited about the evening's concert. They wanted to know more about me and the Ensemble and practically begged me to sing something just for them.

I explained to them that I did have to conserve myself for the concert, but I would be glad to extend myself to them for just a few more moments. The place became our little private chamber room, and I sang very easily—just for us. They loved it, and so did I. I explained just a little about the Ensemble, about me, and about my role on *Mister Rogers' Neighborhood*. I also shared with them that I knew deep within that our little communion, our coming together, was no accident. I wasn't sure what it meant, but I knew it was special.

All the way back to the Inn, I felt so radiant. Everything seemed to go that way during that first trip to Middlebury. Something mystical was present in the most common of activities. The feeling carried through to the green room as the president of Middlebury College, Dr. John McCardell, and his wife came to greet us and wish us well for the concert. They told us about a special reception they had planned at their home following the concert and said they hoped we'd all attend. We expressed our gratitude, and they proceeded to their seats.

During the concert, I allowed myself to take a good look around. The lovely chapel was packed as full as possible. Members of the audience informed us that it was so full that family members had to sit outside on the lawn, where the sound was amplified especially for them. In addition, so many community members had wanted to hear the concert that arrangements had been made to pipe the sound into the Family Hall in the Student Union building about thirty yards down the college passageway.

Years ago, I learned to talk to my audience to warm them up and get them into the spirit of the occasion. This night was no different. "Why are so many folks here tonight?" I asked. "Are your concerts always so well attended?"

"No!" they answered. "We came to hear the Ensemble and to see Officer Clemmons live!" When my brain registered the message, I stood center stage, stock still in shock!

Someone on stage and in the audience had the presence of mind to start singing "Won't You Be My Neighbor," and I joined in. As I stood there, I was aware of the entire audience singing and the echo that followed our sound that came from outside. We all stopped and cheered when it finally ended. I imagined from comments that I heard later that the folks at the Student Union had been singing along too. We had shared something special, like a communion, and it had bonded us in a way too deep and riveting to describe.

After the concert, we proceeded to the lovely reception at the president's house, where I was approached discretely by Mrs. McCardell and asked whether I would consider coming upstairs and reading a story to her two sons and maybe singing a song with them. They were not yet ten years old and still watched the program all the time. They knew that I was downstairs and ordinarily they should have been asleep much earlier. Well I wasn't exactly new at this, so I quietly went upstairs and was introduced to two starstruck young fans. I sat, and we read some stories for a while, and then sure enough we all sang several *Mister Rogers'* songs.

All in all, it was indeed a full day of magical feelings. When I finally managed to get back to my hotel room, I was exhausted, and my head was still spinning. This wonderful day had totally fulfilled itself, and I was so grateful to be at this little New England college. I still didn't know exactly why all this magic should be happening here at Middlebury, but I was content to let it be for now. Maybe someday it would all come together and mean something, but for now it was enough just to witness and enjoy the experience.

✦

I RETIRED FROM *MISTER ROGERS' NEIGHBORHOOD* IN 1993, and it was 100 percent my decision to leave. I realized that I was starting to get requests for tours with the Harlem Spiritual Ensemble for weeks at a time, and I couldn't do both anymore—I was needed in another way, in another place. Plus, I could do all the things with the Harlem Spiritual Ensemble that I hadn't been allowed to control on *Mister Rogers' Neighborhood*, including song choice, final decisions about what to wear, choreography, scheduling of repertoire, arrangements of songs, etc. I had freedom and autonomy in a way that I didn't when I was on someone else's show. I was full of ideas and needed more creative freedom.

When I told Fred that I was leaving the show full-time, he was very understanding. I even agreed to come back periodically and perform operas. And I still toured with Fred sometimes. To be honest, my last day on the show was not intensely emotional because it simply wasn't goodbye forever. I knew that I was still going to see Fred and other cast members, so it was just continuing in a different capacity.

On my last full show, I sang "I'm Going Away" as well as "There Are Many Ways to Say I Love You."

> *I'm going away*
> *I'm going away*
> *And then come back*
> *I'm going away*

I'm going away
And then come back

There was a good sense of closure, and none of the cast or crew took my departure personally. And, since the Harlem Spiritual Ensemble was really taking off, I was making enough money as a performer that I could fly to Pittsburgh and visit whenever I felt like it.

✦

WE WERE ASKED TO RETURN TO MIDDLEBURY FOUR years in a row, rare for a visiting ensemble unless you're in residence. Then, in 1996, I received an honorary doctorate at Middlebury and was offered a teaching job as choral director and a position as Alexander Twilight Artist-in-Residence. For the first time in my professional career, I did not have to travel full-time to make a living.

In truth, all of this came about because of persistent health problems. My doctor basically said I was working myself to death. It sounds a bit dramatic, but I was getting tired and couldn't get rested. I developed a cough that wouldn't go away. It required strict vocal rest, which I could not get since I was the prime tenor singer and conductor for the group. If I didn't perform, the Ensemble essentially couldn't perform. All of this along with the mounting financial difficulties—the Ensemble was a brilliant success artistically, and yet continually struggled to make ends meet.

From asking around, I knew many other arts organizations that were perpetually having the same problem. Some like Alvin

Ailey American Dance Theater, Dance Theater of Harlem, Boys Choir of Harlem, and the Harlem Opera Theater actually took a sabbatical, realigned their board of directors, and started over again. None of those Band-Aid approaches would have solved our problem. So, we—the management and I—made the painfully difficult decision to dissolve the Ensemble.

This did not go over well with my singers. After all, they were the ones who had worked the hardest and had the most to lose. But at the same time, no one provided a financial solution to our persistent, recurring problem of mounting debt.

When I arrived at Middlebury full-time, I didn't exactly come empty-handed. I certainly had all my musical skills for solo and choral preparations, which were on regular public display, but I also came armed with superb public relations, touring, managing, grant-writing, hosting, networking, and mothering skills. My years as founder and director of the Harlem Spiritual Ensemble and CEO of the American Negro Spiritual Research Foundation had served me well. I was ready.

Right from the start, I was drawn to this little village with its unique flavor waiting to be discovered. At first glance, the remote, pristine college set on top of a hill was almost old-fashioned and conservative. But it wasn't any of these things once you got to know the folks! Everywhere I went, I felt at *home*. I was determined to be myself, and everyone knew I had a special artistic relationship with the president. He came to all my concerts—solo and choral—and usually with his wife and a little entourage. The acceptance all over town was like an explosion of goodwill.

After New York, this little town seemed perfect for me, and I thrived in its "countrified" farmer-in-the-dell atmosphere. As I got to know it better (and fully experienced the weather), I found lots of interesting things to do during the long, almost bleak Vermont winter: there were lectures and plays to enjoy; concerts to attend and give; and lots of writing, arranging, and research to fill my time.

It was no easy task to sometimes teach all week and then hop on an airplane at unusual hours from Burlington and travel by sometimes very circuitous routes, usually through New York or Montreal—nothing was direct—and wind up in Vienna or some part of Italy to sing a full concert the next day. I'd sometimes leave immediately, right after the concert on a red-eye, maybe by an even more circuitous route, so I could be back in Vermont on campus to greet my eager choristers for our intense rehearsals as we prepared for seasonal concerts and semester-ending obligations.

Through all these activities, I stayed in touch with Fred and Joanne. We spoke at least once a month, if not more often, depending on our hectic schedules and the issues that could arise in the normal life of artists on the road. As soon as I got back home, I'd call him to catch up and report on the success and expected ups and downs of the tour. He was my constant mental and emotional support.

Taking over the Middlebury College Choir was no chore at all. I had been substituting for almost two years and knew the routine fairly well. The former choir director and members of the music faculty made the transition as easy as possible for me, and I began by teaching them some of my arrangements of spirituals and other sacred repertoire I liked. Because they were not professional musicians, they didn't learn as fast as the Harlem Spiritual Ensemble, but they held on to the arrangements forever. I was always amazed at their retention and youthful eagerness.

All through my tenure as Artist-In-Residence, questions would come up: What's Mister Rogers really like? Is he as nice as he seems on TV? Did you like working with him? What are the other Neighbors like? How long have you been with him?

I suggested that those who wanted to know more about him should come to my home for dinner, and we'd have an informal chat about *Mister Rogers' Neighborhood* and Fred. I casually threw out the invitation and said yes when someone wanted to know if they could bring a friend. Needless to say, I was not prepared when some fifty-plus college kids showed up at my home Sunday afternoon to hear me chat about Fred Rogers! I didn't have enough food or chairs for everybody. Fortunately, these kids didn't mind lounging around informally on the floor along with paper plates and plastic spoons, knives, and forks for the food I had prepared for dinner. They had lots of questions, and I tried as best as I could to answer them. When I didn't know the answer, I said so. When the day came to a close, no one seemed to be unhappy, and I started making plans for our next get-together.

Once I got settled into my new routine—my rehearsals, my office hours—and knew my way around, it was only natural that I should invite Fred to come to Middlebury. He agreed, and we began to look seriously at his schedule. The fates were not on our side, and we spent more than a year going back and forth with suggestions, none of which worked for us either because of his prior commitments or my forays to do solo concerts or the frequently rigid academic calendar that was simply not kind to us.

I had done numerous visits to college campuses with Fred over the years, and it occurred to me that it would be just the thing for Middlebury College to give him an honorary doctorate. Plus, it hadn't hurt that they had already given me an honorary doctorate of the arts. So, I approached President John McCardell with the idea, and he took it to the board of directors.

Everyone agreed that it was a great suggestion, and I presented it to Fred. Happily, he agreed, and we were finally getting somewhere on this visit.

I remember suggesting that Fred stay with me. After all, I lived a short block from our historic, restored downtown, and I thought it would be a nice, simple, comforting atmosphere for Fred. As it turned out, the board and John McCardell had very different ideas about how Fred should be feted during his brief visit to our little town and campus! Frankly, the more I thought about it, the more I realized that they were totally right. The college went out of its way to make sure that Fred and Joanne knew full well how much they and the entire larger community appreciated his taking the time to come and visit our little village. It was easy to see and hear how proud everyone was of their two-hundred-year-old New England history, and they shared it at every opportunity.

Before the ceremony, in keeping with their desire for things to go smoothly, the graduation committee often checked with me to make sure that things were the way Fred would like them to be. All kinds of details were presented to me. I either checked with Fred, his office in Pittsburgh, or just said, "I don't know!" I clearly remembered that he was a vegetarian, so all meals had a no-meat menu, and I knew that he'd probably want to go swimming every day that he was here. That was easy to fulfill since we had an Olympic-size pool that a buddy of mine, Coach Peter Solomon, oversaw. He and the teams, both men and women, were equally excited, as were their families and friends, when I told them that Fred was coming. I daresay they were making plans for the whole team to practice at 6:00 a.m.—for as long as Fred was in the pool, I was told.

The banquet prepared for the day before the graduation was a feast. I lovingly teased Fred and Joanne when we arrived at Kirk Alumni Center and observed that the college had spared no expense. In practice, Fred was naturally more modest than I am, and it was adorable to see him blushing at this kind of lavish attention. There were flowers on every table and candles to match. As I looked around, I couldn't help but have a deep feeling of pride and joy.

John McCardell, our beloved president, tapped the microphone as he quieted the crowd and presented a stately and warm welcome fit for the occasion. At his signal, several campus a cappella groups sang a meaningful tribute for Fred, and my Middlebury College Choir dedicated a lovely arrangement of spirituals that I had prepared for the occasion; Peter Nilsson, my undergraduate assistant, conducted. Lastly, I introduced and sang a medley of songs from *The Neighborhood* and ended it with a hopping arrangement of "Ride on, King Jesus!" By then, all of us were ready for this very specially prepared banquet. John signaled to the student waiters, who had been standing, peeking, and listening by the kitchen doors, to begin serving. Where only seconds ago, it was quiet in rapt attention to the speeches and singing, the room now burst forth into a cacophony of dancing waiters negotiating trays full of coffee, water, bread, and other goodies.

The culmination of the graduation the next day was a simple moment when Fred invited everyone to sit quietly while we remembered, with gratitude, everyone who was responsible for our being here at that moment. I was fine for about twenty seconds. After all, I'd been through this before when I had traveled with

Fred and attended graduations where he had received honorary doctorates. I usually sang a medley of his songs from the *Neighborhood*. But somehow, for some reason, that graduation was different. I felt particularly vulnerable, and my only comfort was that I could hear all the unabashed, obvious sniffling going on around me.

It was cleansing for me. Deeply cleansing. The way you'd feel if you could have washed yourself out and hung your insides out to dry. I felt lighter, stronger, and better. And in this moment, I also seemed to have released lots of pent-up anger and angry memories. I bunched them all together and just threw them out. I recognized that it was a new day, and I had been blessed to sing for millions and millions of folks all over the world. Not too bad, if you ask me.

Then I heard Fred speaking again and he called my name! He mentioned my value and growth on the program. He played a song over the entire sound system from the *Neighborhood* where I sang "There Are Many Ways to Say I Love You."

> *There are many ways to say I love you*
> *There are many ways to say I care about you.*
> *Many ways, many ways, many ways to say*
> *I love you.*
> *There's the singing way to say I love you*
> *There's the singing something someone really likes*
>   *to hear,*
> *The singing way, the singing way, the singing way*
>   *to say*
> *I love you.*

Cleaning up a room can say I love you.
Hanging up a coat before you're asked to
Drawing special pictures for the holidays and
Making plays.
You'll find many ways to say I love you.
You'll find many ways to understand what love is.
Many ways, many ways, many ways to say
I love you.
Singing, cleaning,
Drawing, being
Understanding,
Love you.

When the ceremony was over, and the awards presented, we proceeded off the stage and into the audience. Fred was mobbed, and I was semi-mobbed. I got the better part of that deal. Since I knew he would be hard to get to, I gathered a few of my students and suggested they come with me to where he was staying. We could say our farewells there. This would be our last chance to see him before he headed back for Pittsburgh.

This was truly a small town, as evidenced by the fact that I poked around and found an unlocked door and let everybody in. We settled in among the few bags of luggage and waited. Sooner than I expected, I heard the wheels of several cars turning into the driveway and doors slamming. I heard keys in the front door lock, and Fred and his small entourage of escorts entered, looking a bit surprised to see me and my gang sitting comfortably waiting for him.

We all moved over expectantly and surrounded the source

of our excitement. Fred was his unexcitable self, unperturbed and receptive. The gang took full advantage and started in right away:

"Oh, Mister Rogers, I used to watch you all the time when I was little."

"My mom and dad told me about the show, and Lady Aberlin was my favorite."

"I always loved it when the trolley went over to the Neighborhood of Make-Believe and visited with the puppets and the castle."

"I liked Daniel and Henrietta in the big tree in Make-Believe."

Somebody was even kind enough to say, "I loved the operas and when Officer Clemmons sang."

Fred replied, "We loved it when Officer Clemmons sang too! I'd love to stay and visit more, but we do have a plane to catch. Won't you all understand and allow us this time to say goodbye just a bit early? We don't want to have to drive so fast to get to the airport."

With those simple words, we released our captive and he walked over, looking searchingly around for where he had placed his luggage. I said, "The guys who are driving you to the airport took all the luggage out to the car. Why don't I walk you to your car, Fred? Guys, wait here for me for a few minutes and I'll take you home."

I was true to my word and got everyone home pronto. Within the hour, I was sitting in my living room, relaxing, and mentally going over the packed events of this graduation weekend. I wasn't tired, but there was definite melancholy in the air. This was hardly the visit I had imagined, but so much had happened that I could hardly complain. Our time, when Fred and I were together, was intensely wonderful and fulfilling, but it wasn't enough. What had happened to quiet, easy, laid-back, unhurried, thoughtful, and mindful sharing of ideas and opinions? I wanted my old Fred back.

◆

I HAVE BEEN TALKING TO THE SO-CALLED DEAD SINCE my darling sister, Lawanna, committed suicide in March of 1975. Talking to her brought me comfort. Amazingly, I felt that we were actually communicating. Oh, not in words but in nonspecific ways: in feelings, smells, air textures, and sounds that I couldn't explain; I noticed shadows that reminded me of her. At other times, her presence seemed to gently envelope me, offering comfort and understanding. It was never a threatening or intimidating experience in any way. I loved thinking about her; maybe I was just daydreaming. She had been my "pet," and my longing for her would sometimes approach the painful.

My mother and Warren had one child between them. Lawanna Jeannette Boswell was born June 1, 1955, when I was ten years old and in the fourth grade. Typical of any older brother, I used to tease her and call her Lackawanna for fun. She was the apple of my eye. We shared a special bond, and it was a joy to play with her and watch her grow. I didn't teach her to walk or read or write, but I sure helped her to practice.

As she grew, I detected a real musical gift in her and encouraged her to sing with me. She also displayed an amazing ability to remember lyrics that I struggled to memorize. She had a clear, lovely soprano voice that blended quite well with mine. We could harmonize together for hours along with my other siblings.

Later, she learned to play the piano and used to pretend that she was accompanying me for my singing engagements. She had a natural sense of humor, and we laughed a lot in spite of my growing differences with my mother and stepfather. Sometimes she would even let me rock her to sleep in my arms at night; I felt like I had a living teddy bear to love.

I found her body the day after I had had a very productive day filming *Mr. Rogers' Neighborhood* in Pittsburgh. Because I was tired after I had flown home, I decided to contact her the following day after I had rested some. Early the following morning, her best friend, Sheila, called to ask if I knew where Lawanna was. She didn't answer her phone, and she hadn't come in to work that morning, and Sheila was concerned. I said I did not, but I'd get back to her just as soon as I could go over and find out. I had been able to secure her an apartment in the same building where I lived, only a few doors down the hall. We had exchanged keys, and I saw her frequently. So, I grabbed the keys, put on my bathrobe, and headed over.

There really are not, and perhaps never will be, sufficient words to express my grief for the loss of this beloved sister-child. I knocked on the door, but she never opened it. As I called out her name and put my ear to the door, I heard quiet pastoral music playing softly. It sounded eerie. That was strange because it was not her musical taste. I used the key but found it equally as strange: the chain was on from the inside. The door opened perhaps an inch. I could see her bare legs as she lay on the bed on her stomach, not moving. I called to her several times, becoming more and more hysterical as she didn't respond. By then neighbors had come out of their apartments to ask what was going on. Why was I yelling? Frankly, I told them I didn't know.

In desperation, I kicked the door in, and I desperately tried to rouse my sister. Through all this chaos, she remained calm and unmoved. It was then that I knew she was dead.

Someone called out that they had called 911 and help was on the way. I shook her shoulders and tried in vain to revive her. In the process, I discovered the cause of her death: stabbing. I couldn't bear the sight of the suicide utensil in her body, gripped so tightly in her sweet, baby-sister hands, so I took it out. I did everything you're not supposed to do. In my grief, I held her and kissed her and hugged her and rocked her and sang to her and cried. She was covered in blood, and soon, I was too.

✦

IN ADDITION TO MY YOUNGEST SISTER, I MEDITATED and prayed to be able to forgive my daddy and stepfather for their alcoholic abuse of our family. In my twenties and thirties I became painfully aware of the unmitigated damage each of them had done to all of us children, not to mention my mother, with their drinking and philandering. I set out to try to under-stand them better and ultimately forgive them. I urge anyone to not take such a task lightly. In my case, it felt necessary! Many very painful and unmentionable memories flooded my soul during those years. I ultimately spent some five years in therapy trying to free up and heal the damaged young spirit my daddy and stepfather had nearly destroyed by their brutal treatment of my mother.

During that process I summoned them up more times than I can count and struggled to understand why they behaved the way they did. Suffice it to say that I learned a lot from this deep analysis about me and my "fathers." I did, after many tries, forgive both of them. It was painful, and I slipped back into hate several times before the forgiveness stuck. Two powerful thoughts stand out from that experience for me. First, I realized that forgiveness for me is an ongoing process. I grew into understanding and loving from hatred and anger. It did not happen all at once, but when I finally got there, I felt such a sense of being purged and cleansed that I can hardly explain it. It was like letting go of some one hundred pounds of organic poison I had been infected with for some forty-five years.

✦

WHEN FRED DIED IN 2003, I WAS SHATTERED. I WAS caught off guard and wanted to sit and grieve and feel my pain, but circumstances forced me to keep moving. I was the guest conductor of a musical organization in Vermont preparing an all-state musical festival at Green Mountain College. I was in charge of the choral presentation. Many students, parents, and community folks had gathered together and were depending on me to lead them in a major statewide concert in three days.

After some serious consideration with all the folks gathered in Pittsburgh for Fred's funeral, it was agreed that for me to cancel the musical preparations and performance with the children and fly to Pittsburgh was unthinkable. Fred would never do something that deliberate to disappoint so many children. I agreed, and I knew that as soon as I could, I'd make my way to Pittsburgh and travel up to Latrobe, Pennsylvania, where Fred was interred, and pay my respects. But I was miserable and remained that way for several years.

✦

I OFTEN THINK OF FRED TODAY IN LIGHT OF ALL THAT IS
happening in our world. There is violence against children everywhere. Guns, war, and random attacks against unarmed civilians
seem to be the order of the day. On the daily newscasts we see
the tortured faces of young and helpless children as they reflect
the full story of these battles, sometimes about religion, or race,
or political systems. Time and again we see that the children are
traumatized in the midst of these adult conflicts, while they desperately search in vain for their parents or someone who will help
them.

Fred would certainly not be happy. Much of the time, I'm not
very happy. Many times, I'm not sure we're necessarily meant to
be happy in this life. There's so much work to be done. There are
times I feel a deep sense of contentment, and I have known satisfaction from a job well done. But happiness is another matter
altogether. There's simply too much going on that is not caring
or kind or considerate of other people. Fred not only talked the
talk; he walked the walk. His life was an example for everyone—
one cannot just sit around and pretend we don't know what's going on and do nothing.

In my humble opinion, our society has evolved in such a way
that Fred would hardly recognize it. Fred was simply a man concerned about society, and he left a legacy of care for his fellow
men. Everyone had value as far as he was concerned! What people said and how they behaved was important to him; it is important to me too. I will never understand the hurt we inflict on
one another because of our differences in religion, sex, skin color,
hair color, eye color, what games we play, what continents our

families came from, how long we've been citizens, our culture, language, on and on. None of these matter when it comes to being a good human being.

✦

ONCE, WHEN I RETURNED TO NEW YORK FROM ONE OF my tours, I naturally took some R & R time before catching up on my daily chores. I sat down and began to write out some checks. Looking back at this time in my life, I knew that I owed a deep debt of gratitude to Fred and his relationship to me career-wise and personally. I wanted a way to say a profound thank-you. It is important to show gratitude when life-has been kind to you. So many folks have been kind to me and continue to contribute to the success of my career. But in my mind and in my heart, Fred's contribution was special right from the start.

It seemed only natural to me to send a check to Fred's 501(c)(3) company to show my gratitude. In some ways, I didn't give it much thought. I wrote out a check, enclosed a special note to him, and sent it off to Pittsburgh. I thought that would be the end of it, and I went on about organizing my life again after a wonderful, hectic tour.

Several weeks went by when I heard from Fred . . . most unexpectedly. His first words were, "Franç . . . I hardly know what to say. I'm so thankful for the gift you sent to me for my work."

I was a little embarrassed. "Well, yes, Fred," I stammered. "I believe in you and your work and wanted to show my appreciation. You're always giving to me. This was just one way I could say thank you for all you've done for me."

"Let me tell you something, Franç," he said. "In all the years

I've been working with children and sharing my vision for PBS and our program, no one who worked for me has ever given me such a contribution like this. I can't tell you what this means to me. I will never forget it."

After that, we chatted a bit, but words couldn't really convey our deep mutual love and respect. When we hung up, I sat there a long time repeating the words he had just spoken to me. I found myself talking out loud to him because I couldn't help myself. It was like he was there with me, in my living room, and we were communing about the need for the world to love one another and show their care and appreciation. And, of course, Fred never cashed that check.

EPILOGUE

Well Fred,

Now I am seventy-five years old. I will be seventy-six in April. It's so strange to imagine that now I'm older than you were in earth years. Boy, I wish you were around to feel and touch. Listen to and smell. Smile and laugh with.

Frankly, these days I'm very lonely, but I'll survive! The nation, and indeed the world, is thoroughly embroiled in a fierce campaign to end the reign of a COVID-19 pandemic. It afflicts all nations and societies across the globe and travels through the air most invisibly. I find it quite painful and depressing at times.

As if the pandemic were not enough, the social and political climate all over America is more and more contaminated. Black people are still experiencing a nightmare perpetrated by those you called "the Helpers." Those who are supposed to be protecting black communities—the black ghetto, where I was raised—are killing us. Life in America frequently doesn't seem to be any safer than it was when John Kennedy, Martin Luther King Jr., Medgar Evers, and Bobby Kennedy were assassinated. Seems like everybody has a gun! Folks, white men, whether uniformed or not, frequently kill at will and do not have to give an account. I am tired of this withering pain and grief.

But while I long for physical touch and a healed nation, iron-ically at this lonely point in my life, I feel the whole world wrap-ping its gigantic arms around me in one soul-smothering, cosmic hug. Sometimes I wonder if the state of the world has made the responses to my story—*our* story—so tremendous. It's opened up the floodgates to having meaningful conversations with read-ers from all walks of life.

All this activity makes me feel like maybe I've finally "made it." Kurt Vonnegut's words remind me of what you would say:

> I don't think being good at things is the point of doing them. I think you've got all these wonder-ful experiences with different skills, and that all teaches you things and makes you an interesting person, no matter how well you do them.

My work, and indeed experience, is of a thinking man who is neither doctor nor therapist of any sort. In academic circles I consider myself rather common. But I'm not unaware of other gifts the Universe has bestowed on me: compassion, communi-cation, kindness, empathy. And I live a life of enormous cosmic excitement. I've forged deep connections with new readers and longtime fans in a way I never anticipated. I was amazed when I fully realized how much love would find me once I honestly exposed my true self.

There have always been many songs ringing around in my head, particularly American Negro spirituals. These songs make me feel good and have been a part of my intimate life since child-hood. They also make me feel closer to God. I wondered, is this the same God that so forcefully fills my singing and now my quiet meditative time? So I began to create my own version of singing-meditation. I didn't consult any known metaphysical teachers or old, wise Christian sages. I just began! It was gentle at first, gentle and quiet, but very deeply felt. Sure enough, I eventually began to see and feel *you*. And ultimately, I felt that both of you were somehow connected. The feeling was not intimidating or threatening in any way. In fact, the presence of the Great Unknown began to present Itself more and more often. It encouraged me as though it were you!

At least twice a day I sing *There Are Many Ways to Say I Love You*, and you seem to appear, or rather descend upon me! You never seem to run out of confidence-giving warmth and love. I began to call it "Fred-Love"! By channeling you and your legacy, I know my readers feel this, too. I think we're giving them a heaping dose of Fred-Love *and* François-Love.

The bottom line is that I feel you'll always be with me. You'll be with me to continue our collaboration on many projects I've begun or am still formulating in "our" mind! I know that sounds a bit unhinged to lots of folks, but it's as close to the truth as I can get. I'm not writing my books alone. That needs to be clear.

We've been receiving beautiful letters from dear readers across the country. Wherever you are, I hope you enjoy them as much as I do.

FRANÇOIS-LOVE

ACKNOWLEDGMENTS

It truly took a village to bring *Officer Clemmons: A Memoir* into the world, and I profoundly thank each and every one of you who had a hand in helping me share my story.

I want to offer my sincere thanks to my earliest editor and book doctor, Peter Alson, who is simply the best. He visited my secret pains and joys often, and probably knows my manuscript as well as I do, but he never left the slightest fingerprint to reveal his visit!

In addition, history has spoken well of literary agents who have launched many a career. I want to add my voice to that chorus of praise: I thank my agent suprema, Lady Elizabeth Copps, and the entire team at Maria Carvainis Agency from the bottom of my heart. They will be spoken about as among the very finest. It was Elizabeth who had faith in me from the beginning and kept introducing me to real possibilities—she believed that a wonderful book could be fashioned from my humble yet challenging life experiences. There would be no publishing contract if it were not for her boundless, ever-positive, deeply centered, creative, faithful, and pointed encouragement of my work. Because of her, a childhood dream is coming true: to one day be a singer *and* a published writer.

I also want to sincerely thank Carolyn Kuebler and her crew at the *New England Review* who were the very first to publish a story about my family's roots in the Deep South. If I hadn't needed the money, I would have framed the check!

Let me humbly thank Frances and Paul Stone, my very special friends, sage advisors, and intrepid travel companions. Their unwavering support has kept me going through personal and professional challenges. I treasure our frank discussions about the serious social and political issues our society faces and how we can all be better citizens of the world. Both of you mean the world to *me*.

To my Brokeback Mountain lunch ladies—thank you for listening to my very early drafts, especially Michael Warner and Joseph Watson.

To my Cosmic Children. You know who you are. I love you all tremendously. And particularly to my beloved Cosmic Son, Ross Carbone—he may be over six foot four on the outside, but to me he is a *seven*-foot-four giant on the inside!

To Marichal Gentry, the friend of a lifetime who listens to me on the phone until the wee hours. I used to think that he was asleep until I asked him questions that he answered with academic accuracy! He suffered through all of the iterations of *Officer Clemmons* and celebrated with me when I finally landed the long-awaited publishing deal. Marichal, I always think about you when I sing "There Are Many Ways to Say I Love You."

And to my dear Marni Willms, who showed up whether it was sunny or cold and braved my dictation. If she preferred to be somewhere else, she never let on. She is my sister.

Thank you to all of my families, including the very special folks I've had the pleasure of knowing through Oberlin

College, Carnegie Mellon University, *Mister Rogers' Neighborhood*, WQED, the Metropolitan Opera Studio, the Harlem Spiritual Ensemble, and Middlebury College.

And of course, THANK YOU to the most marvelous team at Catapult who saw my story as something truly special and who have worked tirelessly to pave the way to publication—especially my fearless editor, Mensah Demary, who championed the book from the start. Jonathan Lee, Andy Hunter, Jennifer Abel Kovitz, Megan Fishmann, Elizabeth Ireland, Katie Boland, Carla Bruce-Eddings, Sarah Jean Grimm, Hope Levy, Dustin Kurtz, Dory Athey, Kendall Storey, Wah-Ming Chang, and Nicole Caputo: I appreciate your hard work and your faith in me immensely! I also offer my sincere gratitude to Elaine Trevorrow, who opened the door to incredible speaking opportunities, and to Gary Sweeney, who designed my beautiful website.

And to you, dear readers, thank you for choosing my book!! I want you to know that I am very excited about the next phase of this journey, and I hope you will take the time to come out for an in-person event—I promise we'll find lots of things to talk about. Come to think of it, Fred used to say that!

Much love,
FRANÇOIS "DIVAMAN" SCARBOROUGH CLEMMONS

DR. FRANÇOIS S. CLEMMONS received a bachelor of music degree from Oberlin College and a master of fine arts from Carnegie Mellon University. He also received an honorary doctor of arts degree from Middlebury College. In 1973, he won a Grammy Award for a recording of Porgy and Bess; in 1986, he founded and directed the Harlem Spiritual Ensemble; and from 1997 until his retirement in 2013, Clemmons was the Alexander Twilight Artist in Residence and director of the Martin Luther King Spiritual Choir at Middlebury College in Vermont, where he currently resides.